INDONESIA

Number 113 — April 2022

Published by Southeast Asia Program Publications • Cornell University Press

Submissions: Submit manuscript as double-spaced document in MS word or similar. Please format citation and footnotes according to the style guidelines in *The Chicago Manual of Style*, 17th edition.

Address: Please address all correspondence and manuscripts to the managing editor at sg265@cornell.edu. We prefer electronic submissions.

Reprints: Contributors will receive one complimentary copy of the issue in which their articles appear.

Abstracts: Abstracts of articles published in *Indonesia* appear in *Excerpta Indonesica*, which is published semiannually by the Royal Institute of Linguistics and Anthropology, Leiden. Articles appearing in this journal are also abstracted and indexed in *Historical Abstracts* and *America: History and Life*.

Subscription information: Contact subscriptions@dukeupress.edu for more information. Digital subscriptions for individuals and institutions are handled by Project Muse (muse@jhu.press.edu).

INDONESIA online: All *Indonesia* articles published at least five years prior to the date of the current issue are accessible to our readers on the internet free of charge. For more information concerning annual print and online subscriptions, pay-per-view access to recent articles, and access to our archives, please see: seap.einaudi.cornell.edu/indonesia_journal or http://ecommons.cornell.edu

Managing Editor   Sarah F. M. Grossman

Cover credit: Photographer unknown. Leiden University Library Special Collections, KITLV A1420, 4763

ISBN 978-1-5017-6778-4
ISSN 0019-7289
©2022 Cornell University

Special Issue: Disaster in Indonesia

Disaster in Indonesia: Along the Fault Line toward New Approaches   1
Susie Protschky

Portents of Power: Natural Disasters throughout Indonesian History   9
Wayan Jarrah Sastrawan

The Toba Super-Catastrophe as History of the Future   33
Faizah Zakaria

Processions: How the Spiritual Geographies of Central Java
Shaped Modern Volcano Science   51
Adam Bobbette

Military Responses to and Forms of Knowledge About Natural Disaster
in Colonial Indonesia, 1865–1930   67
Susie Protschky

Plague Rat or Anopheles: Health Disasters and Home Improvement in   91
Late Colonial Java
Maurits Bastiaan Meerwijk

The Public Politics of Supplication in a Time of Disaster   113
Julian Millie and Dede Syarif

Book Reviews:
Leiden, *Authoritarian Modernization in Indonesia's Early Independence Period:*   127
The Foundation of the New Order State (1950–1965)
Mattias Fibiger

Judith E. Bosnak and Frans X. Koot, *The Javanese Travels of Purwalelana:*   131
A Nobleman's Account of His Journeys Across the Island of Java 1860-1875
Peter Carey

Disaster in Indonesia: Along the Fault Line toward New Approaches

Susie Protschky

Abstract

This article posits that examining Indonesia as a locus of global learning begins to answer Greg Bankoff's critique (2001, 2018) of "resilience" and "vulnerability" in contemporary disaster studies as stagist, neocolonial frameworks for recasting developmental concerns. It proposes working "along the fault line" to examine how Indonesia's disaster sites have generated diverse forms of knowledge about catastrophe, from deep time to the present day. Counter to Anthony Reid's (2013, 2015) contention that discontinuity must punctuate the past and future of an archipelago located along the Pacific Ring of Fire, this article argues that catastrophic events in Indonesia should not be principally understood as acute episodes triggering rupture and change, but also as occasions for tracing important continuities. These become evident when foregrounding the key preoccupation of the plural communities that have occupied and studied Indonesian sites of catastrophe: that is, how to *live with* disaster, not just survive it. This article provides an overview of new research from historians, geographers, and anthropologists on how that concern is evident in ancient oral traditions that inform current work on geomythology, in premodern Javanese and Balinese sources on time and power, in state and scientific attempts to mitigate disaster that bridge colonial and postcolonial regimes, and in contemporary religious practices in Indonesia.

Keywords: disaster, Indonesia, environment, disease

Susie Protschky is Associate Professor of History and an Australian Research Council Future Fellow at Deakin University (Melbourne, Australia). I am grateful to the anonymous reviewers and to Ruth Morgan for commenting on earlier versions of this article, the research for which was funded by an Australian Research Council Discovery Grant (DP170100948).

Our starting assumption in this issue is that disasters are "socionatural" phenomena, reflecting the entanglement of humans with their environments.[1] The Indonesian archipelago lies along one of the world's great subduction zones, with a population that has grown five-fold in the last two centuries and is increasingly susceptible to natural disasters as deforestation and climate change progress.[2] We seek to move beyond the established observation that the Indonesia's location on the Pacific Ring of Fire bestows a deep past and certain future of earthquakes, volcanic eruptions, and tsunamis that shape its culture as well as its geology and environment. Borrowing from the historical ethnographer Ann Laura Stoler's precept of following "along the grain" of archives, this article proposes working "along the fault line" to examine how Indonesia's disaster sites have generated diverse forms of knowledge about catastrophe, from deep time to the present day.

Stoler intended to outline a postcolonial methodology for attending to the "thickening" of colonial archives, their accumulation and activation around problems of governance in Indonesia, in order to identify the epistemic frames and ethnographic sites that produced forms of "common sense" around Indonesian "problems."[3] While several authors in this issue (Bobbette, Protschky, Meerwijk) explicitly examine colonial modes of disaster governance, the sources and time periods others cover range far beyond colonial chronologies and epistemologies. We investigate forms of knowledge generated at disaster sites—the loci of pandemics (Meerwijk, Millie, and Syarif) and Indonesia's volcanoes and subduction zones (Sastrawan, Bobbette, Zakaria, Protschky)— to demonstrate how such locations have generated not only theories of causation for and possible solutions to catastrophe, but more profoundly, disciplined understandings of past and future, power and agency, just rule and morality. We investigate forms of disaster-knowledge as frameworks not only for receiving but also *producing* knowledge that has shaped a range of responses: predicting immediate and long-term dangers, cultivating morality, propitiating cosmological forces out of balance, assisting victims, and legitimizing regimes.

While critical theorists have deployed the concept of "disaster speak" to understand how cultural scripts constrain the "possibilities for thought and exchange that might resolve social and environmental crisis,"[4] our approach of situating forms of knowledge along the fault lines of disasters in Indonesia grounds these scripts at the sites where they have arisen, in plural forms whose coexistence and intersection are yet to be elucidated. Over millennia, the existential threats posed by pandemics and tectonic disasters in Indonesia have impelled the explanatory powers of animistic folklore, Hindu and

---

[1] Phillip Drake, *Indonesia and the Politics of Disaster: Power and Representation in Indonesia's Mud Volcano* (New York: Routledge, 2016), 3; Greg Bankoff, "Under the Volcano: Mount Mayon and Co-Volcanic Societies in the Philippines," *Environment and History* 26 (2020): 7–29.

[2] Anthony Reid, "Population History in a Dangerous Environment: How Important May Natural Disasters Have Been?" *Masyarakat Indonesia* 39, no. 2 (2013): 507; Anthony Reid, "History and Seismology in the Ring of Fire: Punctuating the Indonesian Past," in *Environment, Trade and Society in Southeast Asia: A Longue Durée Perspective*, ed. David Henley and Henk Schulte Nordholt (Leiden: Brill, 2015), 68; Christopher Small and Terry Naumann, "The Global Distribution of Human Population and Recent Volcanism," *Environmental Hazards: Human and Policy Dimensions* 3 (2001): 95.

[3] Ann Laura Stoler, *Along the Archival Grain: Epistemic Anxieties and Colonial Common Sense* (Princeton: Princeton University Press, 2009), 3, 22, 35, 50–51.

[4] Drake, *Indonesia and the Politics of Disaster*, 10.

Buddhist cosmology, Islamic theology, colonial science and contemporary scholarship, and global systems of knowledge converging on Indonesian sites where problems of epidemiology, biology, and geology originate. It is along Indonesia's geological and metaphoric fault lines—in the earth's surface and between disciplines—where spiritual, governing, and scientific knowledges of local as well as foreign derivation have attracted, accrued, and congealed. Indonesian disaster sites are the contiguous field that have brought these accretions together. In this special issue, we therefore build new categories of location into Marieke Bloembergen's work on "sites of knowledge," which has broken fresh ground for understanding Indonesia's connectedness to global spiritual, intellectual, and population movements through its heritage sites.[5] To the spiritual geographies that traverse locations such as Borobudur, Prambanan, and the great mosque of Demak, the contributors to this volume add methodological and geological fault lines that cross: the villages of Java where colonial authorities tested technical solutions to bubonic plague (Meerwijck); the public situations in which Islamic organizations cultivate religious responses to contemporary disasters, including the COVID-19 pandemic (Millie and Syarif); and the volcanoes and other sites of tectonic tumult in Java, Sumatra, and Bali that host intersecting spiritual, scientific, and governing geographies (Sastrawan; Bobbette; Zakaria; Protschky).

To center Indonesia as the site of plural forms of disaster-knowledge is, on the one hand, to share with disaster studies the many decades of scholarship that positions Indonesia specifically, and perhaps Southeast Asia more generally, at the crossroads of civilizations: a place that has absorbed and recreated Indic and Islamic cultures, been colonized by Europeans and drawn into international capitalism, and defined the terms of its sovereignty and independence in the context of Cold War and global decolonization movements.[6] More than that, however, this volume seeks to address an international, interdisciplinary field of disaster studies that has only recently begun to grapple with the intellectual challenges of decolonization. Greg Bankoff, focusing on the Philippines, has posited that the central concern with "vulnerability" and "resilience" in postcolonial disaster scholarship—concepts arising in and after the Cold War transition from colonialism to developmentalism—revives stadial models of civilization and ascribes dependency to people living in disaster-prone places.[7] To center Indonesian sites of catastrophe is to answer the critique of disaster studies as stagist and neocolonial by positioning Indonesia as a locus of global learning.[8] To work along the fault lines of disaster in Indonesia illuminates the colonial genealogy of developmentalist

[5] Marieke Bloembergen, "New Spiritual Movements, Scholars, and 'Greater India' in Indonesia," in *Modern Times in Southeast Asia c. 1920s–1970s*, ed. Susie Protschky and Tom van den Berge (Brill: Leiden and Boston, 2018), 57–86. See also Marieke Bloembergen and Martijn Eickhoff, *The Politics of Heritage in Indonesia: A Cultural History* (Cambridge: Cambridge University Press, 2020), 3, where the authors discuss "a dual approach that is both site-centred and mobile" for understanding heritage formation in Indonesia.

[6] Jean Gelman Taylor, *Global Indonesia* (New York: Routledge, 2013); Jean Gelman Taylor, *Indonesia: Peoples and Histories* (New Haven, CT: Yale University Press, 2003).

[7] Gregory Bankoff, "Rendering the World Unsafe: 'Vulnerability' as Western Discourse," *Disasters* 15, no. 1 (2001): 19–35; Greg Bankoff, "Remaking the World in Our Own Image: Vulnerability, Resilience and Adaptation as Historical Discourses," *Disasters* 43, no. 2 (2018): 221–39; Greg Bankoff, "Blame, Responsibility and Agency: 'Disaster Justice' and the State in the Philippines," *Environment and Planning E: Nature and Space* 1, no. 3 (2018): 363–81.

[8] Adam Bobbette, Ruth Gamble, Cin-Ty Lee, and Christopher Wilson, "Decolonizing Geology: A Discussion," *GeoHumanities*, June 7, 2021, https://doi.org/10.1080/2373566X.2021.1896373.

concerns with vulnerability and resilience to disaster (Bobbette; Meerwijk; Protschky). It also elucidates much longer disaster histories—incorporating ancient stories that accumulated around the problems of living with catastrophe—that resonate now, in the contemporary scientific engagement with geomythology, an interdisciplinary field that recognizes how major geological events have been passed down orally and through ritual over thousands of years (Bobbette; Zakaria).[9]

This brings us to a further intervention of this special issue on disaster in Indonesia. Several authors here cast catastrophic events in Indonesian history not only as turning points but also as occasions for tracing important continuities. They do so by foregrounding the key preoccupations of those who have passed over and resided by Indonesian sites of catastrophe: how to *live with* disaster, not just survive it. Demographers have established that, globally, population density typically decreases with distance from volcanoes,[10] a telling insight into some of the benefits and opportunities that local populations perceive in a life lived along the fault line. The articles in this issue demonstrate how researching strategies for living with disaster— which includes recognizing the prospects that hazards herald, as well as the tragedies they signal—opens new views into major continuities in Indonesian history. In doing so, we query Anthony Reid's contention that, "in a zone as seismically active as Indonesia[,] we must expect history to be discontinuous."[11] The articles in this issue suggest that we must perhaps distinguish between, on the one hand, neoliberal uses of "resilience" in Disaster Risk Reduction (DRR) scholarship, where the term glosses measures of success at "development"[12] and, on the other hand, frameworks for accommodating disaster that are autochthonous to Indonesia. Far from arguing that Indonesia is surreptitiously located at the heart of all disaster histories, we suggest that centering place offers new views into disaster studies elsewhere and does more to push Western-centric, neoliberal discourses of disaster to the margins than theoretical work alone can accomplish.

Wayan Jarrah Sastrawan's opening contribution to this issue distills these themes in a critical survey of Indonesian sources over the past millennium of tectonic disasters. A historian of premodern Southeast Asia, Sastrawan sifts through Javanese and Balinese legal charters, calendars, divination manuals, royal chronicles, temple ruins, augury paintings, and the findings of archaeological research to show how local sources on disaster, from the ninth to nineteenth centuries, did not "simply consist of a factual core wrapped in layers of cultural meaning."[13] Rather, they reveal complex conceptions of political and spiritual power and its ambivalent workings in the world. Disasters augured bad harvests and disease and heralded new kings, but it would be simplistic

---

[9] Dorothy B. Vitaliano, "Geomythology: Geological Origins of Myths and Legends," in *Myth and Geology*, ed. Luigi Piccardi and W. Bruce Masse (London: Geological Society, 2007), 2; Patrick D. Nunn, Loredana Lancini, Leigh Franks, Rita Compatangelo-Soussignan, and Adrian McCallum, "Maar Stories: How Oral Traditions aid Understanding of Maar Volcanism and Associated Phenomena during Preliterate Times," *Annals of the American Association of Geographers* 109, no., 5 (2019): 1619, 1627.

[10] Christopher Small and Terry Naumann, "The Global Distribution of Human Population and Recent Volcanism," *Environmental Hazards: Human and Policy Dimensions* 3 (2001): 102, 104–5.

[11] Reid, "History and Seismology in the Ring of Fire," 77; Reid, "Population History in a Dangerous Environment," 507, 509.

[12] Reid, "History and Seismology," 507, 509.

[13] Wayan Jarrah Sastrawan, "Portents of Power: Natural Disasters throughout Indonesian History," *Indonesia* 113 (2022): X-X.

to interpret Javanese and Balinese notions of tectonic catastrophe merely as signs of discontinuity. Both Indic and Islamic conceptions of time normalized disasters as *predictable* components of life—even if the futures they heralded were uncertain—rather than as calamities that disrupted from beyond culture. Importantly, Sastrawan outlines a continuous labor of rebuilding and resuming after disaster in Java and Bali. Historical sensitivity to narratives of resilience in sources left by the communities that lived along the fault lines, he argues, may yet overturn some pervasive rupture narratives in Indonesian history, including the theory that royal power shifted from Central to East Java in the 930s CE because of a major eruption in the Merapi-Merbabu complex. The silence of written sources on this topic, together with the fact of Gunung Merapi's almost incessant eruption over two millennia, suggests that local populations had probably habituated to tectonic instability and that a single volcanic disaster may not have been the catalyst for geopolitical change after all.

Lest the reader settle comfortably into a millennial timeframe, Faizah Zakaria, also a historian, pushes the chronological boundaries of Indonesian life on the fault lines into the deep past, to the Toba super catastrophe that occurred 73,000 years ago. Her article explores how a tectonic rupture located in what is now Sumatra draws geomythology together with Cold War global nuclear and climate science. These two fields converged, in the twentieth century, to focus on the distribution and impact of particulate matter in the atmosphere. "[T]ools to model *future* nuclear winters helped us visualize a *past* Toba volcanic winter," producing interlocking spheres of science that "made past, present and future climate changes visible."[14] Zakaria demonstrates how a similar concept of disaster events as a "history of the future" emerged in the folklore that has accrued along the Toba fault line, in geomyths that recast "prehistory to promote values that could prevent future disaster."[15] The common thread linking recent and ancient stories of the Toba catastrophe is what Zakaria terms a thematics of "estrangement" between humans and nonhumans that has the potential to permanently remake a landscape. Her findings chime evocatively with the earthly and spiritual functions of historical time-keeping that Sastrawan argues disasters perform in Java and Bali. Zakaria develops the metaphor of Toba's "tremor" across space and time, which she gives a musical resonance, "the echo of a long past experience still audible in the form of a new one."[16] Music is perhaps more than a metaphor given, as Margaret Kartomi's research has shown, its profound and restorative power after the 2004 Indian Ocean tsunami among communities in the neighboring Sumatran province of Aceh.[17]

Picking up on the resonance of Indonesian geomyths in global science, Adam Bobbette's article takes us to Central Java, where Gunung Merapi, like Toba, has generated new forms of local as well as international knowledge. Bobbette is a geographer, and like Zakaria, he demonstrates how Indonesian locales of seismic catastrophe should in fact be recognized as global sites of learning. Using the framework of "processions" at Merapi

[14] Faizah Zakaria, "The Toba Super-Catastrophe as History of the Future," *Indonesia* 113 (2022): XX.

[15] Zakaria, "The Toba Super-Catastrophe," X.

[16] Zakaria, "The Toba Super-Catastrophe," X.

[17] Margaret Kartomi, "Toward a Methodology of War and Peace Studies in Ethnomusicology: The Case of Aceh, 1976–2009," *Ethnomusicology* 54, no. 3 (2010): 452–83; Margaret Kartomi, "Responses to Tsunami and War Trauma through the Musical Arts in Aceh, 2005–12," *Wacana Seni / Journal of Arts Discourse* 13 (2014): 2–28.

to bring scientific research and local Hindu, Buddhist, and Islamic spiritual geographies into a contiguous field, Bobbette reveals "how these spiritual infrastructures shaped and enabled scientific volcanology."[18] Colonial scientists and ethnographers observed with interest the Labuhan processions at Merapi in the nineteenth and twentieth centuries. They also relied on the ritual paths that locals trod for their own fieldwork and depended on the labor of Javanese guides, translators, and assistants. After Indonesian independence, Yogyakarta became the new hub for volcanological research, merging the "cosmic center of the *keraton*" with the axis of state efforts to sponsor science.[19] The global descendants of colonial volcanology have since developed a theory of plate tectonics at volcanic archipelagos that originated with connecting the Indian Ocean trench to Merapi's quakes and eruptions. That theory accords remarkably with an ancient, continuous Javanese cosmology linking the sacred volcano (via the sultan) with Nyai Ratu Kidul, the goddess of the Southern Sea. Bobbette's article raises the question of whether geomythology is really just geology's discovery of "culture," a post hoc attempt to integrate older forms of knowledge into "modern" science. Following along the fault line, Bobbette uncovers how a Central Javanese volcano was at the origin of a "new scientific narrative of lithospheric evolution and history" in the twentieth century, with older "roots in the ritual pathways and spiritual geographies of Merapi."[20]

Gunung Merapi is also central to other forms of knowledge about tectonic crises in Indonesia, as Susie Protschky demonstrates in her article on the development of colonial military praxis in disaster response. A historian, Protschky traces the shift in the mid-nineteenth century from a colonial army caught up in and reacting to local earthquakes and volcanic eruptions, while it was otherwise occupied with the violent subjugation of the Indonesian archipelago, to a military largely "done" with conquest by the early twentieth century and therefore prepared to launch more coordinated operations focusing on humanitarian assistance for Indonesian victims of disaster. At the end of the First World War, Dutch colonial authorities in Indonesia articulated a new will to divert military resources toward disaster, just in time for the Kelud eruption of 1919. However, the new policy was not fully expressed until the 1930 Merapi eruption. What accounts for the change in the intervening decade is the colonial state's investment in a military air force with the capacity for reconnaissance and remote operations, a venture taken in preparation for defending against the rising regional threat of Japan. Protschky argues that special attention to photographic sources, particularly the development of military aerial photography and its imbrication with aestheticized and scientific ways of seeing, provokes comparisons between colonial and post-independence governmentality on disasters in Indonesia as "'crises' requiring state control" and the humanitarian assistance they necessitate as veiling "state driven territorialization strategies."[21]

Maurits Meerwijk's historical research extends this special issue's investigation of colonial forms of knowledge about disaster in Indonesia toward new understandings

[18] Adam Bobbette, "Processions: How the Spiritual Geographies of Central Java Shaped Modern Volcano Science," *Indonesia* 113 (2022): XX.

[19] Bobbette, "Processions," XX.

[20] Bobbette, "Processions," XX.

[21] Christina Griffin, "The Dieng 'Hazardscape': A Political Ecology of Vulnerability to Natural Hazards in Java's Highlands," *Environmental Hazards* 18, no. 1 (2019): 38.

of "tropicality" as a medical trope with its origins in colonial forms of governance.[22] Moving from the physical fault lines and tectonic terrain of the other articles toward the tense metaphoric fault lines of public health debates, Meerwijk's article interrogates the biological disasters that, as COVID-19 has reminded us, periodically arise from human-animal relations. Particularly, he investigates colonial authorities' technical solutions for eradicating pandemic plague on Java, solutions that had the unexpected effect of exacerbating endemic malaria. The Dutch colonial government's major response to the Third Plague Pandemic, which hit East Java in 1911, was a large-scale program of *woningverbetering* (home improvement) to modify rural bamboo dwellings so that they were less accommodating to rats. In the process, they became more susceptible to mosquitoes. As with Protschky, following along the grain of colonial archives leads Meerwijk to a clearer view of the problems that preoccupied Dutch authorities in the early twentieth century and that preceded postcolonial developmentalist concepts of disaster-response. He demonstrates how the gap between the wide prevalence and mortality of malaria and its low prioritization in public health campaigns was forged by Dutch colonial authorities during competing crises. He also shows the stubborn endurance of the Dutch commitment to a technical fix for plague, one that persisted in the face of evidence that malaria was exacerbated by "home improvement" in rural areas, perhaps because this program was instrumental to "Dutch efforts to broadcast an image of modern and benign colonial governance."[23] Together, Protschky and Meerwijk demonstrate how global science and public health were grounded in colonial concepts of a volatile tropics prone to the aberrations of tropical disease (malaria) and landscapes (volcanic mountains). Their case studies demonstrate "the persistence of the environment as the decisive quality in determining the condition of danger posed by this 'other' world," the tropics.[24]

Finally, Julian Millie and Dede Syarif bring an interdisciplinary approach to understanding the role of public Islamic supplication practices in community responses to disaster in contemporary Indonesia. Millie, an anthropologist, and Syarif, a sociologist, attend to the "embodied and performative practices of religion" and examine how the COVID-19 pandemic has exposed the connection of "ritual practices and their desired efficacies to social and political fault lines within Indonesian society."[25] Focusing on two mass Islamic organizations, Muhammadiyah (f. 1912) and Nahdlatul Ulama (f. 1926)—respectively, the modernist and traditionalist segments of Indonesian Islam—they trace how the different theological positions of each bears on public disaster-response. Muhammadiyah eschews supplication in favor of reflective practices and secular, scientific, practical responses, preferably through the Disaster Management Centre it founded as a bridge between NGOs and Indonesian communities after the 2004 Indian Ocean Tsunami. Nahdlatul Ulama, by contrast, favors public, often large-scale

---

[22] David Arnold, *The Problem of Nature: Environment, Culture and European Expansion* (Oxford: Blackwell, 1996), 141–69; David Arnold, "'Illusory Riches': Representations of the Tropical World, 1840–1950," *Singapore Journal of Tropical Geography* 21, no. 1 (2000): 6–18; David Arnold, *The Tropics and the Traveling Gaze: India, Landscape, and Science 1800–1856* (Delhi: Permanent Black, 2005).

[23] Maurits Meerwijk, "Plague Rat or Anopheles: Health Disasters and Home Improvement in Late-Colonial Java," *Indonesia* 113 (2022): XX.

[24] Bankoff, "Rendering the World Unsafe," 28.

[25] Julian Millie and Dede Syarif, "The Public Politics of Supplication in a Time of Disaster," *Indonesia* 113 (2022): XX.

gatherings and prayer by distinguished people to seek divine intervention as well as communal introspection to mitigate further suffering. Some of these rituals have recently become enmeshed with public, civic ceremonies in the context of the current COVID-19 pandemic, despite the Indonesian government's official commitment to neutrality on sectarian issues. Millie and Syarif argue these developments follow from the popularization of politics, democratization of the public sphere, and increasing political mobilization of traditionalist Islam in recent decades.

In conclusion, Anthony Reid held, not so long ago, that "for Indonesia, everything remains to be done" in the realm of disaster studies.[26] The articles in this issue are just the tip of the volcano, to Indonesianize the English idiom, and to coin an analogy that is perhaps more suited than the iceberg to characterizing how scholarship builds upon scholarship, only to erupt occasionally and create new formations. We hope, with this special issue, to provoke more activity along the fault line.

This special issue of *Indonesia* is the first interdisciplinary undertaking of its kind, bringing together new research in history, anthropology, and geography on disaster in Indonesia.[27] The articles here arose from a workshop hosted at Monash University (Melbourne, Australia) in mid-2020. It was intended to be in-person, but we were fortunate to be able to quickly move it online in response to the COVID-19 pandemic. For us, as Indonesia scholars working around the world in the midst of a global pandemic that has been devastating for colleagues, students, friends, or family in Indonesia and elsewhere, disciplined thinking and interdisciplinary collaboration seems a more crucial response than ever to understanding and living with disaster.

[26] Reid, "History and seismology in the Ring of Fire," 65.

[27] There has been a recent interdisciplinary collection on disaster in Asia more broadly. See the introductory article by Chris Courtney and Fiona Williamson, "Disasters and the Making of Asian History," *Environment and History* 26 (2020): 1–5.

Portents of Power: Natural Disasters throughout Indonesian History

Wayan Jarrah Sastrawan

Abstract

The Indonesian archipelago plays a major role in the global history of natural disaster. Traditional sources can provide crucial insights into this history, but their full potential has yet to be realized. This paper investigates a diverse range of sources from Java and Bali, spanning the eighth to the twentieth centuries, to ascertain cultural attitudes to disasters, the impacts of disasters on society, and practices of recording disaster events. These sources include royal charters, historical chronicles, temple ruins, traditional paintings, and divination manuals. The paper finds that natural disasters were considered to be signs of power, broadly conceived to include political, spiritual, and natural power. Disasters were therefore closely associated with political change and divine activity. The impacts of disaster, while sometimes severe, were normalized in Indonesian society through practices of augury and tactics of resilience. The paper's culture-focused approach allows for more reliable interpretations of traditional records of specific disaster events, such as a major eruption of Bali's Agung volcano in 1710–11. It can therefore offer valuable insights into how natural disasters have shaped global history in the long term.

Keywords: disaster, Indonesia, power, volcano, earthquake, history

Postdoctoral Research Fellow, École française d'Extrême-Orient (DHARMA Project ERC n°809994). I acknowledge the help of Anthony Reid, Adrian Vickers, Susie Protschky, Arlo Griffiths, and the Sydney Quad intellectual history seminar.

Introduction

Natural disasters loom large in the history of Indonesia. The greatest global disasters of historical times originated in the archipelago: the 1257 Samalas eruption, the 1815 Tambora eruption, and the 2004 Indian Ocean tsunami. Recent advances in the scientific study of the region's tectonic past have raised new questions about how disasters interact with human history.[1] In addition to a scientific understanding of disasters, we want to know how people experienced them at different times and places in history.[2] This growing interest has led to renewed attention to the historical record for disaster in Indonesia. The long-term effects of natural disaster are reflected in a wide variety of textual and material sources from Java and Bali, from the eighth to the twentieth century. Of particular interest are the sources written in indigenous languages of the archipelago, which promise to shed light on disaster events that are not recorded European-language sources.[3]

Indonesian experiences of natural disaster were shaped by a pattern of cultural attitudes. Central among them was the belief that natural disasters were signs of the presence of power in the world. The physical force of natural disaster was intimately connected to other kinds of power, such as those of divine agency and of human politics. Since this power was a natural part of how the world operated, disaster events were considered a normal part of life, and they could be rendered intelligible through practices of augury and chronicle-writing. While the power of natural disasters could be destructive, they also provided opportunities for rebuilding and renewal. The available sources consistently reflect ambivalent attitudes toward the positive and negative social effects of disaster. These attitudes were expressed in a variety of ways in different eras of Indonesian history; for example, the adoption of Islam in early modern Java led to new understandings of the role of divine power in natural disasters. Nevertheless, there were significant continuities of thought and practice that informed Indonesian experiences of disaster over the long term.

This article examines an exceptionally broad range of historical sources that have rarely been tapped for information about natural disasters.[4] These sources from Java and Bali, dating from the eighth century onward, include dynastic chronicles, copperplate inscriptions, divination manuals, classical paintings, and archaeological finds. Drawing on this diverse material, I extend and add nuance to existing analyses of traditional Indonesian ideas about power, such as those of Benedict Anderson and Soemarsaid Moertono.[5] I follow

---

[1] Gillen D'Arcy Wood, *Tambora: The Eruption That Changed the World* (Princeton: Princeton University Press, 2014), 5.

[2] Such concerns are prominent in two important edited volumes on natural disaster history: Greg Bankoff and Joseph Christensen, eds., *Natural Hazards and Peoples in the Indian Ocean World* (New York: Palgrave Macmillan, 2016); Gerrit Jasper Schenk, ed., *Historical Disaster Experiences: Towards a Comparative and Transcultural History of Disasters Across Asia and Europe* (Cham: Springer, 2017).

[3] Anthony Reid, "Historical Evidence for Major Tsunamis in the Java Subduction Zone" (Asia Research Institute Working Paper Series 178, Singapore, Asia Research Institute, 2012); Anthony Reid, "Two Hitherto Unknown Indonesian Tsunamis of the Seventeenth Century: Probabilities and Context," *Journal of Southeast Asian Studies* 47, no. 1 (2016): 88–108; Anthony Reid, "Recognising Global Interdependence Through Disasters," in *Crossing Borders*, edited by M. Miller, M. Douglass, and M. Garschagen (Singapore: Springer, 2018), 23–40.

[4] I restrict my discussion to earthquakes and volcanic eruptions, since these are the types of disaster that appear most prominently in the indigenous historical record.

[5] Soemarsaid Moertono, *State and Statecraft in Old Java: A Study of the Later Mataram Period, 16th to 19th Century*, Modern Indonesia Project Monograph Series (Ithaca: Cornell University Press, 1968); Benedict R.

several key conceptual threads that formed a coherent yet dynamic pattern of cultural attitudes towards natural disaster over the centuries. It is only by properly understanding these attitudes that we can accurately interpret traditional Indonesian sources. This article thus offers new ways of engaging with these challenging but rewarding Indonesian sources that can contribute significantly to a global history of natural disaster.

I consider three overarching themes: cultural attitudes toward natural disaster, the impact of disasters on premodern societies, and practices of recording specific disaster events. First, I examine the central assumption about natural disasters that can be traced in Javanese sources back to the fourteenth century: that disasters are signs of the presence of power and, therefore, that they have ambivalent effects on the world. This assumption is reflected in chronicles of political history as well as in traditions of disaster augury. Second, I argue that the Javanese and Balinese considered natural disasters and their impacts to be a normal part of life. The inscriptional and archaeological record of Central Java, when read in conjunction with stratigraphic data, shows a society that was able to manage the risks and harms of geophysical disaster. Finally, I discuss how to interpret the handful of Javanese and Balinese chronicles that give information about specific disaster events. The indigenous record can offer rich insights into experience of natural disaster, as illustrated by a unique Balinese source on a little-known eruption of Mount Agung in 1710–11. But working with these indigenous sources can be challenging, because they often construe disaster in ways that are unfamiliar to the professional discipline of history. So before proceeding with an examination of these sources on natural disaster, I briefly consider the methodological issues that they pose.

The Challenges of Traditional Indonesian Sources

It can be difficult to work with traditional Javanese and Balinese sources on natural disasters. Most of the texts are written in literary Javanese and Balinese, languages that require specialist training for many present-day readers.[6] The vast majority of them remain unpublished. Even among those Indonesian accounts of disaster that are readily available, it is extremely rare to find sources written before the twentieth century that are both rich in detail and were written soon after the events they describe. The extant primary sources of precolonial times rarely mention disaster events, and most of the surviving indigenous records of disaster were written decades or centuries after

---

O'G. Anderson, *Language and Power: Exploring Political Cultures in Indonesia* (Ithaca: Cornell University Press, 1990).

[6] I draw on textual sources written in several literary languages: Old and Modern Javanese, Classical Malay, and Modern Balinese. I present these texts in transcription into Latin script, in line with the following conventions: for Old Javanese, the *DHARMA Transliteration Guide* (version 3); for Modern Javanese, the *Pedoman Umum Ejaan Bahasa Jawa Huruf Latin Yang Disempurnakan* (rev. ed.); for Classical Malay, the *Pedoman Umum Ejaan Bahasa Indonesia* (4th ed.); and for Modern Balinese, the *Pedoman Umum Ejaan Bahasa Bali*. In quotations of verse texts, single slashes indicate line breaks and double slashes indicate stanza breaks. I indicate the language of the quotation in square brackets, and all English translations of these quotations are my own. Dániel Balogh and Arlo Griffiths, "DHARMA Transliteration Guide," 2020, accessed April 7, 2021, https://hal.archives-ouvertes.fr/halshs-02272407v3; Tim Pengembang Pedoman Bahasa Indonesia, *Pedoman Umum Ejaan Bahasa Indonesia*, 4th ed. (Jakarta: Badan Pengembangan dan Pembinaan Bahasa, Kementerian Pendidikan dan Kebudayaan, 2016); Balai Bahasa Yogyakarta, *Pedoman Umum Ejaan Bahasa Jawa Huruf Latin Yang Disempurnakan* (Yogyakarta: Penerbit Kanisius, 2006); Ida Ayu Mirah Purwiati, Ni Putu Ekatini Negari, and I Wayan Sudiartha, *Pedoman Umum Ejaan Bahasa Bali Dengan Huruf Bali Dengan Huruf Latin* (Denpasar: Balai Bahasa Provinsi Bali, 2013).

the events they describe. Such sources emerged out of complex textual traditions, which means they cannot be treated as firsthand reports on disaster events.[7] Surviving Indonesian manuscripts are almost always the result of many rounds of recopying and recompilation, which must be taken into account when they are mined for historical information.

These sources are not mere repositories of chronological data that can be straightforwardly correlated with scientific findings. Rather, they express the culturally inflected experiences of Javanese and Balinese people as they coped with and responded to disaster. Anthony Reid has warned against simplistic approaches to disaster history that are "out of touch with new research in history, typically reliant on colonial-era compilations and on naively literal translations of texts."[8] By understanding Javanese and Balinese experiences of disaster on their own conceptual terms, we gain richer insights into the role of disaster in Indonesian history.

Traditional sources on natural disaster do not simply consist of a factual core wrapped in layers of cultural meaning. Rather, cultural assumptions are present even in the basic construal and description of disaster experiences in the sources. It is particularly crucial to be aware of this when applying professional historical methods to sources produced in premodern contexts. For a fourteenth-century Javanese chronicler, the 1334 eruption of Mount Kelud was both a real event that destroyed human life and also a sign of the future majesty of a newborn prince. The distinction between historical fact and mythological perception is one that is imposed by the historian's analysis; it is absent in the sources as they were originally produced. It is therefore more fruitful to treat these sources as expressions of people's attitudes toward and experiences of disaster, rather than trying to peel away mythological perceptions from a putative factual core.[9] It is by properly understanding the cultural attitudes that shaped these sources that we can successfully use them as evidence for historical disaster events.

Disasters and the Presence of Power

Indonesian cultural attitudes toward natural disaster were complex, but a key theme can be discerned from sources that span many centuries. Indonesian people have long considered natural disasters to be signs of the presence of power in the world. Such power is not limited to physical forces of the earth, but also includes what we

---

[7] This applies to such sources as the *Babad Lombok* and the *Babad Suwung*, which have been studied in connection to the 1257 Samalas eruption on Lombok. As argued by Mutaqin and Lavigne, the information given in these texts "is not completely original but derived from other sources that are lost." These texts are the product of oral and written transmission, by which they "were compiled, rewritten, and restructured" over centuries. They therefore cannot be read as firsthand eyewitness accounts, but nevertheless, they are very useful as records of collective memories about the impacts of a major volcanic eruption. Bachtiar W. Mutaqin and Franck Lavigne, "Oldest Description of a Caldera-Forming Eruption in Southeast Asia Unveiled in Forgotten Written Sources," *GeoJournal* 86, no. 2 (2019): 557–66.

[8] Reid, "Two Hitherto Unknown Indonesian Tsunamis of the Seventeenth Century," 89.

[9] This interpretive issue is frequently addressed in the scholarship on traditional Indonesian sources. See, for example, Adrian Vickers, "Balinese Texts and Historiography," *History and Theory* 29, no. 2 (1990): 158–78; Nancy Florida, *Writing the Past, Inscribing the Future: History as Prophecy in Colonial Java* (Durham: Duke University Press, 1995), 392–406; Henri Chambert-Loir, "The *Sulalat al-Salatin* as a Political Myth," *Indonesia* 79 (2005): 131–60; Husni Abu Bakar, "Playing Along the Perak River: Readings of an Eighteenth-Century Malay State," *Southeast Asian Studies* 4, no. 1 (2015): 157–90.

could consider political power and spiritual power. The Javanese and Balinese drew connections between disasters, political change, and divine activity because they were all manifestations of the same underlying power. The eighteenth-century Javanese poem "Wiwaha Jarwa," itself a rewriting of the eleventh-century "Arjunavivāha," describes this as "the power of the heart that blazes in the world."[10] This idea of power is found in several different periods of history, though it changed dynamically to suit a variety of cultural and religious contexts. The Javanese theorizations of power studied by Benedict Anderson, largely on the basis of sources written after 1800, may therefore represent relatively recent expressions of much older attitudes.

In Javanese historical narratives, the rise of a powerful new leader was associated with a variety of natural phenomena, such as earthquakes, eruptions, and major weather events. These phenomena did not reflect negatively on this leader's influence, and they were not necessarily considered bad omens. Rather, they signified that power was shifting away from an old order that had lost its luster toward a new focal point. For example, the chronicle *Deśavarṇana* (completed in 1365) describes the birth of the king Hayam Wuruk:

> It is said that, at his birth in Śaka seasons–arrows–sun [1256],[11] the king was already confirmed as the sovereign.

> As a child prince, he was the lord at Kahuripan; the portents that he is a prodigious person were

> Rumbling earthquakes, ash rain, thunder and lightning twisting in the sky.

> Mount Kampud erupted.[12] The criminals and traitors wailed, choking to death.[13]

The disasters are signs that the king is a "prodigious person." The notion of a prodigy (*adbhuta*), which also connotes an "omen in nature,"[14] includes what we would consider positive and negative aspects. In Old Javanese literature, *adbhuta* can mean "wonderful" and "marvelous," but also "terrifying" and "monstrous."[15] The harmful effects of disaster

---

[10] *sektining tyas prabawaning rat* (canto 27, stanza 19) [Modern Javanese]. Bernard Arps, "The Power of the Heart That Blazes in the World: An Islamic Theory of Religions in Early Modern Java," *Indonesia and the Malay World* 47, no. 139 (2019): 325.

[11] There is a seventy-eight-year difference between the Śaka Era and the Common Era, but since the lunisolar Śaka calendar begins around the March equinox, there is a further two-and-a-half-month lag between the two. In this example, the Śaka year 1256 ran from March 1334 to March 1335 CE. In this article, Western dates before 1582 CE are given as Julian dates, and those after 1582 CE are given as Gregorian dates.

[12] Kampud is most likely an archaic name for the present-day Kelud, a very active volcano in East Java. This hypothesis was first proposed in 1919 by P.V. van Stein Callenfels, based on references to Kampud in the fifteenth-century prose text *Tantu Panggelaran*. Further toponymic information from the Old Sundanese *Bujangga Manik*, which also dates from the fifteenth century, confirms the identification of Kampud with today's Kelud. *Oudheidkundige Dienst in Nederlandsch-Indië: Oudheidkundig Verslag 1919* (Weltevreden: Albrecht & Co., 1919), 11–2; J. Noorduyn, "Bujangga Manik's Journey through Java: Topographical Data from an Old Sundanese Source," *Bijdragen Tot de Taal-, Land- En Volkenkunde* 138, no. 4 (1982): 430–1.

[13] *riṅ śāka r̥tu śarena rakva ri vijil nr̥pati təlas inastvakən prabhū / an garbheśvara nātha riṅ kahuripan vihaganiran amānuṣādbhuta / liṇduṅ bhūmi kətug hudan havu gərəh kilat avilətan iṅ nabhastala / guntur taṅ himavān ri kāmpud ananāṅ kujana kuhaka māti tan pagap* (canto 1, stanza 4) [Old Javanese]. Th. G. Th. Pigeaud, *Java in the Fourteenth Century: A Study in Cultural History* (The Hague: Martinus Nijhoff, 1960), 1:3.

[14] David Pingree, *Jyotiḥśāstra: Astral and Mathematical Literature*, A History of Indian Literature, vol. 7, fasc. 4 (Wiesbaden: Otto Harrassowitz, 1981), 67.

[15] P. J. Zoetmulder, *Old Javanese-English Dictionary* ('s-Gravenhage: M. Nijhoff, 1982), s.v. "adbhuta."

are emphasized in this passage, but it is notable that the victims here are not innocent bystanders but "criminals and traitors." This is in keeping with the chronicler's depiction of Hayam Wuruk as imposing discipline on the kingdom: "every single evildoer ceased to be foolish, utterly afraid of the king's valor."[16] The king's power thus expresses itself in the natural disasters that accompanied his prodigious birth.

The association of royal power with natural disaster in Java continued well into the Islamic period. A version of the Javanese dynastic genealogy *Babad Tanah Jawi*, compiled in Surakarta in 1836 out of older materials, describes the natural disasters that accompanied the military victory of Senapati, who became a powerful king in Mataram in the late sixteenth century:

> Then the wind rustled
>
> And lighting shot through the sky
>
> Trees snapped and collapsed
>
> As the storm cut them down
>
> Then came the thundering rain mixed with wind
>
> A sign that *jinns* had come
>
> Immediately there were shrieks in the air
>
> It sounded like the sky was being torn apart
>
> Like the whole mountain was erupting
>
> Everything roared loudly
>
> The depths of Mount Merapi
>
> Echoed and cracked
>
> The crater thundered
>
> Ash rain fell
>
> Boulders and pebbles rolled down
>
> Volcanic mudslides flowed
>
> It is said there were many huge rocks
>
> With volcanic mud in the river Opak
>
> Flowing down.[17]

---

[16] *həntyaṅ durjana mary ābuddhi kala kevala matakut i vīrya saṅ prabhu* (canto 1, stanza 5) [Old Javanese]. Pigeaud, *Java in the Fourteenth Century*, 1:4.

[17] *nulya umyus mesat ing langit / bayu-bajra narajang / sempal kayu erug / pracandhanya amarapal / prapta udan kumerug awor lan angin / pratandha yèn jin prapta // tan antara surak anèng langit / gurnitanya kadi langit rebah / kadya gunung guntur kabèh / prakatha padha umung / antaraning wukir marapi / nauri nulya bengkah / kawah gumaludhug / udan awu ingkang prapta / gumalundhung watu wadhas [padhas] lan karikil / longsor ladhu lumampah // watu ageng kathah kang winarni / sareng ladhu anèng kali umpak / angili ngisor parané* (canto 39, stanzas 25–27) [Modern Javanese]. *Babad Tanah Djawi* (Batavia: Balai Pustaka, 1939–1941), 5:68–69, accessed April 7, 2021, https://www.sastra.org/kisah-cerita-dan-kronikal/babad-tanah-jawi/1014-babad-tanah-jawi-balai-pustaka-1938-41-1024-jilid-05.

Here too the disaster is seen as a sign (*pratandha*) of the presence of power. But there are important differences in the ways that these two sources depict power. Whereas the *Deśavarṇana* attributes divine power to the king's own person, the *Babad Tanah Jawi* externalizes that power to the *jinn*s. This is related to the fact that the *Deśavarṇana* was written by a Buddhist scholar, while the *Babad Tanah Jawi* was the product of an Islamic royal court. In the religious environment of fourteenth-century Java, it was acceptable to attribute aspects of divine power (*śakti*) to living humans like the monarch. For instance, the *Deśavarṇana* speaks of a previous Javanese king's conquest of territory in Sumatra as being "the result of his divine incarnation."[18]

Once Islam became the dominant religion in Java in the sixteenth century, it was more problematic to directly associate humans with divine power. The Islamic doctrine of God's transcendence, and the absolute distinction between Creator and Creation, is emphasized in a Javanese treatise of the late sixteenth century, *The Admonitions of Seh Bari*: "The attributes of the Lord are not like the attributes of created beings, and the attributes of created beings are not like the attributes of the Lord."[19] The notion of a king having a "divine incarnation" (*devamūrti*) would have been heretical to the orthodox author of *The Admonitions*. But Javanese Islam has always been diverse, and it could accommodate different ways of construing the association between human politics and divine power. The notion of natural disaster as a sign of the presence of power in the world is a consistent thread running through the pre-Islamic and Islamic periods of Javanese history. Despite the five-hundred-year gap between them, both the *Deśavarṇana* and the *Babad Tanah Jawi* depict natural disasters and political change as interconnected consequences of the presence of power in the world.

The theme of political change has been studied closely by scholars of Javanese cultural history. Benedict Anderson argued that the Javanese conceived of power as a fluid entity, capable of concentration and dissipation.[20] Soemarsaid Moertono elucidated the term *wahyu* ("the substance of great power"), which was visualized in Javanese texts as a streaking light in the sky that marked an individual's destiny to become a powerful ruler.[21] The downfall of an old king meant the transfer of power to a new challenger, and therefore, it was accompanied by disasters signifying that change.[22] For instance, an eruption of Kelud in 1811 was seen by Javanese people as presaging the British invasion of Java. Similarly, a series of eruptions and earthquakes of Merapi in the years 1822–25 were interpreted as a portent of brewing unrest that eventually led to the Java War (1825–30).[23] The 1901 eruption of Kelud was later interpreted as a portent of the greatness of Indonesia's first president

---

[18] *saṅka ri kadevamūrtinira* (canto 41, stanza 5) [Old Javanese]. Pigeaud, *Java in the Fourteenth Century*, I: 31.

[19] *tegesé sifat ing pangèran tan kadi sifat ing makluk, sifat ing makluk tan kadi sifat ing pangèran* [Early Modern Javanese]. G. W. J. Drewes, *The Admonitions of Seh Bari: A 16th-Century Javanese Muslim Text Attributed to the Saint of Bonang*, Bibliotecha Indonesica 4 (Leiden: KITLV Press, 1969), 46.

[20] Anderson, *Language and Power*, 19–23.

[21] Moertono, *State and Statecraft in Old Java: A Study of the Later Mataram Period, 16th to 19th Century*, Modern Indonesia Project Monograph Series (Ithaca: Cornell University Press, 1968), 56.

[22] Moertono, *State and Statecraft in Old Java*, 74.

[23] Peter Carey, *The Power of Prophecy: Prince Dipanegara and the End of the Old Order in Java, 1755–1855*, Verhandelingen van het Koninklijk Instituut voor Taal-, Land- en Volkenkunde 249 (Leiden: KITLV Press, 2007), 515.

Sukarno, who was born in the same year.[24] In all of these Javanese texts and traditions, disaster indicated the arrival of a new power, in tandem with the dissipation of an old one. This connection between natural disaster and political change existed because both were consequences of the presence of power itself, blazing in the world.

The Ambivalence of Disaster Augury

This cultural attitude is also reflected in Javanese and Balinese practices of augury; that is, the interpretation of natural phenomena as signs to predict the future. The basis of disaster augury is the assumption that disasters indicate the presence of power and that power brings about certain characteristic outcomes. Hints of this practice appear in the description of Hayam Wuruk's birth discussed above, in the use of the term "portent" (*vihaga*). This Sanskrit loanword has the literal meaning of "sky-goer," i.e., "bird." The link between birds and augury is known in many cultures, including Indian traditions in which the term *śakuna*, "bird," similarly refers to omens in nature.[25] The chronicler's use of augury terms like "prodigy" (*adbhuta*) and "portent" (*vihaga*) suggests that the idea of natural disasters as portents may have been familiar to fourteenth-century readers.[26]

Disaster augury in Java and Bali generally involves earthquakes rather than volcanic eruptions. This preference may reflect the influence of Indian disaster augury, which only concerns earthquakes since there are no active volcanoes on the subcontinent. Between the eleventh and fifteenth centuries, Javanese inscriptions use the term "circle" (*maṇḍala*) to refer to the cardinal directions and their presiding deities.[27] The term *maṇḍala* is associated with earthquake augury in the Sanskrit divination treatises *Gargasaṁhitā* and *Bṛhatsaṁhitā*.[28] It is therefore quite possible that these or similar texts were known in Java at an early time.[29] Tenth-century Javanese texts like the *Brahmāṇḍapurāṇa* and *Agastyaparva* reveal a general familiarity with Indic traditions of divination and astrology, though they do not explicitly mention earthquake augury.[30] Later Balinese divinatory tradition traces its origins, via Java, to the legendary Indian sage Garga.[31] This circumstantial evidence

---

[24] Bob Hering, "Soekarno: The Man and the Myth: Looking through a Glass Darkly," *Modern Asian Studies* 26 (1993): 496.

[25] Pingree, *Jyotiḥśāstra*, 67–80.

[26] To my knowledge, the implications of this passage for early Javanese augury practices has not yet been explored by scholars.

[27] J. G. de Casparis, *Indonesian Chronology*, Handbuch Der Orientalistik 1 (Leiden: E. J. Brill, 1978), 21.

[28] Amrit Gomperts, "Sanskrit Jyotiṣa Terms and Indian Astronomy in Old Javanese Inscriptions," in *Fruits of Inspiration: Studies in Honour of Prof. J. G. de Casparis, Retired Professor of the Early History and Archeology of South and Southeast Asia at the University of Leiden, the Netherlands, on the Occasion of His 85th Birthday*, ed. M. J. Klokke and KR. van Kooij, Gonda Indological Studies 11 (Groningen: Egbert Forsten, 2001), 105–7; Audrius Beinorius, "Tracing the Will of the Stars: Indian Astrology and Divination About Natural Disasters and Threats," in *Historical Disaster Experiences: Towards a Comparative and Transcultural History of Disasters across Asia and Europe*, ed. Gerrit Jasper Schenk (Cham: Springer, 2017), 226–28.

[29] Gomperts, "Indian Astronomy in Old Javanese Inscriptions," 119–21.

[30] Jan Gonda, ed., *Het Oud-Javaansche Brahmāṇḍa-Purāṇa: proza-tekst en kakawin*, Bibliotheca Javanica 5 (Bandoeng: Nix & Co., 1933), 167–80; J. Gonda, "Agastyaparwa: Een Oud-Javaansch Proze-Geschrift," *Bijdragen Tot de Taal-, Land- En Volkenkunde van Nederlandsch Indië* 90 (1933): 349–51.

[31] Peter Wilhelm Pink, *Wariga: Beiträge Zur Balinesischen Divinationsliteratur*, Veröffentlichungen Des Seminars Für Indonesische Und Südseesprachen Der Universität Hamburg 13 (Berlin: Dietrich Reimer Verlag, 1993), 422, 453.

raises the possibility that earthquake augury, as prescribed in the Sanskrit treatises, may once have been practiced in pre-Islamic Java.

When we move into the early modern period, there is more extensive evidence for the practice of earthquake augury. Methods for interpreting earthquakes are explained in handbooks called *palindon* in Javanese and Balinese, and *takbir gempa* in Malay, which work by correlating the timing of earthquakes to a particular calendar cycle. The outcomes predicted by this system of augury are not the direct consequences of the disaster. Rather, the timing of disasters allows for the prediction of future outcomes, both positive and negative. While disasters could cause severe harm to life and property, they could equally presage good outcomes: the birth of a just king or a prosperous harvest season. For example, a Malay *takbir* text copied in 1833 in Tegal, North Java, explains:

> And again, if there is an earthquake in the year Zāi and the month Ramadan, so it is a sign that prosperity will be easy and there will be happiness in that year. And again, if there is an earthquake in the year Zāi and the month Syawal, so it is a sign that there will be hard strife, and disease will be severe, and there will be powerful demons in that year.[32]

Early nineteenth-century Javanese *palindon* texts from Yogyakarta and the Merapi-Merbabu mountains present a similar system, with an added distinction between day and night:

> If there is an earthquake in the month Rabī' al-'Ākhir in the day, it is a sign that many people will die in the state; if in the night, it is a sign that much water will emerge.[33]

Balinese *palindon* texts give interpretations for earthquakes that occur on particular weekdays. For example, a divination handbook in verse (*wariga matembang*) copied in 1940 gives:

> If there is an earthquake on a Saturday, much disease and death will come, the world will be in dearth, it will [be] hard to combat sickness.[34]

Earthquake augury is also represented in Balinese paintings, as an illustrated grid corresponding to the months in which earthquakes occur. These paintings associate each of the twelve Indic months with a particular god and give a brief description of

---

[32] *dan lagi jika lindu pada tahun zāi dan bulan ramadan, maka adalah alamatnya itu rezeki murah dan lagi sukacita adanya dalam tahun itu adanya; dan lagi jika lindu pada tahun zāi dan bulan syawal, maka adalah akan alamatnya itu fitnah akan keras dan penyakit akan sangat dan syaitan terlalu keras adanya dalam tahun itu* [Classical Malay]. Surianiah binti Pakih, "Manuskrip 'Ta`bir Mimpi': Analisis Dan Transliterasi Teks" (Kuala Lumpur, Universiti Malaya, 1993), 75.

[33] *lamun lindhu ing wulan rabengulakir ing rahina lamat akèh wong mati ing negara iku; lamun lindhu ing wengi lamat [pa]ḍa metu banyuné* [Modern Javanese]. This wording is found in the manuscript L 328 (Box 29) from the Merapi-Merbabu region, held in the National Library of Indonesia. I have standardized its distinctive spelling. Ghis Nggar Dwiadmojo, "Koneksi Pusat Dan Pinggiran: Perbandingan Teks Primbon Palindon Kraton Yogyakarta Dan Palilindon Merapi-Merbabu," *Jumantara: Jurnal Manuskrip Nusantara* 11, no. 1 (2020): 28.

[34] *lamun linuh ring śori, sasab mrana akéh rauh, jagaté kamranan, éweh ngarepin panyakit* (f. 19r) [Modern Balinese]. *Wariga Matembang* (manuscript), copied by I Ketut Warta of Toya Mumbul, January 8, 1940, accessed March 15, 2021, https://palmleaf.org/wiki/gaguritan-wariga-02.

the event that are augured by an earthquake in that month. The ceiling of the Kṛta Ghoṣa pavilion in Klungkung, painted in the mid-twentieth century by the artist Pan Seken and his assistants, contains a *palindon* illustration with text corresponding to each month (Figure 1). For example, an earthquake in the second month is associated with the goddess Gaṅgā:

Figure 1a and 1b: Two panels from the ceiling of the Kṛta Ghoṣa depicting the prosperity (panel a) that is presaged by the occurrence of an earthquake in the second month, due to the yogic practice of the goddess Gaṅgā (panel b) (photographs courtesy of Adrian Vickers).

The second month, bhaṭārī Gaṅgā is practising yoga, the world is well, all outcomes are achieved, everything is cheap.[35]

Adrian Vickers described the illustration accompanying this month's entry:

> The fruit-picking continues, accompanied by scenes of flirtatious dancing and a prince blessing one of his followers. . . . In the second month there is abundance, a surplus to be used for the god's and the *raja*'s public storehouse, the *gobarāja*. The close relationship between the rice farming of the Sudra [commoners] and the wealth of the raja is present in the juxtaposition of the image of a prince with farmers planting and tilling the soil.[36]

These examples show that, despite differences in language and religious context, the practice of earthquake augury in Java and Bali shared many commonalities. All of these augury systems are based on a twelve-month calendar of either Indic or Islamic origin, though they sometimes make extra specifications of the year, day, or time of day. They predict similar kinds of outcomes, such as political strife, drought, famine, and disease. It is risky to extrapolate back in time from these nineteenth- and twentieth-century materials. Without explicit sources from earlier periods, we cannot determine to what extent the specifics of augury practices may have changed and developed over the centuries. However, the commonalities among these texts make it at least plausible that earthquake augury has old roots in Indonesia, potentially going back to pre-Islamic Java.

Augury practices highlight some important features of Indonesian experiences of earthquakes. They were ambivalent phenomena, presaging both positive and negative outcomes depending on their timing. An earthquake in itself was not considered to be the ultimate cause of each month's outcomes. The Balinese tradition makes it clear that the earthquakes merely indicate the presence of divine agency, which is attributed to specific deities by means of the calendar cycle. This divine power was the ultimate cause of the positive and negative impacts that are summarized in the augury systems. As Vickers argued, "[e]vents, good and bad, are indirect manifestations of divine power working in the world, and are not related to intentions."[37] By treating disasters not as freak events that occurred at random, but rather as interpretable signs of power whose effects were predictable, the Javanese and Balinese may have been attempting to normalize the impacts of those disasters.

The Impacts of Disaster in Early Java

I now turn to a consideration of the impacts of natural disaster on premodern society in Java. Modern historians have tended to emphasize, and occasionally to overstate, the damaging impacts on society that such disasters caused. Though they took disasters seriously, the Javanese traditionally viewed these events as a normal part of life rather than as exceptional calamities. As Greg Bankoff observed in the Philippines, the

---

[35] *śaśih ka 2, bhaṭārī Gaṅgā sira mayoga, rahayunya ikang rat, sarwa phala dadi, sarwa murah* [Modern Balinese]. This text appears directly to the left of the figure of Gaṅgā in Figure 1b. Adrian Vickers, "Kṛta Ghoṣa, the Ordered Realm: A Study in Balinese Narrative Art" (Bachelor of Arts Honours thesis, University of Sydney, 1979), 179n25.

[36] Vickers, "Kṛta Ghoṣa, the Ordered Realm," 169.

[37] Adrian Vickers, *Balinese Art: Paintings and Drawings of Bali, 1800–2010* (Tokyo: Tuttle Publishing, 2012), 65.

frequency of natural disaster has seen them "integrated into the schema of daily life to form what can be called *cultures of disaster*."[38] While it is undeniable that disasters could cause great harm, early Javanese society appears to have been resilient to their effects, rather than being profoundly destabilized by them. Inscriptions and archaeological traces between the tenth and fifteenth centuries provide evidence of the damage caused to property, as well as successful efforts to rebuild and recover from them.

The early Javanese state sought to protect the property rights of individuals and families in the event of disaster. An inscription issued in 907 commanded the village of Rukam to do service for a religious foundation, "because the *sīma* of *rakryān* Sañjīvana, the king's grandmother, was lost in an eruption."[39] The term *sīma* refers to a piece of land whose fiscal revenues and labor obligations are diverted to a particular beneficiary. The destruction of that productive land in the eruption had resulted in a loss of income and labor for Sañjīvana. As compensation for this, the inscription authorized her to claim the village of Rukam and its labor as a benefice. The recently discovered Warunggahan inscription (issued in 1305) describes the loss of a land title document in an earthquake:

> That was the charter lost at the time of the earthquake, which was the reason that the offspring of *pāduka mpungku* Śrī Buddhaketu were sorrowful and did not know what to do. For the benefits of the *sīma* were not secure when the offspring of *pāduka* mpungku Śrī Buddhaketu were coming of age, due to the lack of a charter.[40]

To protect the entitlements of Buddhaketu's heirs, the king issued the Warunggahan charter as a replacement for the one that had been lost in the earthquake. This decision shows that the Javanese legal system was able to mitigate the disruption to property rights caused by disasters.

Pragmatic responses to the impact of disaster is also apparent in the archaeological record. Temple sites affected by disasters exhibit signs of rebuilding and repair, which suggests that their destructive effects could be mitigated. Several shrines (*candi*) in Central Java were covered by volcanic material after their construction.[41] The volcanic deposits that engulfed *candi* Simbisari and *candi* Kedulan are considerably younger (circa thirteenth century) than the estimated period of the shrines' construction (circa ninth century).[42] The absence of volcanic deposits in the intervening four-hundred-year period suggests an ongoing occupation and maintenance of these temple sites, including

---

[38] Greg Bankoff, *Cultures of Disaster: Society and Natural Disaster in the Philippine*s (London: RoutledgeCurzon, 2003), 4.

[39] *saṅka yan hilaṅ deniṅ tuntur* [*recte guntur*] *sīmān rakryān sañjīvana nini haji* (1r.2) [Old Javanese]. The text is a normalized transcription of a reading by Arlo Griffiths and me, to be published as part of a digital corpus of Javanese epigraphy supported by the DHARMA project (European Research Council Synergy Grant Project n°809994).

[40] *ika taṅ praśasti hilaṅ ri kālaniṅ bhūmikampa, nimittani vka pāduka mpuṅku śrī buddhaketu, anśoka tan vriṅ gatya apan tan apagǝh ri kabhuktyaniṅ sīma ri hidǝmni vka pāduka mpuṅku śrī buddhaketu, iniriṅ de samasānak ri tan hananiṅ praśasti* (3v.1–3) [Old Javanese]. I have normalized the text published by Goenawan A. Sambodo, "Prasasti Waruṅgahan: Sebuah Data Baru Dari Masa Awal Majapahit," *Amerta: Jurnal Penelitian and Pengembangan Arkeologi* 36, no. 1 (2018): 25.

[41] Indung Putra et al., "Candi Kimpulan (Central Java, Indonesia) Architecture and Consecration Rituals of a 9th-Century Hindu temple," *Bulletin de l'École française d'Extrême-Orient* 105 (2019): 94.

[42] C. G. Newhall et al., "10,000 Years of Explosive Eruptions of Merapi Volcano, Central Java: Archaeological and Modern Implications," *Journal of Volcanology and Geothermal Research* 100, no. 1–4 (2000): 45.

the cleaning out of fallen ash, until the thirteenth century. Rather than immediately abandoning temple sites that were affected by volcanic eruptions, the Javanese seem to have gone to considerable lengths to remove volcanic material.

Candi Liangan, a temple site on the northeastern slope of the Sindoro volcano, exhibits evidence of rebuilding after structural damage. This site was discovered in 2008 buried under several meters of volcanic deposits. The presence of burned organic materials strongly suggests a major pyroclastic flow that buried the entire temple.[43] But beneath this layer, the retaining wall on the southern part of the site exhibits a heterogeneous arrangement of stones, as well as reuse of several stone blocks. This appearance contrasts with the polished construction of the other retaining walls, which raises the possibility "that the site was partially destroyed—due to a *lahar* or a landslide—while it was still in use and that it was repaired with the means available."[44] These early efforts at rebuilding may have been thwarted by the major pyroclastic events that ultimately buried the site, though a full account of the site's history must await a proper stratigraphic analysis.

I have emphasized here the capacity of early Javanese society to respond pragmatically to the impacts of natural disaster. This historical trend accords well with Michael Dove's observations of present-day communities living on the slopes of Javanese volcanoes, who see eruptions as "routinized catalysts for productive change," thereby "naturalizing, familiarizing, and 'domesticating' the threat from the volcano."[45] I am not seeking to downplay the great harm that earthquakes and volcanic eruptions could cause, but I am suggesting that they did not necessarily cause a fundamental destabilization of Javanese state and society.[46] Through the repair and rebuilding of damaged sites, and through compensation for lost property, the Javanese were able to recover from the effects of natural disaster. The epigraphical and archaeological evidence suggests that it is more accurate to view earthquakes and eruptions as a significant but managed risk in Javanese society, rather than a cause of unmitigated destruction.

Merapi and the Shift of the Royal Center

By recognizing the true extent of the impact of natural disasters, we can gain a better understanding of how they have shaped the course of Indonesian history. One of the perennial problems in early Javanese history is the shift of the center of royal government in the 920s. From the early eighth to the early tenth century, the epigraphic and architectural record shows that the Javanese state was based in Central Java. But from the late 920s onward, royal inscriptions indicate that the center of government had moved to East Java, where it remained for several centuries thereafter. Charters issued

---

[43] Véronique Degroot, "The Liangan Temple Site in Central Java," *Archipel* 94 (2017): 199.

[44] Degroot, "Liangan Temple," 201.

[45] Michael R. Dove, "Perception of Volcanic Eruption as Agent of Change on Merapi Volcano, Central Java," *Journal of Volcanology and Geothermal Research* 172 (2008): 330.

[46] For a less sanguine assessment of early Javanese resilience in the face of natural disaster, see Jan Wisseman Christie, "Under the Volcano: Stabilizing the Early Javanese State in an Unstable Environment," in *Environment, Trade and Society in Southeast Asia: A Longue Durée Perspective*, ed. David Henley and Henk Schulte Nordholt, Verhandeling van Het Koninklijk Instituut Voor Taal-, Land- En Volkenkunde 300 (Leiden: KITLV Press, 2015), 46–61.

by King Siṇḍok, who took the throne sometime between August 928 and July 929, show him occupying a number of royal palaces in the vicinity of present-day Jombang.[47]

It has long been theorized that the shift of royal government was caused by a rapid evacuation of Central Java due to a powerful volcanic eruption. J. W. IJzerman was the first to suggest that some form of natural disaster caused a mass flight of the population from Central to East Java.[48] The eruption theory was further developed in the early twentieth century, culminating in the claim by R. W. van Bemmelen that an eruption of Merapi "depopulated and desorganized [sic] the prosperous Hindu State of Central Java, converting the surrounding fertile fields into barren ash-covered deserts."[49] The most influential proponent of this theory among historians of Indonesia was Boechari, who proposed that a catastrophic eruption of a Central Javanese volcano (presumed to be Merapi) around 925 forced the Javanese state to relocate to East Java.[50] More recently, Jan Wisseman Christie drew on studies of pyroclastic deposits at Merapi, as well as her own archaeological and epigraphical research, in support of this hypothesis.[51]

Despite these efforts, the eruption theory for the shift of government is not conclusive. This is because of two problems with the evidence: first, the radiocarbon age estimates for volcanic deposits are not precise enough to confirm a direct correlation with the shift of government in the late 920s, and second, no epigraphic source explicitly mentions eruptions as the cause of the shifting royal center.[52] Stratigraphic analysis has revealed the ongoing nature of Merapi's eruptions in the late first millennium, showing "evidence that Merapi eruptions have affected temples of the area . . . though not necessarily during a single large eruption" and that "explosive eruptions of widespread impact occurred before, during and after the period of temple construction."[53] More recent research has confirmed that "the eruptive activity of Merapi over the past 2,000 years has been almost continuous."[54] The eruption theory for the shift of government is thereby weakened, because ongoing volcanic activity at Merapi coincided not only with the departure of the

[47] Boechari, "Some Considerations on the Problem of the Shift of Matarām's Centre of Government from Central to East Java in the 10th Century," in *Melacak Sejarah Kuno Indonesia Lewat Prasasti / Tracing Ancient Indonesian History through Inscriptions* (Jakarta: Kepustakaan Populer Gramedia, 2012), 160.

[48] J. W. IJzerman, *Beschrijving der Oudheden Nabij de Grens der Residentie's Soerakarta en Djogdjakarta* (Batavia: Landsdrukkerij, 1891), 4–5.

[49] Van Bemmelen suggested that this disaster happened in 1006, based on a misinterpretation of a reference to a "catastrophe" (*pralāya*) in the Pucangan inscription. The epigraphical record makes clear that the shift of government from Central to East Java happened in the early tenth century, not the early eleventh. Unfortunately, the erroneous 1006 date is still occasionally found in publications on Java's volcanic history. R. W. van Bemmelen, *General Geology of Indonesia and Adjacent Archipelagoes*, vol. IA, The Geology of Indonesia (The Hague: Government Printing Office, 1949), 560.

[50] Boechari, "Shift of Matarām's Centre of Government," 180–1.

[51] Wisseman Christie, "Under the Volcano," 46–61.

[52] By contrast, instances where political conflict was the main reason for evacuating a royal center are explicitly discussed in Old Javanese inscriptions, such as the fall of Dharmavangśa Teguh's palace in 1017 (Pucangan inscription), the temporary ousting of Sarveśvara from his palace at Katang-Katang (Kemulan inscription dated 1194), and the destruction of the Singhasari palace in 1292 (Kudadu and Sukhamerta inscriptions). Boechari, *Melacak Sejarah Indonesia Lewat Prasasti* (Jakarta: Gramedia, 2012), 104, 108, 206.

[53] Newhall et al., "10,000 Years of Explosive Eruptions of Merapi Volcano, Central Java," 45–6.

[54] Ralf Gertisser et al., "The Geological Evolution of Merapi Volcano, Central Java, Indonesia," *Bulletin of Volcanology* 74 (2012): 1227.

royal center from Central Java in the early tenth century, but also with its first appearance there in the early eighth century and its heyday in the mid-ninth century.

There is still not enough evidence for the theory that a volcanic eruption was the primary cause of the shift of government in the 920s. It is certainly plausible that ongoing eruptive activity placed stress on the Javanese state's infrastructure and that such stresses may have contributed to the decision to move the palace. However, the hypothesis of a single catastrophic eruption of Merapi that compelled this shift of government requires stronger physical and textual evidence than is currently available. An alternative may be to look beyond the well-studied Merapi in search of "[a] bigger eruption from a more distant volcano, less given to regular small eruptions than Merapi, [which] may have caused the crops to fail."[55] But the shift of the royal center to East Java does not necessarily mean there was a wholesale collapse of society in Central Java. It may instead be more viable to imagine Javanese society experiencing volcanic eruptions as a harmful but manageable phenomenon, for which they had effective strategies of resilience.

The Recording of Disaster Events

Having taken stock of Indonesian cultural attitudes toward natural disaster and their impacts, we are ready to turn to some historical records of specific disaster events. The Javanese and Balinese paid close attention to the chronological aspects of disaster. Specific occurrences of earthquakes and volcanic eruptions were recorded in chronicles, sometimes precisely to the day. Even though disasters were unpredictable, they were viewed as concrete historical events whose timing was both quantifiable (through dated records) and interpretable (through augury). This shows how disaster events were incorporated into the chronological practices of Javanese and Balinese people. They did not occur in some mythical realm beyond time but were comprehended within the timekeeping of normal life. It is this chronological orientation that makes certain Indonesian sources very useful to historians of disaster, as long as they are handled properly.

Natural disasters are regularly mentioned in Javanese and Balinese chronicles. This was a mindful choice by the compilers of these texts. Eruptions and earthquakes were included because they were signs of power in the world, just like battles and coronations. The chronological precision of these entries reflects close attention to the idea of the "moment" (*duk*).[56] Connections between particular kinds of events and specific moments in time were judged in terms of their "accordance" (*tut*) with each other.[57] Just as earthquake calendars interpreted the timing of earthquakes as presaging certain outcomes, the chronicling of disaster events drew attention to the irruption of power into significant moments in time. An examination of how these chronicles

---

[55] Anthony Reid, "Revisiting Southeast Asian History with Geology: Some Demographic Consequences of a Dangerous Environment," in *Natural Hazards and Peoples in the Indian Ocean World: Bordering on Danger*, ed. Greg Bankoff and Joseph Christensen (Palgrave Macmillan, 2016), 41.

[56] This polysemous word also has meanings of "hit," "strike," "stab," and "meet." At its core, the word refers to the point of encounter between otherwise separate things, whether in time or space. P. J. Zoetmulder, *Old Javanese-English Dictionary*, s.v. "duk."

[57] Vickers, "Balinese Texts and Historiography," 169.

positioned natural disasters within a temporal framework can give us valuable insight into Indonesian concepts of historical time.

A sixteenth-century Javanese chronicle called the *Pararaton* (The Monarchs) gives a precise chronology of disaster events in the pre-Islamic period. The *Pararaton* is a heterogeneous compilation of historical materials spanning the thirteenth to fifteenth centuries.[58] Its central concern is the history of the Rājasa royal dynasty that ruled Java in this period, but it also mentions eleven natural disasters that occurred in the period 1311–1483. The chronicle entries for natural disasters are interspersed among other entries pertaining to political events (see Table 1). The Javanese viewed natural disasters as an effect of power in the world, which is why such events were considered fit for inclusion in a royal chronicle like the *Pararaton*. Each of these entries follows a standard format: the type of disaster, a specifier, the phrase "in Śaka," a chronogram in words, and a year numeral. Of particular interest is the manner in which the disasters are specified, using a label derived from a base word plus a prefix *pa-*. This is the standard way to label events in the *Pararaton*; for example, the Javanese military expedition against the Sumatran kingdom of Malayu is referred to as the *pamalayu*.[59]

The specifiers for six of the eight eruptions are based on the names of weeks in the Javanese *wuku* calendar, which is why I have included "the week" in my English translations. This convention of specifying eruption events by a *wuku*-based label is not unique to the *Pararaton*, as it also appears in the eighteenth-century *Babad ing Sangkala*.[60] A plausible interpretation of these week-based labels is that they indicate the week in which the eruption event occurred. The use of the *wuku* calendar to label eruption events suggests a possible connection to disaster augury. In modern Java and Bali, it is earthquakes rather than volcanic eruptions that are commonly used for augury, as discussed above. Nonetheless, the *wuku* system is closely connected to divination in general, so it is plausible that the *Pararaton* may represent an older type of disaster augury that is no longer known in the modern Javanese and Balinese traditions.

It is tempting to try to match the week name and year numeral given in the chronicle entries, in order to more precisely date each eruption event. Unfortunately, two technical problems prevent this. First, the *wuku* calendar operates on a thirty-week cycle, which runs independently of the lunisolar Śaka year. The short length of this cycle means that any named week (e.g., Watugunung) often occurs twice within a given Śaka year. Second, this section of the *Pararaton* is significantly affected by distortions in the manuscript transmission, thereby impairing the reliability of the Śaka years supplied in the text. For example, the Prangbakat eruption is associated with the chronogram "faces–of–person–bodies–serpents," a corrupt reading equivalent to the nonsensical year 8319 Śaka, which is in conflict with the year given in numerals (1319 Śaka).[61] For these reasons, we should refrain from using the *wuku* labels to assign precise dates to these eruptions, because

[58] Wayan Jarrah Sastrawan, "How to Read a Chronicle: The *Pararaton* as a Conglomerate Text," *Indonesia and the Malay World* 140 (March 2020): 1–22.

[59] Brandes, *Pararaton*, 24.

[60] M. C. Ricklefs, *Modern Javanese Historical Tradition: A Study of an Original Kartasura Chronicle and Related Materials* (London: School of Oriental and African Studies, University of London, 1978), 18.

[61] The numerals are given as 1317 in manuscripts B and F of the text, which further suggests that this particular entry has been distorted in the course of manuscript transmission.

Table 1: List of chronicle entries for natural disasters in the *Pararaton*[62]

Page	Text	Translation	CE Year
25.28	guntur paluṅge i śaka api api taṅan tuṅgal, 1233	Eruption of Lungge[63] in Śaka fires–fires–hands–single, 1233	1311
28.16	guntur pabañupiṇḍah i śaka, 1256	Eruption of moving water[64] in Śaka 1256	1334
29.34	hana gunuṅ añar i śaka naga leṅ karnaniṅ voṅ, 1298	There is Mount Anyar [a new mountain][65] in Śaka serpents–holes–ears–of–person, 1298	1376
29.35	guntur pamaḍasiha i śaka r̥ṣi śūnya guṇa tuṅgal, 1307	Eruption of [the week] Madangsia in Śaka sages–emptiness–qualities–single, 1307	1385
30.27	guntur praṅbakat i śaka mukaniṅ voṅ kaya naga, 1319	Eruption of [the week] Prangbakat in Śaka faces–of–person–bodies–serpents, 1319	1397 [?]
31.18	guntur pajuluṅpujut i śaka kaya veda guṇaniṅ voṅ, 1343	Eruption of [the week] Julungpujut in Śaka bodies–Vedas–qualities–of–person, 1343	1421
31.23	pahilan aguṅ i śaka nāga yugānahut voṅ, 1348	Great famine in Śaka serpents–ages–biting–person, 1348	1426
32.2	paliṇḍu i śaka pakṣa guṇānahut vulan, 1362	Earthquake in Śaka wings–qualities–biting–moon, 1362	1440
32.8	guntur pakuniṅan i śaka velut viku anahut vulan, 1373	Eruption of [the week] Kuningan in Śaka eels–monks–biting–moon, 1373	1451
32.17	guntur palaṇḍep i śaka pat ula teluṅ wit, 1384	Eruption of [the week] Laṇḍep in Śaka four–snakes–three–stem, 1384	1462
32.25	guntur pavatugunuṅ i śaka kayāmbara sagara iku, 1403	Eruption of [the week] Watugunung in Śaka bodies–sky–seas–tail, 1403	1481

[62] I have extracted all the disaster entries and listed them here in chronological order. The column "Page" refers to the first edition by Brandes, in the format [page number.line number]. J. L. A. Brandes, *Pararaton (Ken Arok) of Het Boek Der Koningen van Tumapěl En van Majapahit* (Batavia: Albrecht & Co., 1896).

[63] The interpretation of the term Lungge is uncertain, as it is unknown either as a wuku name or as a toponym. An unpublished manuscript of this text (Leiden University Library collection, Codex Orientalis 20.031, which I have denoted witness N of the Pararaton) gives the reading *guntur paluṅguhe* ("eruption at [the time of] his establishment"). This "establishment" may refer to the ascension of the king Jayanagara in the preceding chronicle entry. If this alternative reading is correct, then this entry demonstrates yet again the link between natural disaster and political power. Sastrawan, "Pararaton as a Conglomerate Text," 22.

[64] This entry probably refers to an eruption of Kelud. The year coincides with that of the Kelud eruption mentioned in the *Deśavarṇana*, as discussed above in connection with Hayam Wuruk. The reference to moving water is consistent with the ejection of water from a crater lake, a harmful eruptive product that is typical of Kelud. The *Tantu Panggelaran* gives an origin story for this crater lake as a physical expression of the anger of the goddess Umā. Th. G. Th. Pigeaud, *Java in the 14th Century: A Study in Cultural History* (Leiden: KITLV Press, 1962), 4:8; J.-C. Thouret et al., "Origin, Characteristics, and Behaviour of Lahars Following the 1990 Eruption of Kelud Volcano, Eastern Java (Indonesia)," *Bulletin of Volcanology* 59 (1998): 462–64; Fukashi Maeno et al., "Eruption Pattern and a Long-Term Magma Discharge Rate over the Past 100 Years at Kelud Volcano, Indonesia," *Journal of Disaster Research* 14, no. 1 (2019): 27–39; Stuart Robson, trans., *Threads of the Unfolding Web: The Old Javanese Tantu Panggělaran* (Singapore: ISEAS Yusof Ishak Institute, 2021), 44.

[65] This summit may have been a recent formation within the Kelud summit vent complex, hence the appellation Gunung Anyar ("new mountain"). In the *Bujangga Manik*, this toponym is listed directly before Kampud/Kelud itself, strengthening the hypothesis that it may refer to a peak in or near the Kelud complex. Noorduyn, "Bujangga Manik's Journey Through Java," 430.

the accuracy of this method cannot be guaranteed. The complexity of the *Pararaton's* manuscript transmission also means that the East Javanese eruption dates given in Table 1 should not be assigned the very high degree of confidence that is sometimes found in databases of volcanic eruptions.[66]

Natural disasters also feature prominently in later Balinese chronicles. Several lists of chronograms collected in Bali in the late nineteenth and early twentieth centuries give entries for eruptions of the major active volcanoes in Bali (Table 2). These chronicles have generally been found to be accurate for events from the late seventeenth century onward, while showing less accuracy and precision for earlier periods.[67] Chronicle entries with precise and self-consistent calendar dates are more likely to be historically accurate, since this indicates the information may well have been sourced from a contemporary record of the event. However, errors in the manuscript transmission mean that the date of an entry cannot always be accurately reconstructed.

Many of these entries are brief, simply indicating which mountain erupted in a particular year, but some of them furnish additional information of historical significance. For example, the entry for the November 20, 1683 eruption of Agung adds that "I Dewa

Table 2: List of chronicle entries for natural disasters from various Balinese chronicles.[68]

CE Dates	Volcano	Sources
circa 1612	Batur[69]	*Babad Bhumi* #62 & #109, *Korn 2* #23, *Korn 4* #24, *Korn 5* #52, *Pangrincik Babad* #31, *Tattwa Batur Kalawasan* #27
circa 1616	Agung	*Babad Gumi* #33 & #34, *Babad Bhumi* #57 & #110, *Korn 5* #54, *Babad Tusan* #29, *Tattwa Batur Kalawasan* #33, *Pangrincik Babad* #35
circa October–November 1665	Agung	*Babad Gumi* #54
November 20, 1683	Agung	*Babad Gumi* #65
February 10, 1696	Batur	*Babad Bhumi* #119, *Pasasangkalan* #15, *Korn 1* #78
October 12, 1703	Batur	*Pasasangkalan* #16, *Korn 1* #79
June 18, 1706	Batur	*Pawawatekan* #77
October 21, 1710 –February 1, 1711	Agung	*Babad Gumi* #77, *Pasasangkalan* #18, *Korn 1* #81
circa 1784	Batur	*Babad Bhumi* #128
June 13–21, 1820	Agung	*Babad Bhumi* #132, *Babad Bhumi* #133

---

[66] For example, in the Smithsonian Institution's *The Volcanoes of the World* database record for Kelud, accessed May 14, 2021, https://volcano.si.edu/volcano.cfm?vn=263280.

[67] Hans Hägerdal, "Candrasengkala: The Balinese Art of Dating Events," Department of Humanities, 2006, accessed 7 April 2021, https://lnu.diva-portal.org/smash/get/diva2:206791/FULLTEXT01.pdf.

[68] The designation of each source and the enumeration of its entries follows that of Hägerdal.

[69] In some of the sources, this eruption is attributed to a mountain called Daya. It is unclear whether the name Daya was considered equivalent to Batur, but it seems that all of these entries do in fact refer to Batur.

at Klungkung as the highest-ranked of Bali's several kings from the mid-1680s through to the 1720s.[70] The entry's juxtaposition of the eruption and Dewa Jambe reinforces the long-standing association between natural disaster and the rise of a new ruler, both of which were signs of power in the world.

The 1710–11 Eruption of Mount Agung

One particular chronicle entry is of unique value for the historical study of natural disasters in Bali. The *Babad Gumi* entry (#77) for the 1710–11 eruption of the Agung volcano is exceptional for its level of descriptive detail, its chronological precision, and the fact that it seems to be a near-contemporary record of the disaster. The entry begins with the word *péling*, "commemoration," which indicates that it belongs to the genre of commemorative notes (*pangélingan*) that were appended to the end of texts.[72] Such notes usually contain information about current events at the time when a text was being written or copied. The level of detail in this record makes it an especially rich historical source:

> A commemoration of the time when Mount Agung was devoured by Kālāgni Rudra.[73] The day it began to burn was 21 October 1710. Eventually, on 2 December, came the ash rain. Then on 12 December, there was an eruption of fire. Then on 16 December,[74] a rain of little stones poured down. It was like the sky was split asunder and the earth was being pulverized. Everyone was in panic and people were fleeing desperately. There was an eruption of big stones and sludge. Many villages were destroyed, as well as the dry rice fields and the irrigated rice fields. Ravines became hills and hills became ravines. The wellsprings were destroyed, engulfed by fire. The number was more than 3 – people of Paleg – 10 – people of Bantas – Kayuaya – Bukit – Tigaron – the number of deaths, young and old, was more than 600 – the village of Tianyar – destroyed as far as its forest – Sukadana as well.[75] Remember the lifetime of the earth, when the earth's lifetime ends, 1,700 years. Devoured by Kālāgni Rudra was Mount Agung, as well as Tulamben, the forest of Batudawa, Muntig, Abang, Pidpid and the forest of Babi.

---

[70] Helen Creese, "Śrī Surawīrya, Déwa Agung of Klungkung (c. 1722–1736): The Historical Context for Dating the Kakawin Pārthāyaṇa," *Bijdragen Tot de Taal-, Land- En Volkenkunde* 147, no. 4 (1991): 408.

[71] *jeneng I Déwa Jambé di Kalungkung* [Modern Balinese]. Hägerdal, "Candrasengkala," 37.

[72] Vickers, "Balinese Texts and Historiography," 170–77.

[73] Kālāgni ("Fire of Time") is an epithet of the god Rudra, identified with Śiva, in his role as destroyer of the world at the end of each cosmic era. The eruption is understood here not merely as a physical phenomenon but as a consequence of the god's power. Stella Kramrisch, *The Presence of Śiva*, 1st Indian ed. (Varanasi: Motilal Banarsidass, 1988), 274–75.

[74] The week name is not specified in this date, so it could have fallen on any conjunction of the weekdays Kliwon and Anggara around this time. I choose December 16, 1710, which is the soonest Kliwon Anggara after the preceding date. I see no strong reason to follow Hägerdal's alternative proposal of January 20, 1711. Throughout this entry, the weekday Anggara is abbreviated to a, rather than the standard abbreviation *ang*. Hägerdal, "Candrasengkala," 40.

[75] Here the grammar of the Balinese text is ambiguous, with short phrases and words separated by punctuation. To propose a grammatical English translation here would involve unjustifiable guesswork about the intended syntax of the Balinese original. I have instead used dashes to more fairly represent how the Balinese is expressed.

The destruction went as far as the betel plants, the fruit trees and the coconut trees, as far as the dry rice fields. The aqueducts were destroyed and could not be quickly rebuilt. Everything was destroyed. The rivers Bungbung and Yeh Lajang both destroyed the paddy fields, and the bathing place of Babi was all filled up. The river Bangkak destroyed dry rice fields of Susut. The rivers Selat and Barak destroyed the paddy fields. It started in 1710 and went to 1711, and it was violently destructive.[76]

A briefer entry (#18) in the *Pasasangkalan* chronicle gives some additional information about this eruption, using the volcano's alternative name, Tolangkir:[77]

The time when a flood of hot water flowed northward from Tolangkir, killing the people of Bukit and the people of Cahutgut, the people of Bantas, the people of Kayuaya. In the end they were destroyed, killed by that torrent, on 1 February[78] 1711.[79]

These descriptions of the 1710–11 eruption invite comparison with the famous 1963–64 eruption of Agung, which was the most powerful Indonesian eruption of the twentieth century.[80] A remarkable feature of the *Babad Gumi*'s description is its breakdown of the emergence of different volcanic products by date, essentially giving us a record of the 1710–11 eruption sequence. Balinese terms like "little stones" (*watu alit-alit*), "big stones" (*watu ageng-ageng*), "ash rain" (*udan awu*) and "sludge" (*nyanyad*) can be identified as

---

[76] *péling duk ing gunung agungé kapangan déning kalagni rudra, dina mimiti geseng, wa, a, wara dungulan, kresnapaksa caturdasi, sasih 4, rah 3, tenggek 3, awekasan, teka ring dina, u, a, kruwelut, udan awu, malih ring dina, u, su, mrakih, guntur apuy, malih ring dina, ka, a, wudan watu alit-alit, kredhek, kaya bentar ikang akasa, kaya bubur ikang prethiwi, gégér ikang kabéh, amrih-mrih awak, mwah guntur watu ageng-ageng mwah nyanyad, akwéh desa rusak, mwah gaga sawah, jurang dadi gunung, gunung dadi jurang, mwah anakan yéh pejah liput apuy, kwéhnya rangkung, 3, wwang paleg, 10, wong bantas, kayuaya, bukit, tigaron, kwéhnya pejah anom wredhah, rangkung 600, desa tyanyar, teka ning alasnya rusak mwah sukhadana, élingakna tuuh ikang bhumi, yan tutug tuuh bhumi ika, sepaha satus temwang, ana kapangan déning kalagni rudra, ikang gunung agung, mwah tulamben, alas batudawa, muntig, abhang, pidpid, mwah alas babi, teka ning basé buah nyuh, teka ning carik rusak, pangalapan rusak, tan kena tangun gelis, kabéh padha rusak, tukad bungbung, yeh lajang, padha mangrusak sawah, mwah kayéhan babi rusak pada urugen, tukad bangkak mangrusak carik, susut, tukad selat, tukad barak, padha mangrusak sawah, mamimiti, rah, 2, teka ning, rah, 3, maksi mangrusak* (ff. 7r–8r) [Old Javanese/Modern Balinese]. Kirtya manuscript 808 (shelf Va). See also Hägerdal, "Candrasengkala," 40–41.

[77] The equivalent entry #81 in the *Korn 1* chronicle expands on the information about this eruption given in the *Pasasangkalan*. However, *Korn 1* appears to be a late copy of the *Pasasangkalan* and deviates considerably from its original. It may even be the case that a previously separate entry, concerning the nobleman I Gusti Ngurah Balé Agung, has been interpolated into *Korn 1*'s account of the 1710–11 eruption. Due to its uncertain reliability, I have excluded this entry from the discussion. Hägerdal, "Candrasengkala," 88–89.

[78] In his conversion of this date, Hägerdal interpreted the solar element Suryāgni as "one of the days in the Balinese calendar which are associated with Surya" and went on to suggest Sukra Pahing falling on February 6, 1711 as such a day. A more plausible interpretation, supported by Damais's study of Balinese calendars, is that Surya is a synonym of Radité (Sunday), which gives Radité Pahing falling on February 1, 1711. Louis-Charles Damais, "Études d'épigraphie Indonésienne, V: Dates de Manuscrits et Documents Divers de Java, Bali et Lombok," *Bulletin de l'Ecole Française d'Extrême-Orient* 49, no. 1 (1958): 26; Hägerdal, "Candrasengkala," 170.

[79] *duk balabur wédang mily angalor saking tolangkir amatyani wong bukit miwah wong cahutgut, wong bantas, wong kayuaya, samapta éntya pinatyan déning lwah ika, wara ugu suryāgni palguna lék, swanita ro, tri sirah, i śaka siki guṇa karenga awani* [Old Javanese/Modern Balinese]. Hägerdal, "Candrasengkala," 169–70.

[80] Stephen Self and Michael R. Rampino, "The 1963–1964 Eruption of Agung Volcano (Bali, Indonesia)," *Bulletin of Volcanology* 74 (2012): 1522–24.

typical products of this volcano in modern eruptions.[81] Of particular interest is the chronicle's claim that the first observed phenomenon was that the mountain "began to burn" (*mimiti geseng*) on October 21, 1710. Similarly, lava was the first major product to be observed on February 18, 1963.[82] Such detailed information on the 1710–11 eruption sequence can be used in conjunction with stratigraphic and other kinds of scientific analysis to better discern historical patterns in Agung's eruptive behavior.

The extent and severity of damage caused by Agung's eighteenth-century eruption was similar to that of the twentieth-century eruption. The chronicle's estimated death toll of "more than 600" in 1710–11 is comparable, as a proportion of total population, to the 1963–64 toll of approximately 1,700 deaths.[83] Most of the villages where the chronicles report deaths are located to the northeast of the Agung summit, overlapping closely with areas affected by pyroclastic and lahar flows in 1963. The chronicles describe flash flooding and damage to irrigation systems along rivers that flow southeast and southwest, mapped in Figure 2. The damage to farms, gardens, and waterworks is strongly emphasized in these accounts, since it directly threatened food security in the affected districts. These descriptions confirm that the 1710–11 eruption was a major event, which prompts us to reevaluate the geological data for Agung's early modern eruption history.

Conclusion

In this article, I have explored how Indonesians experienced earthquakes and volcanic eruptions over more than a thousand years. For many people, disasters signified the presence of power in the world. Such power included not only the geophysical power of the disaster itself, but the political power of great leaders and the spiritual power of deities and supernatural beings. Since disasters were a sign of the presence of power, they could be interpreted as signs of future events using calendar-based augury. Indonesians were not passive in the face of disasters, nor did they conceive of them as wholly negative. Instead they pragmatically responded to disasters as a normal part of life. The Javanese state in the ninth and tenth centuries had the means to compensate or repair property that was damaged by earthquakes and eruptions. This encourages us to reconsider some of the grander claims about the catastrophic impacts of natural disaster in Indonesian history. For example, modern arguments that the tenth-century Central Javanese state was destroyed by a volcanic eruption are not well supported by the available geological and textual evidence.

Traditional records can offer useful information about specific disaster events in Indonesia, especially those that are not mentioned in foreign sources. The *Pararaton* chronicle provides a dated list of disaster events in East Java through the fourteenth

---

[81] Self and Rampino, "The 1963–1964 Eruption of Agung Volcano," 1524–28; Karen Fontijn et al., "A 5000-Year Record of Multiple Highly Explosive Mafic Eruptions from Gunung Agung (Bali, Indonesia): Implications for Eruption Frequency and Volcanic Hazards," *Bulletin of Volcanology* 77 (2015).

[82] Self and Rampino, "The 1963–1964 Eruption of Agung Volcano," 1524.

[83] "Angka2 terachir: 1476 Orang tewas, jg. tertimbun lahar belum dapat diambil," *Suara Rakjat*, April 1, 1963; M. T. Zen and D. Hadikusumo, "Preliminary Report on the 1963 Eruption of Mt. Agung in Bali (Indonesia)," *Bulletin Volcanologique* 27 (1964): 275–82; M. Poffenberger, "Toward a New Understanding of Population Change in Bali," *Population Studies* 37 (1983): 46.

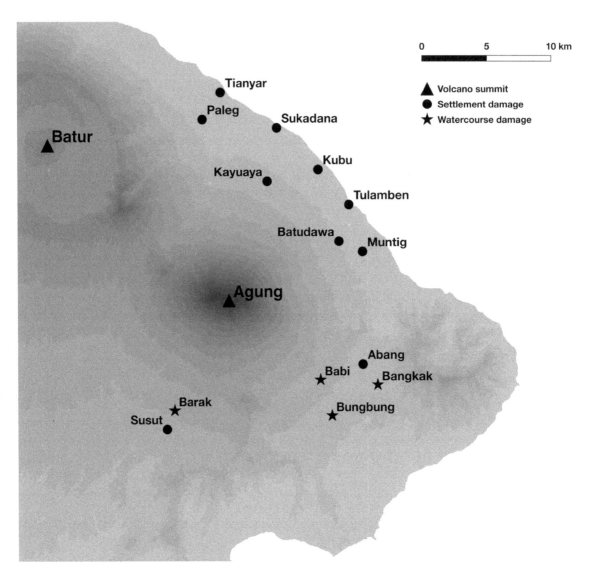

Figure 2: Map of the impacts of the 1710–11 eruption of Agung as mentioned in Balinese chronicles. Altitude os shaded in increments of 200 meters

and fifteenth centuries. However, these dates cannot necessarily be taken at face value, due to the unstable transmission of this text through its manuscript copies. Balinese chronicles similarly offer a historical record for eruptions of the Agung and Batur volcanoes during the seventeenth and eighteenth centuries. Of these, the *Babad Gumi*'s detailed account of the mighty 1710–11 eruption of Agung can help us to reevaluate the volcanic history of the island. While they can be immensely useful, these sources have their own complex histories and cannot be interpreted in a naively literal way, as if they were straightforward repositories of historical fact ready to be synthesized with scientific findings. Rather, the very construal of disaster events in these chronicles are shaped by the cultural assumptions embedded within them.

In keeping with recent approaches that stress the relevance of culture in how people have experienced disasters in history, I have demonstrated how an in-depth understanding of cultural attitudes is crucial to properly interpreting the available evidence for natural disasters in Indonesia. Such an approach allows us to include a much broader range of sources than are usually considered in studies of natural disasters: legal charters, divination manuals, royal chronicles, temple ruins, and augury paintings. When interpreted in ways that are sensitive to their cultural assumptions, all of the sources discussed in this article can give us valuable insights into Javanese and Balinese experiences of disaster. These insights can fruitfully contribute to the comparative and transcultural approaches that have shown such promise in recent studies of natural disaster in global history.

The Toba Super-Catastrophe as History of the Future

Faizah Zakaria

Abstract

This article considers Lake Toba's origins through global science and local folklore to examine how volcanic eruptions in the deep past are accessed, remembered, and understood. The eruption of the Toba volcano circa 73,000 years ago was theorized by some scientists as a "Super Catastrophe" that nearly extinguished the human population. At a local level, folklore of the Toba Batak peoples articulates this disaster in the form of morality tales. In these stories, nature is anthropomorphized as an act of memory to warn against the future impact of wrongful action. This article argues that both historical memories index a history of the future. While seemingly disparate, each narrative—scientific and folkloric—contains a meta-narrative on how the future has shaped our questions of the past and vice versa. In both epistemes, the writing of the distant past emerges with the writing of the future to define ethical choices for the present.

Keywords: Toba eruption, volcano, extinction, disaster narratives, future, climate science, nuclear science

Introduction

Circa 73,000 years ago, a volcano near the equator erupted and spewed more than twenty-eight square kilometers of volcanic tuff on a massive scale, remnants of which

Faizah Zakaria is Assistant Professor of History at Nanyang Technological University. Special thanks are due to all interlocutors at the Gatty Lecture in 2018 where this paper was first presented and to Susie Protschky, Peter Lavelle, and Emiko Stock for their insights.

were still found in parts of the Indian Ocean, Arabian Sea, and South China Sea today. The implosion of its magma chambers collapsed the volcano's top and sides, creating a deep depression known as a caldera. Over the next 20,000 years or so, in what geologists described as the "afterparty to the big dance," volcanic activity rumbled on, even as water filled the caldera while subterranean molten rock reconfigured into an uplift that pushed a dome-shaped island above the surface of the water.[1] Located in the northern part of the island now known as Sumatra, that caldera lake and the island are respectively called Toba and Samosir.

The Toba eruption was the most destructive known in history, qualifying for super-volcanic status more than twice over and causing a long period of global cooling that possibly decimated the human population.[2] How did we come to retrieve the Toba eruption from prehistory and understand its significance? This article investigates this question through two modalities of knowledge. The first is trace evidence gradually made visible by scientists and the second is everyday sensing of tremors, intergenerationally translated into folklore that posits a past crisis. To fully understand how Toba came to be perceived as catastrophe is to braid together two histories: its global impact made evident through eruptions and local knowledge of risk in the time between eruptions.

In so doing, this article examines the Toba eruption as a history of the future: a Janus-faced narrative where the writing of the long past emerges *with* the writing of the future. "History of the future" is a term that has acquired multiple valences in recent literature but essentially represents diverse stories about humans negotiating uncertainties. Such histories include chronological examinations of how societies envisioned future technologies and its applications,[3] critical analyses of past visions of the future,[4] and, most suggestively for this article, stories of future-making, the latter being the tools that we use to hedge against uncertainties of the future.[5] On the latter, Matthew D. O'Hara, writing about colonial Mexico, adopts a stance I take in this article: that future-making leverages on tradition (e.g., religious divination rituals) *and* innovation (e.g., hedging risk through insurance). Given this inclination to look both ways, perhaps Christopher Bonneuil's suggestion that historians may make the best futurists should be taken seriously.[6] As will be shown in this article, knowledge of Toba in prehistory is simultaneously afforded by glimpses of future climate change and alters views of the latter.

---

[1] Shanaka L. de Silva, Adonara E. Mucek, Patricia M. Gregg, and Indyo Pratomo, "Resurgent Toba, Field Chronologic and Model Constraints on Time Scales and Mechanisms of Resurgence at Large Calderas," *Frontiers in Earth Science* 3 (2015): 1–17.

[2] To qualify as a supervolcano eruption, the amplitude of eruption should measure 8 on the Volcanic Explosive Index and emit deposits over an area larger than 1,000 km3. See Oregon State University, "Aftermath of Super-Eruption Shows Toba Magma System's Great Size," *ScienceDaily*, May 16, 2017, http://www.sciencedaily.com/releases/2017/05/170516143417.htm.

[3] Peter J. Bowler, *A History of the Future* (Cambridge: Cambridge University Press, 2017); Blake J. Harris, *The History of the Future: Oculus, Facebook and Revolution that Swept Virtual Reality* (New York: Dey Street Books, 2019).

[4] Daniel Rosenberg and Susan Harding, *Histories of the Future* (Durham: Duke University Press, 2005).

[5] See David J. Staley, *History and Future: Using Historical Thinking to Imagine the Future* (Lanham, MD: Lexington Books, 2007) on how historians contribute to scenario planning; Matthew D. O'Hara, *The History of the Future in Colonial Mexico* (New Haven, CT: Yale University Press, 2018).

[6] Christopher Bonneuil, "Do Historians Make the Best Futurists?" *History and Theory* 48 (2009): 98–104.

O'Hara's insight on the entanglement of traditional religion and secular innovation—generally seen as opposites—underscores the need for the braided histories that this article examines. Science and folklore, the two knowledge domains that are centered here, present analogous relationships between past and future catastrophes where the past feeds into warnings of impending disaster even as the prospect of future disaster in turn modifies our narratives about the past. Both sets of narratives can be used to embed moral imperatives for present action to mitigate an uncertain future. However, these conversations currently take place in separate domains. Humanity's future is shared but conversations about what this shared future could or, indeed, should look like take place in independent spheres at multiple scales. Without juxtaposition of these narratives as a first step toward identifying intersecting concerns from which we can build a common moral agenda, discourse about future disaster will likely be framed only through a fractious binary between perceived superstition and hegemonic science.

A long-ago disaster like Toba is peculiarly well-positioned to complicate not only epistemic but also temporal binaries. As Jason Phillips noted, "Anticipating the future changes it."[7] In a similar vein, Reinhart Koselleck observes how human reactions to possible disaster were conditioned by our "horizon of expectation," shaped by history.[8] This view of the horizon leans partly on Kant's quest for a "predictive history" where we can see the future from our own standpoint in the present because historical institutions orient in a very specific direction. The possibility of seeing both ends from the present is independently indicated in Braudel's concept of the longue durée, where mental and geologic structure "forms the stabilizing ground against which cyclical variations of other temporal structures are established."[9] The difference between Kant and Braudel, Phillips argues, is that "German temporality sees the future as a formative era that shapes the past and present, while American and French temporality sees the future as a pliable period that is shaped by the past and present."[10] This article acknowledges both temporalities, demonstrating that tools that used the past to model future catastrophe simultaneously shaped values that could prevent it. Moreover, controversy over how to interpret Toba was made urgent by a looming global climate crisis. Whether Toba represents an unmitigated catastrophe, an avoidable disaster, a testament to human negligence, or a tale of human resilience might counterintuitively depend on how we *forecast* such a crisis playing out.

Retrieving Toba through Trace Evidence

The Toba eruption, or, as geologists put it, the "73 ka Toba Event," was the latest of at least three previous eruptions, occurring approximately 500,000, 1.2 million, and 1.5 million years ago.[11] All these eruptions left traces of tephra in the layers of Earth's soil. The specific

[7] Jason Phillips, "Harpers Ferry Looming: A History of the Future," *Rethinking History* 18, no. 1 (2014): 10–27.

[8] Reinhart Koselleck, *Futures Past: On the Semantics of Historical Time* (New York: Columbia University Press, 2004), 263.

[9] Dale Tomich, "The Order of Historical Time: The *Longue Durée* and Italian *Microstoria*," in *The Longue Durée and World Systems Analysis*, ed. Richard E. Lee (Albany: SUNY Press, 2011): 53.

[10] Phillips, "Harpers Ferry Looming," 13.

[11] C. A. Chesner et al., "Eruptive History of Earth's Largest Quaternary Caldera (Toba, Indonesia) Clarified," *Geology* 19, no. 3 (1991): 200–3.

volcanic tuff linked to the 73 ka Toba Event was thus called the Youngest Toba Tuff (YTT) and was first discovered in 1978.[12] How did we develop the capacity to find, date, and distinguish trace evidence? How did then we come to connect tephra with global cooling? The technology required to do so emerged from an entanglement of climate science and nuclear research, both of which have a common interest in the distribution and impact of particulate matter in the atmosphere. Such research looked both ways: knowledge of past conditions both generated and validated models about future impact.

Climate scientists pioneered research into particulate movement; they were early collectors of data from clouds, ice, and deep-sea cores. This data had potential offensive and defensive military uses. Clouds held the clue to the capacity to forecast and potentially control precipitation, while oxygen bubbles, volcanic ash, pollen, uranium decay, and plankton fossil contained key information about past temperatures, precipitation, atmospheric composition, wind patterns, and volcanic activity of the past.[13] Military programs helped the progress of climate science research by facilitating access to ice and deep-sea cores. In 1960, for instance, the US started Project Iceworm and built a military base in Greenland under long ice tunnels known as Camp Century.[14] Concerned about whether these tunnels were secure from the elements, Danish and American polar climate experts were invited to Camp Century to obtain and study ice core samples. The scientists predicted that the tunnels would eventually collapse under the weight of melting ice—a prediction borne out in the late 1960s when the tunnel ceilings lowered dramatically and the base was abandoned—but the collapse did not herald the end of international research in the area.[15] It was from a Greenland ice core Greenland Ice Sheet Project 2 (GISP2) that a team led by climate scientist Greg Zielinski noted high levels of sulphuric acid in air bubbles dating about 74,000 years ago, leading him to posit a past volcanic eruption of uncertain origin that affected global climate.[16] Contemporaneously and independently, geologist Michael Rampino, in a quest for past extinctions, noticed that the oxygen isotopes in his planktonic microfossil samples in deep sea cores showed evidence of the area cooling suddenly by about 5 to 6 degrees Celsius. He noted that the cooling coincided with the 73 ka Toba Event but was initially cautious about positing a causal connection as it was possible that the change in climate caused Toba's eruption rather than the other way around.[17] His paper with volcanologist Stephen Self a few years later was more confident of a causal link, suggesting a "climate-volcano feedback" loop where climate cooling induced volcanism, which in turn caused further cooling.[18]

---

[12] D. Ninkovich et al., "K-Ar Age of the Late Pleistocene Eruption of Toba, North Sumatra," *Nature* 276 (1978): 574–77.

[13] J. Jouzel, "A Brief History of Ice Core Science over the Last 50 Years," *Climate of the Past* 9, no. 6 (2013): 2525–47.

[14] Donald Prothero, *When Humans Nearly Vanished: The Catastrophic Explosion of the Toba Volcano* (Washington, DC: Smithsonian Institute, 2018), 11–2.

[15] On Project Iceworm, see Nikolaj Petersen, "The Iceman That Never Came: 'Project Iceworm,' the Search for a NATO Deterrent, and Denmark, 1960–62," *Scandinavian Journal of History* 33, no. 1 (2008): 75–98.

[16] Greg Zielinski et al., "Record of Volcanism since 7000 BC from GISP2 Greenland Ice Core and Implications for the Volcano-Climate System," *Science* 264, no. 5161 (1994): 948–52.

[17] Michael R. Rampino, Stephen Self, and Richard B. Stothers, "Volcanic Winters," *Annual Review of Earth and Planetary Sciences* 16 (May 1988): 73–99.

[18] Michael R. Rampino and Stephen Self, "Volcanic Winter and Accelerated Glaciation Following the Toba Super-Eruption," *Nature* 359 (1992): 50–52.

The concept of "feedback" came from parallel inquiries unfolding in the field of nuclear research over the second half of the twentieth century, which modeled how devastating the Toba Event could have been. In the 1940s and 50s, anxieties over future nuclear war motivated such work. Even after detonating atomic bombs over Japan, scientists had no clear idea of how far and fast particles from nuclear weapons could travel through the atmosphere or spread over water and land. Two examples illustrate this perilous floundering. In the mid-1940s, the Kodak Company in Upstate New York was mystified by the problem of its film mysteriously warping in their cardboard boxes. Scientist Julian Webb in Kodak's research department eventually concluded the contamination originated from radioactive river water in Indiana where its cardboard packaging had been pulped.[19] The water had been polluted by nuclear weapons testing in Los Alamos, thousands of miles away; a finding that led to Kodak threatening to sue the Department of Defense. Testing without knowledge had even more disastrous consequences in 1954. That year, the United States detonated a bomb in the Marshall Islands. Its designers miscalculated the yield of the device, which generated so much radioactive ash that without warning, it reached the Rongelap Atoll where children played with the sediments falling from the sky. "No one knew it was radioactive fallout,' testified Senator Jeton Anjain, on behalf of the Rongelap Atoll Local Government in a belated inquiry at the US Congress some fifty years later. "The children played in the snow. They ate it."[20]

Even in the 1950s, interdisciplinary research in nuclear, climate, and geological sciences intimated a picture of global crisis on the horizon. From 1953 to 1959, the Argonne National Laboratory, the United States Weather Bureau, and the University of Chicago's Fermi Institute for Nuclear Studies collaborated on a large-scale data collection exercise in which hot-air balloons were sent up to collect air samples at altitudes of 45,000 to 100,000 feet over a large geographic area.[21] The results showed that gases mixed quickly and evenly across all altitudes; a spike in carbon dioxide levels in one locality, for instance, quickly diffused through the air at all altitudes such that its concentration become nearly uniform throughout.[22] The findings were alarming for nuclear scientists and policymakers as it spotlighted that the range of nuclear fallout (the residual radioactive material propelled into the upper atmosphere and falling out of the sky following a nuclear blast) might have been severely underestimated. With this new finding, it seemed likely that the impact of a nuclear strike could not be contained at its site; a bomb set off in the Northern Hemisphere would even impact those in the Southern Hemisphere.

---

[19] J. H. Webb, "The Fogging of Photographic Film by Radioactive Contaminants in Cardboard Packaging Materials," *Physical Review* 76, no. 3 (1949): 375–80.

[20] Committee on Natural Resources, "Statement of Senator Jeton Anjain on Behalf of the Rongelap Atoll Local Government," in *Radiation Exposure from Pacific Nuclear Tests: Oversight Hearing Before the Subcommittee on Oversight and Investigations of the Committee on Natural Resources House of Representatives* Serial No. 103-68 (Washington, DC: US Government Printing Office, 1994), 57.

[21] French Hageman, James Gray Jr., Lester Machta, and Anthony Turkevich, "Stratospheric Carbon-14, Carbon Dioxide and Tritium," *Science* 130, no. 3375 (1959): 542–52. Note that 100,000 ft. was the estimated height of the 73 ka Toba Event cloud column, so while the experiments were not designed to study volcanic eruptions, the data collected could be used to do so.

[22] Hageman, Gray, Machta, and Turkevich, "Stratospheric Carbon-14," 49–52.

If the consequences of a nuclear strike could well be global, how bad could it get? Research on volcanoes helped to clarify the question. What was common to both research agendas was an interest in the magnitude of the impact of a potential ejection of massive amounts of sulphuric particles into the atmosphere. Before taking into consideration data from volcanic eruption, military research on nuclear weapons were hampered by what historian of science Paul Edwards characterized as "self-inflicted organized blindness," as such research did not move much beyond a consideration of radiation effects.[23] The US government remained invested in the idea that nuclear weapons can be made "clean" (that is, produce far less radioactive fallout) and used in tactical, surgical strikes well into the 1970s and 80s.[24] However, volcanologists provided alarming clues. In a landmark 1970 paper, English climatologist Hubert Lamb synthesized the scientific research with extant historical data on major reference eruptions: Vesuvius in 1631, Laki in 1783, Krakatau in 1883, Etna in 1886, Mt. Spurr in 1953, Bezymjannaja in 1956, and Agung in 1963.[25] During the eruptions of Laki and Krakatau in particular, contemporary witnesses had noted a "brilliant rosy or fiery red colored glow which lingers near the horizon long after the Sun has set."[26] Leveraging data on how bomb test particles transferred from one point to another, Lamb reconstructed a model of "volcanic dust veils" that blanketed the atmosphere causing these changes in color at sunset and concluded that explosive volcanic activity during the last thousand years was accompanied by regionally widespread episodes of *cooler* climate, of which the Little Ice Age is the best-known example.

This data was key to predicting future catastrophe. A team of scientists led by atmospheric scientist Richard P. Turco published a pioneering paper in 1984 that outlined an apocalyptic "nuclear winter" scenario that could ensue even from a small first strike where the opposite party did not hit back.[27] The catalyst for destruction here was not radiation but smoke—urban smoke from burning cities, fire storms, and wildfires—all of which would send a blanket of aerosols into the atmosphere and plunge the world into a period of cold that would last for more than a year. While the team discounted the possibility of a new Little Ice Age, the prolonged subfreezing temperature, drier climate, low light coupled with radiation spelled massive casualties through starvation. Evidence for volcanic and nuclear winters was entangled: where Lamb had cited projected bomb fallout data, Turco and his team cited data from historic eruptions.

The notion of nuclear winter attracted its fair share of detractors, with several studies contending that Turco's team had disregarded some mitigating variables such as the altitude at which the smoke enters the atmosphere and the effect of soot in creating "dirty snow" that would offset the drop in temperature.[28] But on the whole, the nuclear winter hypothesis—built on data from historic volcanic eruptions as a proxy for burning

[23] Paul N. Edwards, "Entangled Histories: Climate Science and Nuclear Research," *Bulletin of the Atomic Scientists* 68, no. 4 (2012): 34.

[24] For idea of "clean" bombs, see Toshihiro Higuchi, "Clean Bombs: Nuclear Technology and Nuclear Strategy in the 1950s," *Journal of Strategic Studies* 29 (2006): 83–116.

[25] H. H. Lamb, "Volcanic Dust in the Atmosphere with a Chronology and Assessment of Its Meteorological Significance," *Philosophical Transactions of the Royal Society of London* 266, no. 1178 (July 1970): 425–533.

[26] Lamb, "Volcanic Dust," 432.

[27] R. P. Turco et al., "Nuclear Winter: Global Consequences of Multiple Nuclear Explosions," *Science* 122 (1983): 1283–92. These large-scale perturbations later came to be known as "climate forcing."

[28] Alan Robock, "Snow and Ice Feedbacks Prolong the Effects of a Nuclear Winter," *Nature* 310 (1984): 667–70.

cities—effectively ended the idea that a clean nuclear war was possible. The literature on future human annihilation through nuclear war burgeoned in the 1980s. Close on its heels were revised projections about the impact of past volcanic eruptions. Rampino and Self's 1988 model of "volcanic winters" drew heavily on Turco's work on "nuclear winters," in which they directly linked Toba to a 1992 paper that theorized a mechanism where the climate-volcano feedback led to accelerated glaciation in the 73 ka Toba Event. The idea of nuclear and volcanic winters therefore emerged in parallel, both resting on a bedrock of data about how a massive injection of sulphurous particles induced climate change.

That climate science was closely connected to military science is not a new finding. What is less well established, though, is the feedback loop between future and past. Examining research on Toba allows us to see how science made past, present, and future climate changes visible. Data to write the future writes the past. Moreover, such data collection originated from a moral grappling with the problem of containing foreseeable nuclear disaster such that it would exact only an acceptable toll of sentient lives. Such a quest for controlled damage was futile, only making clear the unpredictable scope of past and future catastrophe, further raising the stakes of our moral reckoning. Science was not the only ontological tool that could access and utilize this double perspective. Religious folklore, too, approximates this approach to knowing disaster, not through employing sophisticated tools to detect trace evidence but by postulating an anthropomorphic history consistent with human senses.

Tremors: Sensing Toba

Is the 73 ka Toba Event only accessible through the traces made visible by scientists? This question parallels anthropologist Peter Rudiak-Gould's seemingly simple query: is climate change visible or invisible? He found a dichotomy between physical scientists who emphasize invisibility and climate change's inaccessibility except through instruments, and Indigenous advocates who stressed that their communities at the frontlines were already seeing local changes such as increasing frequency of flash floods.[29] His findings indicate not an ontological gap but a convergence around *seeing*, albeit with different tools. Climate change and attendant impacts on the physical environment are part of a long tail of consequences from a volcanic eruption such as Toba. Volcanologists Donald T. Sanders and Jelle Zeilinga de Boer characterized such consequences stemming from an eruption as "the plucking of a long tight-stretched string representing time."[30] This impact encompassed cultural energy that could last through generations of human lives in the form of narratives, stories, and artifacts that transmogrify the eruption into social memory. Toba's vibrating string entangles the science of seismology with religion and culture.

The Toba Batak are the Indigenous people of northern Sumatra. Their origin stories provide a glimpse into how past eruptions of Toba became folded into a cultural matrix that enmeshed history with future-making. Their version of history-telling was not predicated on events unfolding over linear time; rather, history was lineage tied to storied

---

[29] Peter Rudiak-Gould, "'We Have Seen It With Our Own Eyes': Why We Disagree About Climate Change Visibility," *Weather, Climate and Society* 5 (2013): 120–32.

[30] Donald T. Sanders and Jelle Zeilinga de Boer, *Volcanoes in Human History* (Princeton: Princeton University Press, 2015), 17.

ancestors. For generations, such stories were told orally. Documentation of these oral histories of lineage began with missionaries trying to understand the Batak conception of God. Early documents containing origin stories include a *pustaha* (bark book) in the collection of Herman Neubronner van der Tuuk, a translator sent to the Batak uplands in the 1840s and 1850s by the Netherlands Bible Society (Nederlands Bijbelgenootschap) to learn the language, and a set of papers by a Batak Toba elder called Guru Sinangga who wrote them down at the behest of German missionary Ludwig Nommensen in 1872.[31] Some decades later, Waldemar Hutagalung published a pioneering ethnohistory of the Batak, *Pustaha Batak: Tarombo Dohot Turi-Turian Bangsa Batak*, followed by a similar work by a Dutch scholar and colonial officer, W. K. H. Ypes, in 1932.[32] These works formed the basis for a later Batak history that grafted family history with myth. *Tarombo* (genealogy) was central in all these tellings and helped to explain how a Batak *marga* (patri-clan) came to be situated as they were in the present.

The *tarombo* of each *marga* began similarly, with a common ancestor, Si Boru Daeng Parujar, facing catastrophic earth-shaking.[33] At the beginning of the world, the High God made the universe and ruled over its three tiers of the world where he was known by different names: He was Mulajadi Na Bolon in the upper world, Siloan Na Bolon in the middle, and Pane Na Bolon in the netherworld. Mulajadi Na Bolon created a magical chicken that laid eggs that hatched three children: Batara Guru, Soriosohalipan, and Balabulan.[34] Si Boru Daeng Parujar was the daughter of the first child, Batara Guru. She descended into an empty world to a mountain called Pusuk Buhit on the banks of Lake Toba to escape a marriage to her cousin Raja Odapodap. Life in the middle world was challenging; it was empty and unsteady because of a *naga* called Naga Padoha that swirled through the underworld, leaving tremors in his wake. With the divine help of Mulajadi Na Bolon, Si Boru Daeng Parujar battled Naga Padoha and won. She struck the *naga*'s head with a magical sword and stilled him. Mulajadi Na Bolon then sent down Raja Odapodap to marry her and, newly reconciled with this marriage, Si Boru Daeng Parujar and Raja Odapodap populated the Batak world through their descendent, the eponymous Si Raja Batak, whose progeny founded all the major Batak *marga*. They then returned to the heavens where Si Boru Daeng Parujar could sometimes be seen in the light of a full moon, weaving a cloth that represented the world she was still building.

Does this Indigenous religious folklore—which tells of a formative, earth-shaking event and personifies human experiences of earthquakes in the form of a serpent—refer

---

[31] See Johann Angerler, "Images of God in Toba Batak Story-Telling," *Wacana* 17, no. 2 (2016): 312–16. Parts of Guru Sinagga's text was later translated and published in Sandra Niessen, *Motifs of Life in Toba Batak Texts and Textiles* (Dordrecht: Foris, 1985).

[32] Waldemar M. Hutagalung, *Pustaha Batak: Tarombo Dohot Turiturian Ni Bangso Batak* (1926; repr., Medan: Tulus Jaya, 1991). See also W. K. H. Ypes, *Bijdrage tot de kenis van de stamverwantschap, de inheemsche rechtsgemeenschappen en het grondrecht der Toba-en Dairibataks* (Leiden: Adatrechtstichting, 1932).

[33] There are many written sources of the story of Si Boru Daeng Parujar, with slight variations. Besides sources in the preceding two footnotes, see also P. Lumbantobing, "The Structure of Toba Batak Belief in the High God" (PhD diss., Utrecht University, 1956), 35, 137; Batara Sangti, *Sejarah Batak* (Balige: Karl Sianipar, 1977), 43–47; Yves Bonnefoy, ed., Wendy Doniger, trans., *Asian Mythologies* (University of Chicago Press, 1993), 166. In this paragraph, I present parts of the stories on which all these sources agree and discuss variation later.

[34] Soriosohalipan and Balabulan were taken from the Toba rendition; they were also known as Soripada and Mangalabulan, respectively, in different versions of the tales.

directly to a massive eruption from the Toba volcano? Perhaps not *the* 73ka Toba Event specifically, but it does indicate *a* Toba Event of the past that connects volcanic instability to the community's existence. It is a foundational tale that emerges from postulating disaster as a beginning centered at the lake's caldera in the horizon of the past as an explanation for the peopling of the region and their beliefs in a three-tiered cosmology. It emerges from experiencing life in between eruptions where tremors reminded one of the past eruptions and foreshadowed future ones. A major Toba eruption was thus *sensed* even though it was not concretely defined or dated. The sensing of past disaster through folklore was framed through a notion of history that was not chronological. Rather, it is more productive to think of this history as "antiphonal," as Toba musicologist Julia Byl expresses it, "answering back and forth to each other . . . the echo of a long past experience still audible in the form of a new one."[35] Toba music today performs histories *and* their legacies in alternate beats. Toba poet Sitor Situmorang noted that Si Boru Daeng Parujar's story was embedded in a wedding ritual where the father of the bride would drape a traditional woven cloth (ulos) over a newly wedded couple to bless their union and future progeny; the cloth symbolizing the world that Si Daeng Parujar had populated, still being woven to connect heavens and Earth.[36] The patterns on the *ulos* represented the "motifs of life": Earth, flora, fauna, humans, sun, rain, and cultivated fields.[37] Similarly, Angerler explicates on a pre-Christian Toba Batak ritual dance performed at the founding of a new endeavor: the building of a new house or irrigation canal, for example, as a "renewal of the original relationship with the autochthonous spiritual being originally forged by Boru Daeng Parujar."[38]

Disaster still shadowed life on Earth. This was embodied in the figure of Naga Padoha. The netherworld *naga* chasing its tail was a common trope in folktales and its figure featured not just in illustrations in Batak bark books but in manuscripts of several communities in insular Southeast Asia.[39] From one angle, this dynamic ubiquity was reflective of ongoing religious displacement where Naga Padoha—like the *trimurti* (three forms) of Batara Guru, Soriosohalipan and Balabulan—were part of a complex of Hindu-inflected Indigenous deities that were adapted into Christian beliefs from the late nineteenth century onward. Intriguingly, in a few interpretations of Batak pre-Christian beliefs, Naga Padoha and Pane Na Bolon, the High God's manifestation in the underworld, were understood to be one and the same; source and symbol of how creation and destruction were intertwined.[40] Their intertwining points toward a second

[35] Julia Byl, *Antiphonal Histories: Resonant Pasts in the Toba Batak Musical Present* (Middletown, CT: Wesleyan University Press, 2014), 33.

[36] Sitor Situmorang, *Toba Na Sae* (Jakarta: Yayasan Komunitas Bambu, 2004), 23–36.

[37] Sandra Niessen, *Legacy in Cloth: Batak Textiles of Indonesia* (Leiden: KITLV Press, 2009), 43.

[38] Angerler, "Images of God," 328.

[39] Farouk Yahya, *Magic and Divination in Malay Illustrated Manuscripts* (Leiden: Brill, 2016), 194. Page 206 mentions the talismanic figure 8, known as Solomon's ring entwined with a turtle and two naga that was found buried on a plaque under a post where a sacrificial buffalo was tethered. The mixing of Solomon from monotheistic tradition, the turtle from the Hindu myth of the churning of the ocean of milk, and the Shivaite naga demonstrated the adaptability of each symbol to religious synthesis of the concept of formless power.

[40] On the *naga* as an ambivalent figure, see Robert Wessing, "Symbolic Animals in the Land between the Waters: Markers of Place and Transition," *Asian Folklore Studies* 65 (2006): 208. This interpretation of Naga Padoha and Pane Na Bolon as one and the same has been contested by scholars of Batak religion who considered the High God to be more transcendent than immanent. A brief synopsis of the debate can be found in Angerler, "Images of God," 303–5.

perspective on how to read the *naga* in Si Boru Daeng Parujar's story as simultaneously past and future. Si Boru Daeng Parujar's story puts the present between the parentheses of a challenging natural environment of the past and a supernatural being shaping possible futures. Within these parentheses are moral obligations entailed by such a cosmology in the production and reproduction of human lives.

Such obligations are not static. As with most histories of future-making, this story contains an implicit compass from the past to serve a better future. From the late twentieth century, a few renditions of Si Boru Daeng Parujar's tale acquired an addendum that more explicitly connected her to the status of Toba's natural environment. In these versions, Si Boru Daeng Parujar's firstborn was a formless hunk of flesh that she was understandably grieved and repelled by. With the guidance of her grandfather, the High God, she buried him near the lake, after which the barren landscape became populated with trees. In this variation, trees were, therefore, the elder siblings of humans. This version, emerging in Marpondang's 1992 vernacular publication and then circulating online through separate reiterations by Monang Naipospos and Thompson Hutasoit,[41] was cited in Siburian's academic paper on Batak ecological wisdom of the past.[42] This arboreal firstborn was not mentioned in earlier versions of the story where the ending emphasizes maintaining ritual connection with the ancestor gods of the upperworld. Which version is the true one matters less than the tale's capaciousness in integrating fresh thematic resonances with present deforestation concerns in North Sumatra. The balding slopes overlooking Toba's caldera renews the moral message embodied in Si Boru Daeng Parujar even as the latter offers the past as a way forward in the present crisis, imbricating tradition and innovation. These multiple reinterpretations of what the long past is, what our present duties are, and their implications for our future orientation are also evident in scientific retracing, as the next section will demonstrate.

From Event to Catastrophe

In 1947, the *Bulletin of the Atomic Scientists* began publishing a "Doomsday Clock" that sought to quantify our proximity to "midnight," a metaphor for an impending global catastrophe. For a time, it was thought that nuclear disaster was the most acute direction of danger. That year, when memories of the atomic bomb in Hiroshima and Nagasaki were fresh, it was seven minutes to midnight. In 1983, when the notion of nuclear winter was established, the *Bulletin* moved its Doomsday Clock forward to three minutes to midnight, stressing that "the superpowers . . . are collaborating in an assault upon the basis of the only true security to be had at this point in history: mutual deterrence grounded on the knowledge that to wage nuclear war is to commit national suicide."[43] From 2007, however, the direction of perceived danger shifted to climate

---

[41] Gultom Raja Marpondang, *Dalihan Na Tolu Nilai Budaya Suku Batak* (Medan: CV Armanda, 1992), 198; Naipospos Monang, "Kearifan Budaya Batak Melindung Lingkungan," *TanoBatak*, June 6, 2007, https://tanobatak.wordpress.com/2007/06/20/kearifan-budaya-batak-mengelola-lingkungan/; Hutasoit Thompson, "Pusuk Buhit, Gunung Leluhur Batak," *Naipospos Monang* 2007; Monang Naipospos, "Kearifan Budaya Batak Melindung Lingkungan," *TanoBatak*, June 20, 2007, https://tanobatak.wordpress.com/2007/06/20/kearifan-budaya-batak-mengelola-lingkungan/.

[42] Robert Siburian, "Kearifan Ekologi dalam Budaya Batak Sebagai Upaya Mencegah Bencana Alam," *Masyarakat Indonesia: Majalah Ilmu-Ilmu Sosial Indonesia* 34, no. 1 (2008): 63–86.

[43] Editorial Team, "Three Minutes to Midnight," *Bulletin of the Atomic Scientists* 40, no. 1 (1984): 2.

change. The Doomsday Clock, long based on an evaluation of nuclear proliferation, began to pay attention to the climate crisis. In the intervening decades, Toba's eruption and the specter of species extinction that it raised became important as a representation of the past that could become our future.

Evidence that the 73 ka Toba Event caused a demographic catastrophe came from within the human body. Tracking mitochondrial DNA, biologists sought a family tree that could explain our human ancestry and migration in the distant past. The period around the Toba eruption was particularly interesting in the history of human evolution because it shortly preceded a wave of migration out of what is now Africa and subsequent elimination of every group other than *homo sapiens*, *homo neanderthalensis*, *homo heidelbergensis*, and *homo floresiensis* over the next 25,000 years for reasons that are yet unclear. Some scholars have posited that warfare between *homo sapiens* and other groups induced by migration and competitive contact over resources led to their extinction,[44] while others suggest traces of Neanderthal DNA in the modern human genome point toward interbreeding between Neanderthals and early modern humans to the detriment of the former and the ascendency of the latter.[45] Still others drew our attention to the possibility that the environment also played a significant part; *homo sapiens* might have been the most successful in adapting to a major change in climate.[46] The successful dispersion of humans must have involved small-scale failures and extinctions, experiments that did not work and environmental changes that were too daunting to deal with. While it is not taken as fact that modern humans were relatively more successful in navigating the vicissitudes of a major climatic perturbation, that outcome was by no means certain. At certain points in prehistory, genetic evidence shows that human populations worldwide dropped to a few thousands, forming a "genetic bottleneck" that linked our shared ancestry closer together, including around 70,000 years ago.[47]

Rampino and Self's 1992 paper on Toba was picked up by science journalist Ann Gibbons, who tied this evidence of the "genetic bottleneck" to Toba and raised the possibility that the eruption's climate impact was akin to a "Big Bang" or the impact of a meteorite.[48] Rampino and Self expressed support for Gibbons's notion in a letter to the same magazine and, in 1998, Rampino teamed up with paleo-anthropologist Stephen Ambrose to scientifically flesh out the idea. The resultant paper, published in

[44] P. Hortola and B. Martinez-Navarro, "The Quaternary Megafaunal Extinction and the Fate of Neanderthals: An Integrative Working Hypothesis," *Quaternary International* 295 (2013): 69–72.

[45] Martin Kuhlwihm et al., "Ancient Gene Flow from Early Modern Humans into Eastern Neanderthals," *Nature* 530, no. 7591 (2016): 429–33. For interbreeding, see also Rebecca Rogers Ackermann, Alex Mackay, Michael L Arnold, "The Hybrid Origin of Modern Humans," *Evolutionary Biology* 3 (2015): 1–11.

[46] A theory similar to Toba but explaining the demise of Neanderthals posits that the eruption of Campanian Ignimbrite 40,000 years ago in what is now Italy was a significant reason for their decline. See Benjamin A. Black, Ryan R. Neely, and Michael Manga, "Campanian Ignimbrite volcanism, climate and the final decline of the Neanderthals," *Geology* 43, no. 5 (2015): 411–14.

[47] Russell Lande, "Genetics and Demography in Biological Conservation," *Science* 241, 4872 (1988): 1455–60. The idea of a "genetic bottleneck" was first identified among nonhuman species by conservation biologists interested in the demographic patterns that could result from it. On the existence of such bottlenecks in human or homo groups' history, see John Hawks, Keith Hunley, Sang-Hee Lee, and Milford Wolpoff, "Population Bottlenecks and Pleistocene Human Evolution," *Molecular Biology and Evolution* 17, no. 1 (2000): 2–22.

[48] Ann Gibbons, "Pleistocene Population Explosions," *Research News*, October 1, 1993, 27

Nature in 2000, formally connected genetic bottlenecks in human prehistory to the Toba eruption; a causal link that imputed both disaster and rebirth. The idea that modern humans had emerged in the wake of this demographic disaster was reflected in the provocative title, "Volcanic Winter in the Garden of Eden: The Toba Super-Eruption and the Late Pleistocene Human Population Crash."[49] This was the first time a superlative was attached to the Toba Event and the designation stuck in popular reports of findings related to the volcano for the next two decades.

The discovery of one genetic bottleneck was swiftly followed by scientists working on many different species. Prothero refers to such a preponderance of parallel scientific evidence as a "consilience," a moment when "varying lines of evidence jump together and agree."[50] Primate scientists discovered genetic bottlenecks among orangutans, geneticists studying pandas discovered the phenomenon in panda DNA, and biologists researching tigers found a similar historical trajectory. Through DNA evidence, it appeared that the populations of all these species crashed dramatically about 70,000 years ago before rapidly regaining in numbers about 20,000 years later.[51]

How much agency did and could we have in forestalling the deadly impact of a changing climate? The demographic crashes of our long past painted a dire picture. However, some scientists at work forecasting our future see potential in little steps we could take to set off a cascade of impactful consequences that might eventually allow us to control the atmospheric world system. Others viewed the unintended consequences of such large-scale human action with more trepidation. Cecil Leith, a retired mathematician who had worked on numerical methods to enable modeling of a nuclear winter, summed up the polar ends of this debate when he recounted a conversation with Edward Teller, a meteorologist, on how far science could influence the atmospheric world system. In Leith's telling:

> I always had to argue with Edward about this matter. He would say, "either the atmosphere is very stable in which case it is very predictable . . . or it's unstable, in which case it's controllable." Because he thought, I can do a little thing and have a big consequence. Well . . . [to me], it's chaotic. You can do a little thing and have a big consequence but it's an unpredictable consequence.[52]

Unpredictable consequences in the future informed imaginations of the distant past. In recent years, the Toba super-catastrophe theory of major eruption followed by a species population crash has been challenged by some archaeologists and paleoanthropologists, who observed that they were finding unchanged levels of artifact production in the Earth's strata before and after Toba and that the direction of ash travel could not be determined.[53] In other words, in some archaeological sites of study, Toba's eruption appeared to have made little difference to the communities there; in South

[49] M. R. Rampino and S. H. Ambrose, "Volcanic Winter in the Garden of Eden: The Toba Super-Eruption and the Late Pleistocene Human Population Crash," *Special Paper of the Geological Society of America* 345 (2000): 71–82.

[50] Prothero, "When Humans Nearly Vanished," 137.

[51] Prothero, "When Humans Nearly Vanished," 143–44.

[52] Edwards, "Entangled Histories," 32.

[53] On the objectors to the Toba Catastrophe Theory, see Clive Oppenheimer, "Limited Global Change Due to the Largest Known Quaternary Eruption, Toba," *Quaternary Science Reviews* 21, no. 14–15 (2002): 1593–609;

Africa they even thrived.[54] Proponents of the theory, in response, regarded this evidence as inconclusive since artifact production was not directly related to population levels. News media reporting on the new evidence, however, present a third way to imagine human organization after the Toba Event. Some sites may have become refuge zones with thriving communities even as others were decimated by the volcanic eruption.[55] It was a picture that re-centralized human resilience in the face of crisis and spotlighted survival over mass death. The Toba theory reformulated as such steered away from a catastrophic fall from Eden and projected onto the past the murky possibilities of survival into the future. Less depressing than humanity's extinction, this depiction of species-level survival was nonetheless anemic as an inspiration, lacking a meaningful purpose to survival since the latter was almost randomly allocated. For survival to be meaningful, it had to be positioned in a web of symbiotic inter-species relationships, interpreted through a subjective lens of what was good and what was not in everyday life. Folklore offers a path to that view.

Samosir's Legacy

Indonesia has had its local anxieties about nuclear proliferation and the state's interest in nuclear energy, but such discourse was not prevalent in North Sumatra.[56] Existential anxieties instead center on quotidian activities such as pollution from tourism and fish farming. Recent years have seen periodic mass death of fish; their glistening carcasses a forbidding portent.[57] In Sumatran folktales, a lake's origin is often tied closely to the fates of fishes, birds, and other animals that augur disaster. Mass fish death—or more generally, changes in animal behavior—could be signs of an impending volcanic eruption. This was indicated in folklore of the past, for example, in early modern Javanese manuscripts on the eruption of Kelud in the 1500s, the death of small fish presaged imminent eruption.[58] Scientists such as Martin Wikelski, director of the Max Planck Institute of Ornithology in Radolfzell, have also begun exploring how animal behavior could give warning of imminent earthquakes, eruptions, and tsunamis.[59] In Toba specifically, folktales describe about how the formation of Toba

M. Petraglia et al., "Middle Paleolithic Assemblages from the Indian Sub-continent Before and After the Toba Super-Eruption," Science 317, no. 5834 (2007): 114–16.

[54] Eugene I. Smith et al., "Humans Thrived in South Africa through the Toba Eruption About 74,000 Years Ago," *Nature* 555 (March 28, 2018): 511–22.

[55] Michael Greshko, "These Ancient Humans Survived a Supervolcano," *National Geographic*, March 13, 2018, https://www.nationalgeographic.com/science/article/toba-supervolcano-eruption-humans-south-africa-science; Ed Yong, "Supervolcano Goes Boom. Humans Go Meh?" *The Atlantic*, March 13, 2018, https://www.theatlantic.com/science/archive/2018/03/supervolcano-goes-boom-humans-go-meh/555356/.

[56] For a survey of local nuclear development in Indonesia, see Sulfikar Amir, "The State and the Reactor: Nuclear Politics in Post-Suharto Indonesia," *Indonesia* 89, no. 1 (2010): 101–47.

[57] Ayat S. Karokaro, "Another Mass Fish Kill Hits Indonesia's Largest Lake," *Mongabay*, August 24, 2018, https://news.mongabay.com/2018/08/another-mass-fish-kill-hits-indonesias-largest-lake/; Binsar Bakkara, "How Pollution Is Devastating an Indonesian Lake," *Yale Environment 360*, October 26, 2016, https://e360.yale.edu/features/how-pollution-is-devastating-an-indonesian-lake#:~:text=Farmers%20remove%20thousands%20of%20dead,of%20oxygen%20in%20the%20water.

[58] Adis Imam Munandar and Arjun Fatahilah, "Disaster Mitigation: Case Study of Kelud Volcano Eruption," *IOP Conference Series: Earth and Environmental Science* 436 (December 1, 2012).

[59] Max-Planck-Gesellschaft, "The Sixth Sense of Animals: An Early Warning System for Earthquakes?" *ScienceDaily*, accessed May 23, 2021, www.sciencedaily.com/releases/2020/07/200706101837.htm.

was linked to a natural disaster stemming from an animal's personal tragedy. These stories are of uncertain provenance and their circulation during the second half of the twentieth century demonstrate a timelessness that captures past, present, and future environmental anxieties.

Today, tourists planning a visit to Toba would likely come across variations of the following story about how the lake and island within it came into being. In times unknown, a man called Toba caught a large fish at a river. Upon capture, the fish transformed into a beautiful young woman. The woman agreed to marry him if he promised never to refer to her aquatic origins. The couple lived in harmony and had a child called Samosir. One day in a fit of rage at Samosir, who had eaten up his lunch instead of bringing it to him, the fisherman Toba reproached the child by calling him by the epithet "the son of a fish." Grieved at her husband's broken promise, the woman transformed back into a fish, rent the land apart, and dived into the waters of the river, which spilled over the banks and drowned her husband. At his mother's bidding, Samosir ran for the hills for refuge. A long period of perpetual rain and subsequent floods ensued, submerging most of the lands. What remained in the middle of the newly formed lake was an island called Samosir.[60] We find in this fable, once again, a moral from the past embedded in an explanation about how the lake came to be. The emergence and circulation of this story as well as its contemporary popularity suggests its resonance with twentieth-century local anxieties about the future. Leveraging on a Toba eruption in the long past, the story set a template for the future that could be read and repurposed as a warning amid present environmental anxieties. The fisherman Toba broke his promise to treat his nonhuman wife well; the eruption was a consequence of that broken compact between the human and the nonhuman.

Elements in this story recall the scientific narrative of global cooling, heavy rainfall, and geological subsidence that formed the present Lake Toba and Samosir over thousands of years. Compressed into a domestic drama taking place over a few days, the story spoke of an eruption that rent the earth and created a crater, causing the weather to cool dramatically. A prolonged period of rain filled the crater with water and drowned the original landscape, part of which reemerged from the waters in a new form. Like the narrative of Si Boru Daeng Parujar, the myth of Samosir indicated a prehistorical enactment of a major catastrophe that could be sensed and anthropomorphized in its telling rather than experienced, documented, and related as shared historical memory.

How, why, and for whom the story was narrated might reveal its moral imperatives. Interestingly, I could not find any trace of this story prior to the 1970s. In none of the documented sources generated through colonial encounters could I find a story of a shape-shifting fish that created Lake Toba, including missionary reports of origin stories

[60] I first heard this story while on a guided tour of Lake Toba and find it on many websites and Youtube videos. See, e.g., "The Origins of Lake Toba," Indonesian Folk Tales Wiki, April 20, 2019, https://indonesianfolktales.fandom.com/wiki/The_Origin_of_Lake_Toba "Lagenda Danau Toba Dalam Bahasa Jawa," *Cerita Wayang Bahasa Jawa*, August 3, 2017, https://ceritawayangbahasajawa.blogspot.com/2015/08/legenda-danau-toba-dalam-bahasa-jawa.html; "History of Lake Toba," *The Land of Batak*, accessed April 2, 2021, https://sites.google.com/site/thelandofbatak1/history-of-lake-toba. Geologists studying Toba's resurgence cite it as an interesting aside, e.g., Oregon State University, "Toba—The Rising Super Volcano," *Volcano World*, August 2, 2018, http://volcano.oregonstate.edu/toba-rising-super-volcano.

that could help the cause of conversion.[61] Rather than indicate the recency of such a story, this absence was perhaps a testament to the limited circulation of various stories among Indigenous communities, which might relate certain tales within their own circles but restrict their telling to outsiders.[62]

A 1970s folktale documentation project appeared to be the first to access pieces of this story on the fish and Lake Toba—and here, how these tales were used to shape morality in the public sphere was clearer. Dispatched by the Ministry of Education and Culture to North Sumatra, investigators in this group project articulated a desire on the part of the Indonesian state to leverage on prehistorical oral community stories to form a bulwark that embodied values that the state wished to inculcate in future generations. They noted that it was still quite challenging to encourage these groups to share their oral traditions and encountered suspicion and concerns about commercialization among the community, especially when they probed narratives about the genealogies of specific patriclans.[63] Nonetheless, the public emergence and subsequent popularity of folk stories about the formation of lakes and other natural landmarks in the 1970s reflected the Indigenous Bataks' new leaning into academic documentation that could preserve the capacity of these stories to explain the slow catastrophes of the present, such as overfishing and deforestation, among others.

Comprising a largely non-Batak writing team collaborating with Batak informants, the group published a collection of folktales gathered during fieldwork in 1979 and 1980. These works were written in Bahasa Indonesia, often translated from Toba Batak. In the volume's foreword, Director-General of Culture, Prof. Haryati Soebadio highlighted that the project aimed to collect myths and legends that embody values "consistent with the values of the Pancasila" so as to protect culture and heritage from "the penetration of outside influences."[64] Similar aims were stated in the many other publications resulting from work in diverse areas in Indonesia: Kalimantan Timur (1978), Betawi (1979), Riau (1982), Bengkulu (1982), Aceh (1984), Nusa Tenggara Barat (1984).[65] The project was not the first to draw on the Pancasila (Indonesia's Constitution), which was a complex document usually invoked at the center of debates over what Indonesia was, its values, and its constituencies. In the context of the 1970s and 1980s, at the height of the New Order Regime, the Pancasila became a focal reference for the state's quest for ideological

---

[61] On Toba Batak encounters with missionaries and the sources generated, see Johan Hasselgren, *Rural Batak, Kings in Medan: The Development of Toba Batak Ethno-religious Identity in Medan, Indonesia, 1912–1965* (Uppsala: Studia Missionalia Upsaliensia, 2000), 21–30.

[62] On storytelling tradition among the Batak, see Clara Brakel-Papenhuyzen, Dairi *Stories and Pakpak Storytelling: A Storytelling Tradition from the North Sumatran Rainforest* (Leiden: Brill, 2014), 19–36.

[63] Mangantar Napitupulu, ed., *Ceritera Rakyat Daerah Sumatera Utara* (Jakarta: Departemen Pendidikan dan Kebudayaan, Proyek Inventarisasi dan Dokumentasi Kebudayaan Daerah, 1982), 4.

[64] Napitupulu, *Ceritera Rakyat Sumatera*, 1–2.

[65] See Proyek Penelitian dan Pencatatan Kebudayaan Daerah, *Cerita Rakyat Daerah Kalimantan Timur* (Jakarta: Departemen Pendidikan dan Kebudayaan, Proyek Inventarisasi dan Dokumentasi Kebudayaan Daerah, 1978); R. R. Dwiantri, *Cerita Rakyat Daerah Riau* (Jakarta: Departemen Pendidikan dan Kebudayaan, Proyek Inventarisasi dan Dokumentasi Kebudayaan Daerah, 1982); *Cerita Rakyat Daerah Bengkulu* (Jakarta: Departemen Pendidikan dan Kebudayaan, Proyek Inventarisasi dan Dokumentasi Kebudayaan Daerah, 1982); U. U. Hamidy and Erli Yetti, ed., *Cerita Rakyat Daerah Istimewa Aceh* (Jakarta: Departemen Pendidikan dan Kebudayaan, Proyek Inventarisasi dan Dokumentasi Kebudayaan Daerah, 1984); Firmana Angela Nai, ed., *Cerita Rakyat Daerah Nusa Tenggara Barat* (Jakarta: Departemen Pendidikan dan Kebudayaan, Proyek Inventarisasi dan Dokumentasi Kebudayaan Daerah, 1984).

hegemony. Rapid development enabled by foreign direct investment and natural resource extraction—feeding a growing middle class while enriching a small elite—sparked questions about Indonesia's moral values and how these swift changes to the economy rendered Indonesia susceptible to becoming "Western."

Therefore, the stories collected through the documentation projects were narrated with a view to cultivating the "right" values for the future. We can find pieces of Toba, the fisherman and his wife, in two stories the Ministry team published in the North Sumatra volume. The first is in a tale called *Balige Raja* (The King of Balige), where a human king married the sister of Si Boru Daeng Parujar. He achieved this magical union by stealing the clothes she needed to fly back to the heavens while she was bathing in a lake. Naked and trapped, she promised to marry him if he would, in turn, promise never to bring up the fact that she could fly. One day, however, angry with their son who wouldn't stop crying, he reproached the son by calling him "the son of a flying being." She thus left him and departed to the heavens with their son. After many trials, he managed to meet her in the upper realm and begged to be allowed to stay, which he did after bringing his son down to Earth to perpetuate his bloodline.[66] *Balige Raja* is thus similar to Toba and his fish-as-wife, although its happy ending departs from the former. In both stories though, the flight of birds and the demise of fishes presage a natural disaster stemming from an estrangement between human and nonhuman. The element of catastrophe engendered by broken promises *between* humans could also be found in a separate folktale in the same collection. Titled *Terjadinya Laut Tador* (The Making of Tador Lake), the tale tells of a king who inadvertently left his daughter with only scraps from a feast. His aggrieved offspring prayed for rain to engulf the kingdom. The repentant king threw himself into the floods that sank his kingdom and turned into an island.[67] Similar to the Toba story, disaster remakes a landscape that was structured by the same moral choices: to be or not to be filial, respectful of the nonhuman, and committed to promises.

These pieces from the oral stories seemed to have been stitched into their present popular form, comprising Toba the fisherman and his fish/wife and bundled into a religious moral blanket, over the next two decades of New Order rule. In 1995, Yayasan Pustaka Nusatama, a Christian foundation based in Yogyakarta, published this version of the Lake Toba story in a collection of moral stories for children.[68] The story persisted in this form; reproduced in children's books and circulated on many websites as well as YouTube travelogues about Toba from the 2000s to the present. Several of these tellings were by tourists for tourists.[69] Tourism in Toba has burgeoned from the late 1990s, affecting everyday as well as ritual life at multiple levels.[70] In this form, the story became a digestible piece about the wonders of Lake Toba, told by travel literature and tour

[66] Napitupulu, *Ceritera Rakyat Sumatera*, 26–39.

[67] Napitupulu, *Ceritera Rakyat Sumatera*, 117–20.

[68] Dra Sujiati and V. Sujiati, *Cerita Rakyat Sumatera* (Yogyakarta: Yayasan Pustaka Nusatama, 1995).

[69] A stand-alone children's tale published later is Suroso and Suhartanto, *Kisah Danau Toba* (Jakarta: Penerbit Bhuana Ilmu Populer, 2016). See, e.g., Martin Johnson, "The Origin of Lake Toba in North Sumatra, Indonesia," Motovlog Indonesia, November 23, 2013, YouTube video, 10:15, https://www.youtube.com/watch?v=pHP_APCFBJQ.

[70] On tourism's impact in Indonesia, see Rithaony Hutajulu, "Tourism's Impact on Toba Batak Ceremony," *Bijdragen tot de Taal-, Land-, en Volkenkunde* 151, no. 4 (1995): 639–55; Andrew Causey, *Hard Bargaining in Sumatra: Western Travelers and Toba Bataks in the Marketplace of Souvenirs* (Honolulu: University of Hawai'i Press, 2003).

guides, peppered among popular invocations of prior cannibalism, spirit communions, folk dances, and woven cloth souvenirs that tourists consumed about the Toba past.

What does this brief history about the circulation, unmaking, and remaking of a popular story about the origins of Lake Toba illustrate about the role of catastrophe as a history of the future? First, it demonstrates a persistent moral trope: a natural disaster resulting from a tense union between the material human and an amorphous, sometimes unseen, divinity as well as greedy acquisition from the unfilial child of that union. Second, it reminds us of local knowledge that the flight or demise of animals signaled impeding disaster for humans and estrangement between human and nonhuman permanently remakes a landscape. State and market capitalization of such stories invests them with anxiety about the future of a society's identity and simultaneously tethers it to a promising future if we remain guided by the values of the past. Third, it is ultimately a story about the capricious power of nature over the human. Folklore about Lake Toba seems to have settled into a shape that stressed a locus of powers outside humankind where survival was selected through personal moral choices.

By stressing that transcendent locus, state-led moralizing through community folktales acknowledges that the actions of tampering with the unseen could result in unforeseen consequences—an acknowledgement that is not unlike Cecil Leith's insight on the scale of unpredictability. But where science tentatively advanced the vision of a resilient humanity in surviving past and future catastrophe in tiny refuge pockets, folklore bound survival to moral choice and underscored how abstract anxiety about the future crisis needed to be made legible through personal options. These stories force us to reckon with the question of precisely *who* will survive; a question that scientific narratives of catastrophe can elide by focusing on *what* will. Building a conversation at the intersection of this common anxiety will require an accounting of both.

Conclusion

A famous scene in Joshua Oppenheimer's important film *The Act of Killing* took place at a restaurant shaped like a giant fish overlooking Lake Toba. The restaurant went bust during the 1997 financial crisis, and Oppenheimer staged dance sequences on its empty premises; sequences whose kitschness underscored the grisliness of the playful reenactments of the orchestrated mass killings in 1960s Indonesia. The choice of Lake Toba for this scene was deliberate. According to Oppenheimer:

> Lake Toba, the lake behind the fish . . . the most important place in our history as a species. It actually was a crater lake from a volcano that erupted 75,000 years ago. . . . We're all much more closely related than we should be and one explanation for this is the Toba super-catastrophe. So in that sense, at the very end of the film where they are dancing with the lake behind them, they really are dancing this sort of *danse macabre* at the edge of the abyss.[71]

That abyss was never far from either our past or our future. The Toba super-catastrophe rendered here as scientific narrative and historical myth, is a history of the

---

[71] Irene Lusztig, "The Fever Dream of Documentary: A Conversation with Joshua Oppenheimer," *Film Quarterly* 67, no. 2 (2013): 55.

future in several ways. As the 73 ka Toba Event, it was reconstructed from tools designed to assess the prognosis for human survival through nuclear war. It gained salience as a moment in history that almost obliterated *homo sapiens*; a moment that could well repeat itself if climate change was not forestalled or nuclear war was not averted. It served as a reminder of the uncertainty of human survival in the distant past and future. As myth and folklore, it presents a motif whose themes beat alternately to the drums of the past, present, and future. It projects from a peopled present to an empty past, embodying the dangers represented by regular tremors into stories where creation and destruction worked in concert. It can be utilized to uphold a set of values that structured life in the region, even as it was sold as part of an effort to secure an economic future. In all its renditions, the Toba super-catastrophe stories recognized how uncertainty loomed on two horizons. Braiding these stories together offers us not just a sense of how the future emerged from the past but also how the past came into being from the future—and urges us to share both.

Processions: How the Spiritual Geographies of Central Java Shaped Modern Volcano Science

Adam Bobbette

Abstract

This paper brings together the spiritual geographies of the central Javanese sultanates and modern volcano science since the early twentieth century. It shows how modern volcano scientists were enabled to undertake their fieldwork along the ritual pathways of Mount Merapi. It shows how colonial scientists relied on Javanese labor to undertake their work and how they engaged with Javanese volcano knowledges. The modern scientific conception of the necessary relationship between volcanism on land and deep water trenches mirrored spiritual geographical concepts of the Yogyakarta sultanate. Colonial and postcolonial scientific work on Javanese volcanoes made crucial contributions to the formulation and adoption of the theory of plate tectonics in the 1960s and 1970s that reimagined the evolutionary history of the lithosphere. The theory of plate tectonics did not fundamentally contradict the spiritual topography of the central Javanese sultanates, rather, this paper demonstrates how they were assembled together.

Keywords: Mount Merapi, spiritual geographies, geology, processions, plate tectonics, infrastructure, cosmology

Mount Merapi is a volcano in Central Java that has long been of interest to Western scientists. Europeans have scaled, measured, painted, and wrote about Merapi at least

Adam Bobbette is a geographer and lecturer in the School of Geographical and Earth Sciences, University of Glasgow.

since 1786 when Francois van Boekhold ascended from the village of Selo.[1] The German naturalist Franz Junghuhn spent two months there in 1844, also in Selo, drawing it and describing its geography.[2] In the late nineteenth century, with a rise of interest in Java's volcanoes, Merapi became of crucial significance for colonial geologists in the Netherlands Indies seeking to understand Javanese volcanism and forge the burgeoning discipline of volcanology. Merapi came to be at the center of debates about why volcanoes erupted, how they were formed, and, even, the role they played in the evolution of Earth itself.

Yet Merapi was not only of interest to Europeans. Long before the appearance of curious Western naturalists, Merapi was at the center of cosmologies of Hindu, Buddhist, and Islamic societies with influence throughout the region. When European geologists and scientists sought to understand and narrate Merapi's history, they did so in a place that had long developed volcano knowledges.

This paper looks at the intersections of these knowledges and their conceptions of volcanism. It investigates how European geological sciences and volcanology were enabled by Central Javanese environmental knowledges. In particular, this paper follows how Javanese Islam shaped scientific volcanology by paying close attention to the infrastructures, the roads and pathways, that connected urbanized sultanates and towns below Merapi to the peak. These paths were originally developed to undertake ritualized processions to give offerings to deities on the volcano and connect them to spiritual geographies further afield in the Indian Ocean. Procession routes were used for pilgrimages, royal rituals, and spiritual tourism, but they also formed spiritual networks between deities in different locations, connecting spiritual topographies, from volcano to ocean, forests, caves, river confluences, and the cosmos. It was along these very same pilgrimage and ritualized procession paths that European scientists traveled to investigate, map, and narrate Merapi. The same routes that were taken by the sultans of Central Java to provide offerings to Merapi deities and deities in the Indian Ocean were then followed by scientists seeking access to the crater. This paper explores how these spiritual infrastructures shaped and enabled scientific volcanology. In doing so, it foregrounds often overlooked forms of Javanese agency—paths, rituals, labor, and infrastructure—and their often subtle, sometimes nonlinear, influence on the emergence of volcano science. This paper contributes to recent endeavors to decenter the West in the formation of modern earth sciences by honing in on the multiple ways that they were enabled by non-Western actors and traditions.[3] It also foregrounds the ways in which those sciences did not represent a radical break or departure from non-Western sources but extended them in key respects.

[1] Newman van Padang, "History of Volcanology in the East Indies," *Scripta Geologica* 71 (1983): 10.

[2] Franz Junghuhn, *Java: sein Gestalt, Pflanzendecke und Innere Bauart* (Leipzig: Arnold, 1857): 328–29.

[3] See for instance, Adam Bobbette, Alison Bashford, Emily Kern, eds. *New Earth Histories* (Chicago: Chicago University Press, 2022); Simon Schaffer, Lissa Roberts, Raj Kapil, and James Delbourgo, *The Brokered World: Go-Betweens and Global Intelligence, 1770–1820* (Sagamore Beach: Watson Publishing International, 2009); James Delbourgo, "The Knowing World: A New Global History of Science," *History of Science* 57, no. 3 (2019): 373–99; Pratik Chakrabarti, *Inscriptions of Nature: Geology and the Naturalization of Antiquity* (Baltimore: Johns Hopkins University Press, 2020); Sujit Sivasundaram, Waves across the South: *A New History of Revolution and Empire* (Dublin: HaperCollins, 2020).

Historians and geographers of Central Java have tended to overlook the relationships between modern Javanese cosmologies and the earth sciences. Central Java is very well represented by scholarship on plantations and the role of the botanical sciences in the formation of the Dutch empire.[4] Environmental historians have appreciated the connections between traditional Javanese social structures, environmental change, and environmental degradation.[5] Anthropologists, at the same time, have long understood the relationships between environmental change and traditional belief systems.[6] Little attention has been paid, though, to the formation of the modern volcanological sciences in Indonesia since their emergence in the late nineteenth century and their interaction with Hindu, Buddhist, and Islamic environmental knowledges. It is a surprising oversight not only because of the number of Javanese volcanoes, but because volcano science was crucial for the maintenance of the Dutch colonial plantation system. Scientists sought to protect the plantations and in doing so developed insights about the nature of volcanism that transformed broader narratives about the evolution of the Earth surface.

Cosmic-Material Networks

Merapi is a stratovolcano bordered on the north by its dormant neighbor Merbabu. To the east is the sultanate and city of Surakarta, to the south is the sultanate and city of Yogyakarta. The spiritual geography under consideration here emerged with the creation of the Sultanate of Yogyakarta and Sultanate of Surakarta in 1755 through the breakup of the Mataram Kingdom. The reason for this focus is the surplus and generally well-known source material and scholarship based on the *babad* court chronicles. The chronicles describe in great detail the origins of the two sultanates and their predecessor, the sultanate of Mataram, founded by Senopati around 1575 through his enlistment of spiritual forces for his political campaign. Of particular significance for the spiritual geography of Mataram was Senopati's encounter with the goddess of the Indian Ocean, Nyai Ratu Kidul, on the coast, nearly thirty kilometers south of what would later become the city of Yogyakarta. The Surakarta babad, begun in the period of Susuhunan Pakubuwana IV (1788—1820), after the division of the Mataram kingdom, described Nyai Ratu Kidul and Senopati sleeping together and marrying.[7] Future sultans in both kingdoms would also marry the goddess. By at least 1805, but almost certainly much earlier, the beach at the South Sea, nearby caves, and river confluences had been

---

[4] See, Andrew Goss, *The Floracrats: State-Sponsored Science and the Failure of the Enlightenment in Indonesia* (Madison: University of Wisconsin Press, 2011), 1–140; Tanyia Murray Li, *The Will to Improve: Governmentality, Development, and the Practice of Politics* (Durham: Duke University Press, 2007), 1–31.

[5] Peter Boomgaard, Frontiers of Fear: *Tigers and People in the Malay World, 1600-1950* (New Haven: Yale University Press, 2001); Martin C. Lukas, "Eroding Battlefields: Land Degradation in Java Reconsidered," *Geoforum* 56 (September 2014), 87–100.

[6] Lucas Sasongko Triyoga, *Manusia Jawa dan Gunung Merapi: Persepsi dan Kepercayaannya* (Yogyakarta: Gadjah Mada University Press, 1991), 8–10, 115–27; Nancy Lee Peluso, *Rich Forests, Poor People: Resource Control and Resistance in Java* (Berkely: University of California Press, 1994), 3–44.

[7] M. C. Ricklefs, *Jogjakarta under Sultan Mangkubumi* 1749–1792 (London: Oxford University Press, 1974). For Ricklefs's reflections on the genealogy and geography of Ratu Kidul, see 387–413. See also the Indonesian translation of the Meinsma translation based in turn on the Otlof translation of the Surakarta Babad: *Babad Tanah Jawi Mulai dari Nabi Adam Sampai Tahun 1647* (Yogyakarta: Narasi, 2014), 93–99.

major pilgrimage sites to the goddess by sultans, sages, mystics, and revolutionaries.[8] Dipanagara, who led Javanese forces against the Dutch in the Java War in 1825, for instance, not only titled himself the Just King (*Ratu Adil*) and waged a righteous war against colonial oppression, he also enlisted the spiritual forces of the Goddess of the Indian Ocean several times.[9] The significance of Nyai Ratu Kidul was familiar to Dutch colonial geographers and ethnologists, too. In *Java: Geography, Ethnology, and History*, Pieter Veth described "the vast territory of Ratoe Loro Kidul," that stretched across the south of Java, and the cave south of Yogyakarta where the Ratu and Senopati slept together.[10]

In the 1850s, babad accounts describe also the significance of deities in Merapi, north of the Indian Ocean. According to these accounts, the court of Yogyakarta enlisted the support of the deities of both the Indian Ocean and Merapi. Prince Dipasana, for instance, who died circa 1840, was married to the daughter of Raden Sapujagad, the ruling deity of Merapi.[11] Sapujagad translates roughly as "sweeper of the cosmos," or more loosely "cosmic cleaner."[12] Dipasana was apparently skilled in magic and enlisting the solidarity of the spirit world and even drew on his powers to attempt a coup.[13] The origin of Sapujagad, however, is contested. He may have been an Islamization of the much more ancient deity Juru Taman,[14] "guardian of land." There was also a cannon built for Sultan Agung called Sapu Djagad in the 1620s during his pious campaign against the Dutch East India Company.[15] It was perhaps that the Merapi deity was named after the cannon, or the cannon named after the deity. Whatever the direction of influence, Sapu Djagad's home in Merapi was considered a northern border of spiritual and political significance, while the Queen of the Indian Ocean, Nyai Ratu Kidul, ruled the south. This constituted the foundational coordinates of the material and spiritual territory of Yogyakarta.

These coordinates were activated through frequent ritual processions between them. R. Soedjana Tirtakoesoema, a translator at the Java Institute in Yogyakarta, recorded a Labuhan procession in 1921 in which the sultan and his retinue paraded to the Indian Ocean to give offerings to the spirit queen, before they turned toward Merapi.[16] They progressed first by train to Kalasan (near to Prambanan), then to the administrative center at Kejambon, and finally to the village of Ngrangkah (Umbulharjo) on the southern slope. The retinue progressed a few kilometers up the steep slope to the edge of the vegetation line in order to provide the final offerings. They then harvested slabs

---

[8] Peter Carey, *The Power of Prophecy: Prince Dipanagara and the End of an Old Order in Java, 1785–1855* (Leiden: KITLV Press, 2008), 141.

[9] Carey, *The Power of Prophecy*, xi–xxii.

[10] P. J. Veth, *Java, Geographisch, Ethnologisch, Historisch* (Haarlem: De Erven F. Bohn, 1882), 377, 680.

[11] Edwin Wieringa, "The Illusion of an Allusion: A Soothing Song for the Exiled Prince Dipasana (d. ca. 1840) in Ambon," *Journal of the Royal Asiatic Society* 10, no. 2 (2000): 199; Carey, *The Power of Prophecy*, 493–99.

[12] For Ricklefs's geography and genealogy of Sapujagad connected with Ratu Kidul, see n. 9 above.

[13] Carey, The Power of Prophecy.

[14] Ricklefs, *Jogjakarta under Sultan Mangkubumi*, 404n88.

[15] H. J. de Graaf, "De Regering van Sultan Agung, Vorst van Mataram 1613–1645 en die van zijn Voorganger Panembahan Seda-Ing-Krapjak 1601–1613," *Verhandelingen van het Koninklijk Instituut voor Taal-, Land- en Volkenkunde* 23 (1958): 125.

[16] R. Soedjana Tirtakoesoema, "De Verjaring van den Verheffingsdag van Z.H. den Sultan van Jogjakarta (Tingalan Pandjenengan)," *Djåwå* 6, no. 13 (1933): 377–82.

of sulphur for the palace. The gatekeeper, or Juru Kunci, responsible for conducting the ritual on behalf of the sultan said the following: "I have been dispatched by His highness the Sultan of Yogyakarta to present the royal clothing which is being offered to those who rule at the 'navel' of the land of Java, Mount Merapi."[17] He named the following deities as those who rule the navel, Merapi: Sangyang Umar, Kyai Empu Permadi, Kyai Brama Kedhali, Gusti Eyang Panembahan Prabu Jagad, Kyai Sabuk Angin, Bok Nyai Gadhung Mlathi, and Gusti Panembahan Megantara.[18] These names are important because of their honorifics, such as the "the highest" and the "greatest," and refer to titles and rank such as king or kyai (a Muslim scholar). Some deities were local ancestors, figures of historical importance, and deities of Islamic descent, as well as belonging to Hindu genealogies. Kyai Empu Permadi, for instance, was a wayang character of the genealogy of Batara Guru, a variation on characters from the *Mahabharata*. In this instance, the character from the Hindu epic had metamorphosed into a kyai. In the spiritual-material topography of the Labuhan, Merapi was historical and genealogical, reflecting the social hierarchies of the sultanate, and combined the spiritual geographies of Hinduism, Buddhism, and Islam. The ritual pathways that connected the sultan to the Indian Ocean and the volcano materialized those cosmic geographies. Merapi, in 1921, was made of material and spiritual networks that were simultaneously local and cosmic.

Part of governing the sultanate in 1921 was the maintenance of this physical and spiritual geography through rituals such as the Labuhan. The realms of the ocean and volcano were connected, the rumblings and movements of one were understood to be implicated in the other. Deities also traveled between the two realms. The village of Ngrangkah (Umbulharjo) was important not only as the site where offerings were given, but also because of the access it created, the literal paths that extended through the village to the crater for those processions. Those paths later became infrastructure for scientific fieldwork.

Colonial Volcano Science

In 1921 when the Labuhan ritual was recorded by Tirtakoesoema, the spiritual geography of Merapi was becoming legible to an increasing number of colonial scientists. This began with the eruption of Gunung Kelud in East Java in 1919. The crater lake inside the volcano was blown out and created a massive mudslide down the flanks, destroying plantations and even swallowing parts of the market town of Blitar.[19] The colonial government, worried about disruptions to its plantation economy, established the Volcano Observation Service.[20] As a part of this, mining engineers and geologists established permanent observatories on the most dangerous Javanese volcanoes, including Merapi. Scientists built an observatory hut on a hill called Maron across the

[17] R. Soedjana Tirtakoesoema, "The Anniversary of the Accession of His Highness the Sultan of Yogyakarta (Tingalan Panjenengan)," in *The Kraton: Selected Essays on Javanese Courts*, ed. Stuart Robson (Leiden: Brill, 2003), 156.

[18] Tirtakoesoema, "De Verjaring van den Verheffingsdag."

[19] G. L. L. Kemmerling, "De Uitbarsting van den G. Keloet in den Nacht van den 19den op den 20sten Mei 1919," *Vulkanologische Mededeelingen* no. 2 (1921): 6–9.

[20] Van Padang, "History of Volcanology," 24.

river from Umbulharjo where the Labuhan procession took place in 1921.[21] The idea was that the elevation of the hill would shelter observers from eruptions. The hut represented the first permanent installation of state scientists on the remote slopes and resulted in access to the procession routes to undertake fieldwork. Those routes would have been the only paths through the densely forested, uninhabited upper flanks.

George Kemmerling, the head of the Volcanological Survey, undertook a number of fieldtrips to study the causes of Merapi's eruptions and reported in 1922 that they had begun to understand that earthquakes after eruptions were being recorded at a distance in the Indian Ocean 250 kilometers south of Yogyakarta.[22] What Kemmerling and his seismologist colleagues were beginning to suspect for the first time was that volcanism in Merapi and earthquakes in the Indian Ocean were connected. He wrote, "After all, it seemed very possible that the imbalance occurring in the Indian Ocean creates an effect in Merapi."[23] He came to this conclusion while conducting fieldwork on what he called "an old ritual path"—the path of the Labuhan—to make his way up to the southern edge of the crater.[24] He ended his visit, like the Labuhan had before, in the same field where sulphur chunks were harvested for the sultan.[25] It is very likely that Kemmerling had access to the Labuhan path by way of Javanese *mantris*, the assistants who accompanied scientists, conducted fieldwork, carried their equipment, and acted as translators with Javanese locals.[26]

Kemmerling's idea that events in the crater were linked to events in the Indian Ocean had only recently been appreciated. The prevailing framework for many colonial geologists in the Netherlands Indies since the late nineteenth century was that volcanoes were separate individual units that exploded as they fell apart. Rogier Verbeek wrote in his *Geology of Java*, the first complete geological survey of Java from 1896, that volcanoes were ruins of once great mountains.[27] Kemmerling in 1922 was coming to understand that, instead, Merapi's volcanism was somehow connected to the Indian Ocean. This indicated a reorientation of the Dutch imaginary toward topographic and subterranean connectivity between the Indian Ocean and the volcano. It is not insignificant that these insights were being worked out along the pathways of the Labuhan, the very infrastructure for ritual processions that literally connected deities in the volcano with deities in the Indian Ocean. Kemmerling, through seeking to connect seismological evidence with records from observatories and fieldwork, sought to connect the hidden causal relations between the two geographies. While there is no indication that Kemmerling understood the meaning of the Labuhan, its infrastructure, based also on the connection between the Indian Ocean and volcano, enabled his fieldwork.

[21] Van Padang, "History of Volcanology," 25.

[22] George Kemmerling, "Vulkanologische Berichten," Natuurkundig Tijdschrift voor Nederlandsch-Indie 82, no. 2 (1922): 188–94.

[23] Kemmerling, "Vulkanologische Berichten," 188.

[24] Kemmerling, "Vulkanologische Berichten," 194.

[25] Kemmerling, "Vulkanologische Berichten."

[26] See also Susie Protschky and Ruth Morgan, "Historicising Sulfur Mining, Lime Extraction and Geotourism in Indonesia and Australia," *The Extractive Industries and Society* 8, no. 2 (2021). https://doi.org/10.1016/j.exis.2021.02.001, 8-9.

[27] R. D. M. Verbeek and R. Fennema, *Description* Géologique de Java et Madoura tome II (Amsterdam: Stemler, 1896), 1014.

On that same expedition, Kemmerling also visited the crater from the north via the village of Selo to a plateau of large boulders called Pasarboebar (also Pasar Bubrah or Pasar Bubar) that abuts the crater wall.[28] The name Pasar Bubar means in Javanese "ruined market" or "thrown market." Kemmerling's inclusion of the toponym in his contribution to *Volcanological Reports* in 1922 is an early appearance of its usage in geologists' literature. Pasar Bubar was named as such because the boulders were understood to be market stalls for the pantheon of spirits in the volcano who would establish their night market there to trade goods with each other. At around the same time as Kemmerling's presence at the Thrown Market, another toponym of a large hill also appeared in the vocabulary of colonial volcano scientists—"Mesjidanlama," or "old mosque," so named because it was the mosque that volcano deities worshiped in. Dutch attention to these terms not only bears witness to the existence of these spiritual geographies in the 1920s, they also recorded the presence of scientists in these places by way of the processional ritual infrastructures that brought them there. The appearance of these spiritual geographies in their maps begins to indicate the direct manner in which Merapi's spiritual geographies shaped how volcano scientists saw Merapi even if scientists were not always familiar with their spiritual significance.

In the 1920s, colonial scientists had begun to reconstruct the history of Merapi to understand the character of its eruptions and manage future catastrophes. Many colonial geologists were trained as mining engineers and they brought with them an attention to the flows and movements of geological material as well as a stratigraphic way of reading the landscape. They categorized Merapi according to layers of eruptive events so as to reconstruct its past. Features such as Masjidanlama or Pasar Bubar were incorporated into scientific topography as events in the historical evolution of the volcano. Chemical and stratigraphic analysis, for instance, by Ong Tian Siang Masdar suggested that Mesjidanlama was Augite-olivine basalt, a product of nineteenth-century lava, perhaps produced as recently as 1872.[29] Gunung Turgo, on the southwest slope, across a river from where the Labuhan stops to give offerings, came to signify a "parasitic cone," according to Reinout van Bemmelen.[30] For Rogier Verbeek, Plawangan, where Kemmerling joined the Labuhan path, was an ancient volcanic crater from the time when he thought Yogyakarta was submerged under the ocean and its waves lapped all the way to the base of the volcano.[31] Scientists incorporated the toponyms of the spiritual geography of Merapi and gave them new natural histories, often without appreciating their significance.

By the late 1920s and early 1930s, volcano observation posts had begun to forge new networks from the existing spiritual geographies. At Sisir, for instance, a *tongtong*—a wooden gong used for the call to prayer—was repurposed for making warning signals

[28] Kemmerling, "Vulkanologische Berichten."

[29] R. W. van Bemmelen, "Table XIV, Petrography and Chemical Composition of the Merapi Lavas," *Kogyo Jimusho: Bulletin of the East Indian Volcanological Survey for the Year 1941*, no. 95–98 (1943): 72–74, Table XIV.

[30] R. W. Van Bemmelen, "Merapi, no. 41. State During 1941," *Kogyo Jimusho: Bulletin of the East Indian Volcanological Survey for the Year 1941*, no. 95–98 (1943): 70.

[31] R. D. M. Verbeek and R. Fennema, *Description Géologique de Java et Madoura Tome I* (Amsterdam: Stemler, 1896), 372.

for incoming eruptions.[32] Newman van Padang explained that the tongtong could foretell an oncoming mudslide one half to one hour in advance of its arriving in a village.[33] The warning posts were also connected to Muntilan, a market town on the western slope, by telephone.[34] These were some of the earliest installations of telephones on the otherwise impoverished, rural slopes. A permanent post was built at Babadan, on the northwest flank, that included a bunker that would allow scientists to hide in case of an eruption. The bunker included a seismograph and a telephone connection to Muntilan such that the observers could continue to communicate even in the course of eruptions. The bunker also included asbestos overalls, gasmasks, and oxygen tanks, adapting militarized solutions for eruptions.[35] The communication networks between observatories were new not only because of their technologies—telephones and radios— but also because they emerged from and cut across existing spiritual infrastructures. Dutch colonial communication networks made new connections between the north, west, and south and with Muntilan. They were not organized, like the predominant north-south spiritual axis of the sultanate. Yet, at the same time, scientists continued to use ritual pathways of the Labuhan to access, measure, and monitor the crater. As new monitoring networks emerged from these geographies, preexisting deities and their topographies did not disappear. The Sultan of Yogyakarta continued to organize Labuhans as scientists sought to connect their observatories across Java and beyond.

Observatories in the 1920s and 1930s were connected also to the Geological Survey in Bandung. Reinout van Bemmelen, Georges Kemmerling, Johannes Umbgrove, Charles Stehn, and others lived in Bandung and frequently traveled to Merapi. The Geological Survey in 1924, for instance, included thirty-seven trained geologists and nearly one hundred Indonesian staff.[36] They undertook extensive fieldwork and surveys across all of Java and the Indonesian archipelago. A bulletin of volcanological observations was used to consolidate their networks and extensive studies of individual volcanoes or eruptions were published as *Vulcanological Communications* (Vulkanologische Mededeelingen), which was superseded by the *Bulletin of the Netherlands Indies Volcanological Survey*. Published primarily in English, it circulated among European and United States metropoles and was read by burgeoning volcano scientists such as Frank Perret and Thomas Jaggar in observatories on Kilauea and Vesuvius. Dutch scientists in the Netherlands Indies, in turn, were reading the debates of European and American geologists.

Throughout the 1920s and 1930s, Reinout van Bemmelen and Johannes Umbgrove traveled extensively to the Hindu and Buddhist ruins at Dieng and Borobudur to rewrite their history, positing that volcanic eruptions had caused the collapse of the early modern

[32] Newman Van Padang, "The Banjirs at Merapi Volcano in 1931," translation of "Het Gloedwolkgevaar," *Vulkanlogische en Seismologische Mededeelingen*, no. 12 (1933): 102–8. Translation by K. Kusumadinata (July 9, 1987): 1. Perpustakaan Pusat Vulkanologi dan Mitigasi Bencana Geologi.

[33] Van Padang, "The Banjirs at Merapi Volcano in 1931," 1.

[34] Van Padang, "The Banjirs at Merapi Volcano in 1931," 4. The telephone line was between Maron and Amiyang [Bakalan].

[35] Newman Van Padang, "Measures Taken by the Authorities of the Vulcanological Survey to Safeguard the Population from the Consequences of Volcanic Outbursts," *Bulletin Volcanologique* 23 (1960): 181(Amsterdam: Stemler, 1896), 92.

[36] Rab Sukamto, Tjoek Soeradi, and R. Wikarno, *Menguak Sejarah Kelembagaan Geologi di Inodnesia: Dari Kantor Pencari Bahan Tambang Hingga Pusat Survei Geologi* (Bandung: Badan Geologi, 2006), 136.

Hindu Buddhist empires.[37] Their travels from Hindu ruins to Java's craters encouraged them to connect volcanism to Javanese culture and develop a vision of volcanic cultural determinism. As Reinout Van Bemmelen put it, "[m]ountain building provides the very basis of our existence on earth."[38] Umbgrove came to understand that mountain evolution, including volcanism, determined not only the surface of the Earth but also impacted species evolution and differentiation.[39]

Van Bemmelen, Umbgrove, and other geologists and volcanologists were not unfamiliar with the spiritual geographies of the central Javanese sultanates. Van Bemmelen, for instance, came to speculate about the destruction of early modern Java through volcanic cataclysm by way of Dirk van Hinloopen Labberton, a prominent Theosophist and Sanskritist who had interpreted inscriptions on the Calcutta Stone in 1921.[40] The Theosophist lodges in Bandung, Batavia, and Yogyakarta were sites where scientists and Javanese elites from the royal families of Yogyakarta and Surakarta crossed paths. Umbgrove even complained in a letter to his mother that Theosophy was "flourishing" in Bandung and "their 'lodge' has many members, including our boss [A.C. de Jongh] who is better informed about it than he is about geology."[41] A.C. de Jongh, a mining engineer, even contributed an article to the *Theosophist Magazine* in 1914 that sought to lend modern scientific credibility to Annie Bessant and Charles Leadbeater's "occult chemistry."[42] Many Theosophists, including Hinloopen Labberton, encouraged a renaissance of pre-Islamic Hindu and Buddhist traditions of Central Java. This orientalist enthusiasm would have been one source for volcanologists encounters with Central Javanese spiritual geographies.[43]

---

[37] R. W. Van Bemmelen, Kogyo *Jimusho Bandoeng Chishitsu-Chosajo (Kwazan Chosabu) Bulletin of the East Indian Volcanological Survey for the Year 1941* no. 95–98 (1943/1949): 69–72; J. H. F Umbgrove, "Het Ontstaan van het Diengplateau," *Leidsche Geologische Medeelingen* 3 (1929): 131–49.

[38] Reinout vam Bemmelen, *Mountain Building: A Study Primarily Based on Indonesia Region of the World's Most Active Crustal Deformations* [sic] (The Hague: Martinus Nijhoff, 1954), 2. Italics in original.

[39] J. H. F. Umbgrove, *The Pulse of the Earth* (The Hague: Martinus Nijhoff, 1942), 1–20, 146–56.

[40] The Calcutta Stone was a stone inscribed with the history of Airlangga's escape from a series of disasters that befell Java in the early modern period. Stamford Raffles stole the stone during the British interregnum between 1811 and 1815 and sent it to his Scottish patron Lord Minto in Calcutta. Another stone from the same period was also sent to Minto's estate in Scotland. For the current fate of the stones, see Nigel Bullough and Peter Carry, "The Kolkata Stone (Calcutta Stone)," *The Newsletter* 74 (Summer 2016): 4–5. For Johan Kern's reading of the Calcutta Stone and his account of its history, see Johan Kern, "Sanskrit-Inscriptie ter Eere van den Javaanschen vost Er-Langa," *Bijdragen tot de Taal-Land. En Volkenkunde van Nederlandsche-Indië* 34 (1885): 1–21. For Hinloopen Labberton's contrasting interpretation, see D. Van Hinloopen Labberton, "Oud-Javaansche Gegevens Omtrent de Vulkanologie van Java," *Natuurkunding Tijdschrift voor Nederlandsch-Indie* 81, no. 2 (1921): 124–58.

[41] Umbgrove, 15.5.'28, *brief 109 JHFU Java*.

[42] A. C. de Jongh, "On the Valency of the Chemical Atoms in Connection with Theosophical Conceptions Concerning Their Exterior Form," *The Theosophist* (July 1914), 535–71.

[43] Theosophy played a crucial role in the "enchantment" of the geological sciences in many European colonies in the 1920s. See, for instance, Sumathi Ramaswami, *The Lost Land of Lemuria: Fabulous Geographies, Catastrophic Histories* (Berkeley: University of California Press, 2004), 53–97. For studies of Theosophy and geologists in Java, see Adam Bobbette, *At Earth's Edge: Political Geology in Java* (Durham: Duke University Press, 2022); Marieke Bloembergen, "New Spiritual Movements, Scholars, and 'Greater India' in Indonesia," in *Modern Times in Southeast Asia, 1920s–1970s*, ed. Susie Protschky and Tom van den Berge (Leiden: Brill, 2018), 57–86.

Postcolonial Processions

The Japanese occupation of Java and the Indonesian National Revolution caused the work of the East Indies Volcanological Survey to cease in 1941. Geologists and volcanologists were interned in camps, exiled, or repatriated to the Netherlands. Reinout Van Bemmelen collaborated with Japanese authorities to undertake surveys of Merapi and forecast eruptions. Many volcano observatories across Java were abandoned and ransacked.[44] It was not until the early 1950s that the Republican government began to undertake geological and volcanological work and the *Bulletins* began to be published again in the new framework of the postcolonial cause. Some colonial geologists remained, such as Theodore Klompe, and began to teach a new generation of Indonesian geologists at the Institute Teknologi in Bandung.[45] Vladimir W. A. Petrochevsky and George Adrian de Neve also remained in Indonesia.[46] The *Berita Gunung Berapi* (Volcano News), the next iteration of the *Bulletin of the Netherlands Indies Volcanological Survey*, was published in 1952 in Indonesian, English, and Javanese.[47] The head of the Volcanological Survey, G. A. de Neve, wrote in the foreword that the publication was significant because it was the first "since our country was sovereign."[48] "The form," he continued, "is simple like ancient man, but our hopes are grand that the people [*masyarakat*] will receive this publication with the joy and happiness of a tool to use in our era of development."[49]

Yogyakarta had been the location of the Republican government before it was recognized as sovereign by the Netherlands and United States in 1949 and then it moved to Jakarta. During the revolution, the sultan of Yogyakarta allowed Sukarno and Hatta to station their anticolonial government in the city, in effect betraying the Netherlands, and in return for the favor, in 1950 Sukarno granted the sultan the right to remain ruler of his realm. The sultanate eventually became a special region within the republic with borders that broadly reflected those drawn after the Giyanti Treaty of 1755. The Sultanate of Yogyakarta was the only sultanate to be granted such status. Surakarta, for instance, was not. These new geopolitical arrangements brought the realm of Yogyakarta, the sultanate, and its ritual processions together into a new center for postcolonial volcanology.

In 1953, Yogyakarta became the location for a new office responsible for coordinating all observatories on Merapi. This meant that seven observatories and watchtowers on the

[44] Adjat Sudrajat, *Van Bemmelen: Kisah di Balik Ketenarannya* (Bandung: Badan Geologi, 2014), 123–267.

[45] J. A. Katili and A. Ariobimo Nusantara, *Harta Bumi: Biograpfi J. A. Katili* (Jakarta: Gramedia, 2007), 67–87; Sukamto, Soeradi, and Wikarno, *Menguak Sejarah Kelembagaan Geologi di Indonesia*, 51–114.

[46] Petrochevsky, a white Russian soldier, fled the Bolshevik Revolution in 1920 and landed in Java. He held the position of head of volcanology until his retirement and immigration to Australia in 1950. De Neve was born in Banjarmasin to Dutch parents. He considered himself Indonesian and took citizenship upon independence. He became the first Indonesian to hold the post of head of volcanology upon the retirement of Petrochevsky. For details on Petrochevsky, see, P. Tchoumatchenco et al., "Geologists of Russian Origin in Australasia/Oceania," *Scientific Israel-Technological Advantages* 21, no. 5–6 (2019), 197–198; see also Petrochevsky's diaries in Java in 1922 in Vladimir Petrushevsky, "January 1-22, 1922–August 30, 1922," *Vladimir Petrushevsky: An Archive*, Alyssa DeBlasio, Dickinson College, Russian Department, https://blogs.dickinson.edu/vapetrushevsky/category/1922/. For de Neve, see "Akrab Dengan Gunung (Maksud) Hatinya Memeluk Gunung," Tempo, August 27, 1983.

[47] G. A. de Neve, Moh. Slamet Padmokesumo, Surjo, Djajadi Hadikusomo, and M. I. Adnawidjaja, eds. *Berita Gunung Berapi*, no. 1-2, September–December (Bandung: Dinas Gunung Berapi Republik Indonesia, 1952), 1–97.

[48] de Neve, *Berita Gunung Berapi*, 1.

[49] de Neve, *Berita Gunung Berapi*.

southern, western, and northern flanks were connected via radio-telephones to the Radio Republic Indonesia receiver and broadcaster in Yogyakarta.[50] The shift from Muntilan to Yogyakarta included monitoring all observatory posts and organizing evacuations for Surakarta, Magelang, Muntilan, and villages on the slopes. The new network consolidated the monitoring of the whole of the volcano in the sultanate and merged the cosmic center of the *keraton* with the modern technological center for volcanology. The new merger was announced through a procession that included Sukarno, Hatta, G. A. de Neve, and Sultan Hamengkubwono IX to the Babadan observatory in 1954.[51] They visited the newly renovated observatory, including its old bunker, waved to the crowds, had their photos taken, and made a film. They met with local villagers who had experienced the effects of a recent eruption that killed sixty-four people.[52] Sukarno and Hatta were photographed making use of the new radio system that connected them to Yogyakarta, and Sukarno was photographed waving to the crowd from the entrance to the observatory.[53] The event was, in many ways, a conventional Sukarno-era, postcolonial political procession, but in this instance its function was to bring together the sultanate, the Republic, Merapi, and old cosmologies with new technologies. The sultanate as the cosmic center for the spiritual pantheon of Merapi then became also a center for modern technological networks of volcano science in the post-colony.

Merapi's Role in a New Conception of Earth's Evolution

When Kemmerling was walking on the Labuhan trail in 1922 speculating about the connection between eruptions in Merapi and earthquakes in the Indian Ocean, he was beginning to understand a relationship that had only recently been appreciated by colonial scientists. Reinout van Bemmelen at around the same time had speculated about the tectonic structures that connected Java's volcanoes to the ocean floor and had begun to consider how Java was an extension of the sea bed.[54] This appreciation made Dutch scientists sympathetic to theories of continental drift proposed by Alfred Wegener in 1912, when many other European and United States geologists were severely critical of the hypothesis. The Dutch geodesist, Felix Vening Meinesz undertook a series of extraordinarily extensive submarine voyages in the 1920s and 1930s to map gravity anomalies in the Indonesian archipelago and found a massive trench thousands of meters deep south of the archipelago in what Pieter Veth, nearly forty years prior, described as the realm of Nyai Ratu Kidul.[55] For many Dutch colonial geologists, the abiding problem thereafter was understanding if there was a relationship between the trench, the arc of volcanoes on land, and earthquakes. Scientists began to be concerned with deep

[50] Djajadi Hadikusumo, *Report on the Volcanological Research and Volcanic Activity in Indonesia for the Period 1950–1957* (Bandung: Departemen Perindustrian Dasar/Pertambangan, 1961), 35.

[51] Photographs (14 February 1954) Album 1954 photo no. 1–6 & 11, Arsip Balai Penyelidikan dan Pengembangan Teknologi Kebencanaan Geologi.

[52] Photograph no. 3, Arsip Balai Penyelidikan dan Pengembangan Teknologi Kebencanaan Geologi.

[53] *Visual Images of Merapi Volcano* (Bandung: Geological Agency of Indonesia), 192–93.

[54] Reinout Van Bemmelen, "On the Geophysical Foundations of the Undation-Theory," *Proceedings of the Royal Academy of Sciences at Amsterdam* 36 (1933): 337–43.

[55] F. A. Vening Meinesz, "Gravity Anomalies in the East Indian Archipelago," *The Geographical Journal* 77, no. 4 (1931): 323–32.

theoretical questions about the origins of volcanoes, the structure of the lithosphere, and the history of continents and oceans.

These theoretical questions were coupled with technical inventiveness. Vening Meinesz shaped the field of ocean geodesy by developing a new apparatus—the four pendulum gravimeter—dubbed the Golden Calf.[56] Vening Meinesz then taught United States and European oceanographers and geophysicists how to use the instrument, and during the Cold War, they were deployed on many international oceanographic expeditions to map the world's ocean floors. Vening Meinesz, with Harry Hess at Princeton, found the same structure of deep ocean trenches and volcanic arcs in the Caribbean. The Geodetic Committee of Japan also imported a Vening Meinesz gravimeter and found the same structure there, too.[57] The axis that was central to the Labuhan procession between Nyai Ratu Kidul in the Indian Ocean and deities in Merapi, between the Indian Ocean trench and volcanism, was found repeatedly throughout the 1920s, 1930s, and 1940s in island arc–trench systems around the world. Understanding the causal relation between the two became key for United States and British geologists in accepting the theory of plate tectonics.

The theory of plate tectonics became orthodoxy in the 1960s and 1970s, in no small part through the contributions of Vening Meinesz, his Golden Calf, and his maps of the Indian Ocean trench. Plate tectonics was heralded as a "scientific revolution," largely by United States geologists who, as Martin Rudwick has pointed out, had been reading Thomas Kuhn; but, they also had been trained by generations of staunch fixists who rejected the hypothesis of drifting.[58] Dutch geologists, on the other hand, had long been sympathetic to theories of drift because of their attempts to connect Javanese volcanism with the Indian Ocean trench. Those same colonial scientists taught a generation of Indonesian scientists to see the Earth's surface as horizontally mobile. John Katili, a Sulawesian, was taught by Theodore Klompe and was an admirer of Van Bemmelen.[59] Katili became the Head of the Geological Survey and then minister of natural resources under Suharto.[60] He had been publishing enthusiastically on the application of the new theory of global plate tectonics as early as the early 1970s and was a forerunner in applying the theory to Indonesia.[61] In the 1970s he hired the United States geologist Warren Hamilton to undertake the first systematic application of the theory to the region.[62] For Katili, the theory of plate tectonics was inseparable from questions of natural resource exploitation for the developing Indonesian nation. He was particularly interested in the possibilities that deep water trenches could offer for mineral and oil

---

[56] Naomi Oreskes, *The Rejection of Continental Drift: Theory and Method in American Earth Science* (Oxford: Oxford University Press, 1999), 238–49.

[57] Oreskes, *The Rejection of Continental Drift*.

[58] Rudwick, *Earth's Deep History*, 258.

[59] Katili and Ariobimo Nusantara, *Harta Bumi*, 67-87; John A. Katili and H. M. S. Hartono, "Van Bemmelen's Contributions to the Growth of Geotectonics and the Present State of Earth-Science Research in Indonesia," *Geologie en Mijnbouw* 58, no. 2 (1979): 107–16.

[60] Katili and Ariobimo Nusantara, *Harta Bumi*, 317–20.

[61] John A. Katili, "A Review of the Geotectonic Theories and Tectonic Maps of Indonesia," *Earth Sciences Reviews* 7 (1971): 143–63.

[62] Katili and Ariobimo Nusantara, *Harta Bumi*, 134–36.

extraction.[63] Hamilton worked on the *Tectonics of the Indonesian Region* for a decade and in 1979 published the first complete map to apply the theory of plate tectonics to the region.[64] The spirit queen's realm south of Java, in Hamilton's map, became a black line indicating a zone of plate subduction. Without departing from the core principle of the Labuhan, though, and even if Hamilton was unfamiliar with the spiritual geography of the region, he argued that volcanism on Java was the result of forces in the ocean.[65] The subductive trench pushed the ocean floor into Java, where it melted and exploded to the surface through volcanoes. In this interpretation, Merapi was an extension of the ocean, what emerged through its explosions and pyroclastics was, in part, reconfigured ocean floor. That material then eroded down the slopes, through the river valleys, where it was carried back into the trench of Ratu Kidul's kingdom.

The theory of plate tectonics applied by Hamilton and Katili placed Merapi within a new scientific narrative of lithospheric evolution and history. But that narrative contained roots in the ritual pathways and spiritual geographies of Merapi. The pathways of the Labuhan, for instance, were based on the idea that deities in the Indian Ocean and Merapi were related to each other. As legal historian and poet G. J. Resink put it in 1997, "[w]hoever as a child heard the sound of the *kentongan* (slit-drums) along the river Code as drums accompanied Ratu Kidul on her journeys high above the water to the volcano Merapi learned early on to associate the Ratu with fresh as well as with salt water."[66] The river Code connects to the Opak River, which drains from the peak into the Indian Ocean. The river Code connects also to the site where the Labuhan procession made offerings at the crater. The river also carried sediment from the crater into the home of Ratu Kidul, the subduction zone where the ocean floor submerges beneath Java to then remerge through Merapi.

What Resink was pointing out was that Ratu Kidul traveled along those rivers to meet with deities who live on the upper flanks. There is a literal exchange between the pantheon of deities in the volcano and the zone of subduction in the Indian Ocean. Ratu Kidul's movements between fresh and salt water suggested her mobility, but also her chthonic and aerial homes, her capacity to shift between ocean and soil. Moreover, the Opak River is above the Opak Fault, which scientists came to understand in the 1960s was the conduit through which magma moved, "the subsurface plumbing," as it came to be called, that transported material from the subduction zone to the magma chamber inside Merapi.[67] The riverine infrastructure that Ratu Kidul used to connect between the ocean and peak was one part of the system that Hamilton and Katili came to understand defined the plate tectonic structure of Merapi. The theory of plate tectonics surreptitiously acknowledged the geography of the labuhan: the Indian Ocean and Merapi are in an ongoing exchange with each other. The Labuhan brought those two

---

[63] J. A. Katili, *Sumberdaya Alam untuk Pembangunan Nasional* (Jakarta: Ghalia Indonesia, 1983), 75-92.

[64] Warren Hamilton, *Tectonics of the Indonesian Region, U.S. Geological Survey Professional Paper 1078* (Washington: U.S. Geological Survey, 1979).

[65] Hamilton, *Tectonics of the Indonesian Region*, 28–33.

[66] G. J. Resink, "Kanjeng Ratu Kidul, The Second Divine Spouse of the Sultans of Ngayogyakarta," *Asian Folklore Studies* 56, no. 2 (1997): 314.

[67] Surono et al., "The 2010 Explosive Eruption of Java's Merapi Volcano—A '100-Year' Event," *Journal of Volcanology and Geothermal Research* 241–242 (2012): 122.

geographies together in a circular system, the theory of plate tectonics did the same, invoking the same geographies, built from the same pathways of ritual processions.

Processions and the New Global Tectonics

The French volcanologists Maurice and Katia Krafft arrived in Indonesia with the new planetary tectonics as their interpretive framework for the archipelago in 1971.[68] They also brought a powerfully orientalist vision of Indonesia and a highly modernist conception of their science. They went to Indonesia to document its volcanism, and for them, volcanoes represented the violence of the Earth. Volcanoes were spectacles at which to witness the chaotic formation of new lithospheric material. Indonesians were of anthropological interest to the Krafft's because they lived so close and made sense of these violent agents of change. The Krafft's purpose was a procession across Java to document volcanic environments and their people. Renault donated a truck to their cause while the Indonesian government, strapped for scientific funding and eager for international cooperation, gave them visas. They hauled a yellow trailer filled with scientific equipment and the side of the truck had "Volcanoes of Indonesia" emblazoned on it, oddly, in French.[69] There was also a large graphic of a world map that centered on Eurasia, perhaps to show the geographic distance between France and the archipelago. The French text and the map were two small but important features because they indicated that the Krafft's procession was not meant for Indonesians but for their French audiences back home. They also carried cameras, recorded film, and published a book.

The Krafft's traveled across Java taking samples, photographs, and measurements. On Bromo they witnessed the Kesodo, an annual procession for deities in the volcano and with historical links to the Labuhan.[70] The Krafft's described the members of the procession as a cult. They could not see their own presence, which used the same roads as the Kesodo to also arrive at the crater while they also carried equipment and wore special costumes for a public display, as a part of the Kesodo procession. Like many modern volcano scientists, the Krafft's believed in a stark separation between myth and science, belief from knowledge. It was modernist volcanology on tour. When they took their procession to Merapi, they called it an "assault" and proceeded to camp for two days in Pasar Bubar. [71]

It was not long after that that their competitor, also a French filmmaker, Haroun Tazieff, arrived on Merapi. Tazieff was often filmed shirtless, trekking the flanks of world volcanoes, or dressed in reflective protective suites beside gushing lava vents. His 1980 film, *Gunung Merapi*, depicted a similar procession to that of the Krafft's nine years earlier.[72] Tazieff was filmed walking alone with a stick, whistling. We later see that he was accompanied by a line of porters carrying his scientific equipment. They later set up their camp in Pasar Bubar among the large boulders, and his Javanese porters sang to him as he descended into the crater.

---

[68] Katia Krafft and Maurice Krafft, *A L'Assaut des Volcans: Islande Indonésie* (Paris: Éditions G.P., 1976).

[69] Krafft and Krafft, *A L'Assaut des Volcans*, 86–87.

[70] Krafft and Krafft, *A L'Assaut des Volcans*, 91.

[71] Krafft and Krafft, *A L'Assaut des Volcans*, 83

[72] Daniel Cavillon, dir., *Gunung Merapi* (1980, A2/CNRS AV).

These volcanologists on Merapi each brought with them the newly orthodox theory of plate tectonics and its conception of volcanism. They did not indicate their ignorance of the critical role that understanding Javanese volcanism played in the development of the theory. It is also likely they were unaware of the role of ritual infrastructures in ushering scientists up Merapi on the same pathways that they were following. What is particularly stark in the Krafft's and Tazieff's representations of Merapi, however, is how Javanese environmental knowledge traditions were considered to be culture and in contrast to their modern science. At the same time, the Krafft's and Tazieff were also participating in the growing internationalisation of the networks that had emerged around the monitoring of Indonesian volcanoes. French, American, British, German, and Japanese volcanologists had been participating in new monitoring networks between Indonesia, Europe, and the United States. Global seismic networks were connecting world volcanic events to information hubs in Bandung but also the United States Geological Survey. When the Krafft's and Tazieff were undertaking their processions, Merapi was monitored also by the office in Yogyakarta, Bandung, and seismology departments in Europe and the United States.

Anthropologist Lucas Triyoga undertook fieldwork in the late 1980s in Umbulharjo, the village where the Labuhan provided offerings.[73] He recorded the persistence of the Labuhan and that Sapujagad was the spiritual king of the volcano. Sapujagad, however, had gained a spirit army working for him that patrolled the flanks and reflected the militarization of the Suharto New Order regime. He also recorded that the area of Gunung Gajah Mungkur, a protrusion near the crater that W. A. Petrochevsky had surveyed in 1927, had become a haunt for evil spirits from the Indonesian Communist Party and the Merapi Merbabu Complex.[74] Other deities he recorded had remained consistent with those recorded in the 1930s by Tirtakoesoema. Triyoga also noted an origin story of Merapi that did not appear in Tirtakoesoema's account. During the encounter between Senopati and Nyai Ratu Kidul on the south coast, Kyai Sapujagad, who was originally the assistant of Senopati, ate an egg (*endhog jagad*) from Nyai Ratu Kidul. After eating the egg he metamorphosed into a giant and took up residence in the volcano.[75] This new version of the story suggested the persistent belief in the direct causal relationships between the Indian Ocean and Merapi. Moreover, the very connection between the two geographies was also understood as the origin of the polity. Politics and the landscape could not be separated.

Conclusion

In 2016, I met a French engineer who had been working on Merapi with a French state-funded project called DOMErapi.[76] The continued presence of French volcanologists and earth scientists on Merapi was the result, in part, of institutional alliances forged by Tazieff in the 1970s.[77] The French engineer was frequently on Merapi to manage

[73] Lucas Sasongko Triyoga, *Manusia Jawa dan Gunung Merapi: Persepsi dan Kepercayaannya* (Yogyakarta: Gadjah Mada University Press, 1991), 34–65.

[74] Triyoga, *Manusia Jawa dan Gunung Merapi*.

[75] Triyoga, *Manusia Jawa dan Gunung Merapi*.

[76] DOMErapi stands for "dome" "Merapi," referring to the dome or lava plug inside the crater.

[77] Interview with Jean-Philippe Metaxian, 2016.

the many seismic signaling stations that transmitted data by way of orbiting satellites back to the observatory in Yogyakarta. In 2016, Merapi was monitored not only by the observatory in Yogyakarta and the United States Geological Survey in Washington but also satellite internet and radio signals. The engineer had visited Pasar Bubar to repair a faulty seismic signalling station and found that offerings had been placed on it. It revealed for him, he explained, that there were spiritual agencies at work in the volcano. He had begun to take those spiritual agents seriously as having agential power over his instruments. He explained that they may be the reason that his instruments often failed. He said that he was often otherwise unable to explain why they stopped working. The offerings enabled and encouraged, as Nils Bubandt has put it, the possibility of doubt, or in other words, they cracked open the black-box of causality and exposed explanatory mechanisms to spiritual actors.[78] Yet, what the offerings also did was enfold the engineers' monitoring within the older cosmic geography of Merapi. Those spirits may or may not have disrupted his machines, but the offerings certainly flattened the distinction between modern seismology, the spiritual networks of the Labuhan, and the history of deities on Merapi. The offerings also resisted the conventional narrative that modern volcano science was exported to the slopes of Merapi. Instead, the offerings revealed that modern volcano science was enabled in different ways by the spiritual geographies of the volcano.

---

[78] Nils Bubandt, "Haunted Geologies: Spirits, Stones, and the Necropolitics of the Anthropocene," in *Arts of Living on a Damaged Planet: Ghosts and Monsters of the Anthropocene*, ed. Anna Lowenhaupt Tsing, Heather Anne Swanson, Elaine Gan, and Nils Bubandt (Minneapolis: University of Minnesota Press, 2017), G12.

Military Responses to and Forms of Knowledge About Natural Disaster in Colonial Indonesia, 1865–1930

Susie Protschky

Abstract

This is the first study to chart changes in military responses to natural disaster in colonial Indonesia (the Netherlands East Indies). It reveals that, up until the early twentieth century, colonial forces conducting wars of conquest across the archipelago were caught in disasters as they happened, and their responses were localized and reactive. Around 1918, colonial policy shifted toward a more coordinated, interventionist role for the military that attended to the humanitarian needs of Indonesian disaster victims. The groundwork for an integrated, first-responder role for the military in natural disasters was laid during the 1920s, with the establishment of an air force with capabilities in aerial reconnaissance and photography. These new technologies fostered a militarization of colonial knowledge about natural disasters that reached its fullest expression during the Merapi eruption of 1930 and, notably, exceeded operational purposes by shaping colonial science, as well as disaster- and geo-tourism.

Keywords: aerial photography, photography, colonial air force, LA-KNIL, colonial army, KNIL, volcanoes, disaster

Susie Protschky is Associate Professor of History and an Australian Research Council Future Fellow at Deakin University (Melbourne, Australia). The research for this article was funded by an Australian Research Council Discovery Grant (DP170100948) and a 2018 Brill Fellowship at the Scaliger Institute of the Leiden University Library (Netherlands).

Introduction

This article charts, for the first time, changes in military responses to natural disaster in colonial Indonesia (the Netherlands East Indies) from the 1860s to the 1930s, when colonial armed forces were at their most pervasive and forceful in prosecuting subjugation campaigns across the archipelago. In doing so, it aims to unravel the historical entanglement of military forms of knowledge born of war and conflict with modern genealogies of disaster response in Indonesia. With the notable exception of scholarship on the aftermath of the 2004 Indian Ocean Tsunami, which devastated Aceh Province but expedited the end of the civil war, there has been very little research on the imbrication of military actions with natural disasters and their aftermath in Indonesia.[1] This lacuna is particularly striking given the modern history of violence in Indonesia, which spawns a considerable scholarship, and the archipelago's deep past and certain future of natural disasters by virtue of its location on the Pacific Ring of Fire, which is a smaller but growing research area.[2] To date, there is no study that examines the historic role of the military in responding to natural disaster in Indonesia.[3]

Historians thus far have justifiably focused on the military's role as the primary agent of conquest in both colonial and postcolonial Indonesia. For the modern colonial era, Henk Schulte Nordholt's study of the genealogy of violence in Indonesia remains foundational for demonstrating the geographic scope, ubiquity, and intensity of military conflicts. During a period roughly contemporaneous with the Aceh War (1874–c.1903), colonial armed forces additionally subjugated Lombok, Central and South Sumatra,

[1] Edward Aspinall, "Indonesia after the Tsunami," *Current History* 104, no., 680 (March 2005): 105–9; Arno Waizenegger and Jennifer Hyndman, "Two Solitudes: Post-Tsunami and Post- conflict Aceh," *Disasters* 34, no. 3 (2010): 787–808; Paul Zeccola, "Dividing Disasters in Aceh, Indonesia: Separatist Conflict and Tsunami, Human Rights and Humanitarianism," *Disasters* 35, no. 2 (2011): 308–28. See also Han Knapen, "Epidemics, Droughts, and Other Uncertainties on Southeast Borneo during the Eighteenth and Nineteenth Centuries," in *Paper Landscapes: Explorations in the Environmental History of Indonesia*, ed. Peter Boomgaard, Freek Colombijn, and David Henley (Leiden: KITLV Press, 1997), 134.

[2] Anthony Reid, "Population History in a Dangerous Environment: How Important May Natural Disasters Have Been?" *Masyarakat Indonesia* 39, no. 2 (2013): 505–25; Anthony Reid, "History and Seismology in the Ring of Fire: Punctuating the Indonesian Past," in *Environment, Trade and Society in Southeast Asia: A Longue Durée Perspective*, ed. David Henley and Henk Schulte Nordholt (Leiden: Brill, 2015), 62–77; Anthony Reid, "Building Cities in a Subduction Zone: Some Indonesian Dangers," in *Disaster Governance in Urbanising Asia*, ed. Michelle Ann Miller and Mike Douglass (Singapore: Springer, 2016), 45–59; Anthony Reid, "Revisiting Southeast Asian History with Geology: Some Demographic Consequences of a Dangerous Environment," in *Natural Hazards and Peoples in the Indian Ocean World: Bordering on Danger*, ed. Greg Bankoff and Joseph Christensen (New York: Palgrave Macmillan, 2016), 31–53; Anthony Reid, "Recognising Global Interdependence through Disasters," in *Crossing Borders: Governing Environmental Disasters in a Global Urban Age in Asia and the Pacific*, ed. Michelle Ann Miller, Mike Douglass, and Matthias Garschagen (Singapore: Springer, 2018), 21–40; Alicia Schrikker, "Disaster Management and Colonialism in the Indonesian Archipelago, 1840–1920," in *Natural Hazards and Peoples in the Indian Ocean World: Bordering on Danger*, ed. Greg Bankoff and Joseph Christensen (New York: Palgrave Macmillan, 2016), 225–54.

[3] Schrikker has researched Dutch and Indonesian modes of knowledge that shaped disaster responses in the eighteenth and nineteenth centuries but does not discuss military forms of knowledge: Schrikker, "Disaster Management and Colonialism in the Indonesian Archipelago." Anthony Reid, the leading scholar of historical disaster research on Indonesia, while advocating that armed forces in the Asia-Pacific should focus their cooperation on responding to natural calamities, has had little to say on the *historic* role of the military in Indonesia's environmental catastrophes: Anthony Reid, "Lessons of Tambora Ignored—200 Years on from the World's Greatest Modern Eruption," *Asian Currents*, April 14, 2015, http://asaa.asn.au/lessons-of-tambora-ignored200-years-on-from-the/; Anthony Reid, "Fragile Paradise: Bali and Volcanic Threats to Our Region," *New Mandala*, October 3, 2017, https://www.newmandala.org/fragile-paradise-bali-volcanic-threats-region/.

Borneo, Central and South Sulawesi (Celebes), Seram, Flores, Timor, and Bali, all within the space of a generation. Schulte Nordholt counted a total of thirty-two "wars" between 1874 and 1910. At the same time, repressive, violent labor regimes upheld colonial authority on Indonesian plantations and in the burgeoning mining sector.[4] In addition to "wars," Piet Hagen's more recent book examines "expeditions," "actions," and responses to "resistance" and "rebellion" involving the colonial army, navy, and local police across the Netherlands East Indies. In a list that is far from comprehensive, a tally of at least 160 armed encounters occurred across the century from 1840 to 1940, with barely a year passing unmarked by conflict.[5] This means that, in the last hundred years of Dutch rule in Indonesia, there was always a military campaign or an armed skirmish between colonial authorities and Indonesian civilians or militias taking place somewhere. Colonial soldiers were constantly garrisoned or moving across the archipelago. Indeed, from 1870 to 1910 alone, there were 30,000 personnel in the KNIL (Koninklijk Nederlandsch-Indisch Leger), or colonial army, and military spending constituted one third of the colonial budget.[6]

The military was a pervasive social institution in the East Indies. A large portion of the European and Indo-European population in the nineteenth century was employed by the military, and from 1918 every adult European man in the Indies was obliged to perform half a year of compulsory military service. Every major town on Java and in some of the Outer Provinces had its own military club. Elite and middle-class colonial society was significantly constituted by military and ex-military men and their families. Mirroring colonial society (although with less sensitivity to class as a determinant of status), the military elite comprised Europeans and Indo-Europeans, while the rank and file were drawn from Indonesian ethnic groups. Widespread barracks concubinage and marriage between soldiers and Indonesian women contributed to the Indies' large Eurasian population.[7]

The military was also crucial for generating colonial forms of knowledge about the East Indies, including on the environment. The specialized training and skills of military engineers, doctors, draftsmen, cartographers, surveyors, and photographers remained a scarce resource in the East Indies until the late nineteenth century, when immigration was deregulated to allow free entry to those outside the civil service and the armed forces.[8] Histories of Dutch colonial science, art, anthropology, and archaeology amply demonstrate how military expeditions, and the individual proclivities of many soldiers, were the source of major Indonesian collections in the Netherlands' colonial ethnographic, medical, art, and natural history institutions, which form the basis of its contemporary museums.[9] Military

---

[4] Henk Schulte Nordholt, "A Genealogy of Violence," in *Roots of Violence in Indonesia: Contemporary Violence in Historical Perspective*, ed. Freek Colombijn and J. Thomas Lindblad (Leiden: KITLV Press, 2002), 36–37.

[5] Piet Hagen, *Koloniale oorlogen in Indonesië; vijf eeuwen verzet tegen vreemde overheersing* (Amsterdam: Uitgeverij De Arbeiderspers, 2018), 889–905.

[6] Schulte Nordholt, "A Genealogy of Violence," 36.

[7] Ulbe Bosma, *Indiëgangers; verhalen van Nederlanders die naar Indië trokken* (Amsterdam: Bert Bakker, 2010), 8–9, 82, 160–61, 179; C. A. Heshusius, *KNIL 1830–1950; een fotodocumentaire over get dagelijks leven van het koloniale leger in Nederlands-Indië* (Houten: De Haan, 1986), 9.

[8] Scholars often refer to the Agrarian Laws of 1870 and the liberalization of the plantation economy as the turning point in this regard.

[9] Anneke Groeneveld, *Toekang Potret: 100 Years of Photography in the Dutch East Indies* (Asmterdam: Fragment Uitgeverij, Museum voor Volkendunde, 1989), 37–38, 42, 111; Harm Stevens, "The Resonance of Violence in the Collection," in *The Netherlands East Indies at the Tropenmuseum*, ed. Janneke van Dijk and Susan Legêne

draftsmen, surveyors, and photographers created a significant share of the visual archives that exist for colonial-era Indonesia.[10] Military ways of seeing Indonesian landscapes were thus deeply ingrained in colonial visual culture.

To begin plotting the development of military forms of knowledge about natural disaster in Indonesia, this article analyzes images *by* military photographers, and *of* military actions in the wake of natural disasters, to show how colonial armed forces generated understandings of catastrophes through the process of responding to them. I examine these photographs as technologies used by the military for operational purposes, as artifacts that performed commemorative military work and shaped what I will call "campaign memories," and as media for commercial as well as scientific interests. My approach builds on work that demonstrates the significance of photography—a technology quickly adopted and diversified in its applications soon after its inception in 1840—not only in "representing" Indonesia, but in actively *constituting* social, political, and economic relations between powerful colonial institutions and diverse communities through practices of production, exchange, and consumption.[11]

Caught in Catastrophe: Photography Capturing Military Reactions to Natural Disaster

Photographs of natural disasters from the mid-nineteenth century onward demonstrate the historical pervasiveness of the colonial military across the Indonesian archipelago, not because armed forces were purposefully commanding operational responses to catastrophes in this period, but because companies of soldiers became *caught in* the processes of natural disasters by the sheer coincidence of their widespread presence in garrisons and as mobile expeditionary forces. Some of the earliest examples of photographs showing the aftermath of natural disasters from the East Indies provide a view into the intersection of the militarization of the archipelago in the nineteenth century with the production of visual forms of knowledge about natural disaster in this period.

The oldest example I have found is of a series of earthquakes that rippled across Java throughout mid-1865, causing the greatest destruction in parts of Central Java on July 16 and 17.[12] The images were probably made by a KNIL photographer, since they focused entirely on army personnel commandeering clean-up operations in the village of Banyubiru and the extensive damage to Fort Willem I (now Benteng Pendem) near Ambarawa, which had served as a KNIL barracks since its completion in 1853 (Figures 1 and 2). The location was

---

(Amsterdam: KIT Publishers, 2011), 29–38; Fenneke Sysling, *Racial Science and Human Diversity in Colonial Indonesia* (Singapore: NUS Press, 2016), 20, 31–32, 175.

[10] Susie Protschky, *Images of the Tropics: Environment and Visual Culture in Colonial Indonesia* (Leiden: Brill/ KITLV Press, 2011), 74–82.

[11] Karen Strassler, *Refracted Visions: Popular Photography and National Modernity in Java* (Durham: Duke University Press, 2010); Susie Protschky, "Camera Ethica: Photography, Modernity and the Governed in Late-Colonial Indonesia," in *Photography, Modernity and the Governed in Late-Colonial Indonesia*, ed. Susie Protschky (Amsterdam: Amsterdam University Press, 2015), 11–40; Susie Protschky, *Photographic Subjects: Monarchy and Visual Culture in Colonial Indonesia* (Manchester: Manchester University Press, 2019).

[12] Volkenkunde Museum Leiden (Nationaal Museum voor Wereldculturen), RV-A33; P. van Dijk, "Rapport omtrent de aardbevingen, die vooral in Juli 1865 en October 1872 de vlakte van Ambarawa, eiland Java, hebben geteisterd," *Jaarboek van het Mijnwezen in Nederlandsch Oost-Indië*, Nationaal Archief (NL-HaNA), Den Haag, 2.10.55, Inv. Nr. 4, 36.

Figure 1: Photographer unknown. The aftermath of an earthquake at
Banyubiru (Central Java), July 16 and 17, 1865.
Collection Nationaal Museum van Wereldculturen, Coll. no. RV-A33-3.

Figure 2: Photographer unknown. The Fort Willem I KNIL barracks near
Ambarawa, Central Java, following the July 1865 earthquake.
Collection Nationaal Museum van Wereldculturen, Coll. no. RV-A33-10.

insalubrious. "It is incomprehensible," reflected one newspaper report several months after the 1865 earthquake, how "such a site could have been chosen for a fortress," given the volcanic plain shook frequently with tremors throughout the nineteenth century.[13]

The KNIL was an important subject in photographs taken during the aftermath of an earthquake that struck Ambon island on January 6, 1898, once again by virtue of the local garrison at Fort New Victoria becoming caught in the disaster.[14] This time, the photographs were made by a civilian, a local teacher, and commercial photographer named Paulus Najoan (or Na Joan), whom one newspaper identified as "an Ambonese of European-equivalent status."[15] His photographs showed the widespread physical destruction across the town, especially in the commercial "Chinese quarter" and among the stone European buildings of the government district. The effects of the earthquake on "Natives" (Ambonese) were staged in tragic(omic) reenactments (Figure 3).[16] The images also captured the ruination of the KNIL infantry barracks and canteen and, by virtue of their location at the disaster site, KNIL personnel as responders who tended to civilian as well as military casualties (Figures 4 and 5).[17] Contemporary newspaper reports reveal that local army assistance was accepted, since the fort personnel had a stake in the disaster, but civilian authorities remained the key responders, and the Resident (the local Dutch governor) was suspicious of military aid from other islands. While he accepted forced laborers (*dwang arbeiders*) and construction materials brought by naval steamships to assist with the building of temporary shelters for displaced victims, he rejected an offer of fifty-five navy personnel.[18] There was thus no sense, in 1898, of a centrally coordinated military response driving rescue and reconstruction efforts.

Little is known about the photographer who captured the aftermath of the Ambon earthquake other than his work, which was advertised (but not reproduced) in two Indies newspapers, along with exhortations for customers to buy his photographs in order to cultivate empathy for the victims of the disaster—including Najoan himself, whose livelihood suffered after the quake.[19] His photographs also circulated beyond Indonesia to the colonial metropole. An album of his prints was presented (by a Dutch photographer, who must have imported them) to Queen Wilhelmina in 1900, perhaps

---

[13] *Soerabaijasch handelsblad* 16-11-1865. On how the Ambarawa plain was particularly prone to strong shocks, see Van Dijk, "Rapport omtrent de aardbevingen," 43–44, which also contains the long list of frequent earthquakes in that region from 1822 to 1873 alone, 47–48.

[14] Leiden University Library Special Collections, KITLV 104090–104103; Bintang Djaoeh, *Ambon voor en na de ramp* (Amsterdam: Eigen Haard, 1898), 10–11, 13.

[15] *De locomotief*, January 4, 1898.

[16] As Liesbeth Ouwehand has argued, the clean clothes worn by all the subjects suggest the photographs were taken when the first emergency supplies arrived by boat, after mid-January: Liesbeth Ouwehand, "Disastrous Encounters: Photographic Representations of Catastrophe in the Dutch East Indies," *Moving Worlds: A Journal of Transcultural Writings* 14, no. 2 (2014): 56.

[17] References for the other photographs mentioned here are Leiden University Library Special Collections, KITLV A1420, 4762, 4752, 4766, 4767.

[18] Bataviaasch nieuwsblad, January 15, 1898; see especially the "Letter from Macassar" by Papaoe Paoewa in *De locomotief: Samarangsch handels- en advertentie-blad*, January 31, 1898, which bemoans the rejection of "onze Jantjes" ("Jan" was shorthand for a soldier of the KNIL).

[19] *De locomotief*, April 1, 1898; *Soerabaijasch handelsblad*, April 6, 1898; *De locomotief*, March 29, 1898. First discussed in Ouwehand, "Disastrous Encounters," 54–56.

Figure 3: P. Najoan, A reenactment of Ambonese fleeing a
collapsing house after the January 6, 1898 earthquake.
(Leiden University Library Special Collections, KITLV A1420, 4769.)

Figure 4: P. Najoan, Damage to the KNIL infantry barracks following
the January 6, 1898 earthquake on Ambon.
(Leiden University Library Special Collections, KITLV A1420, 4754.)

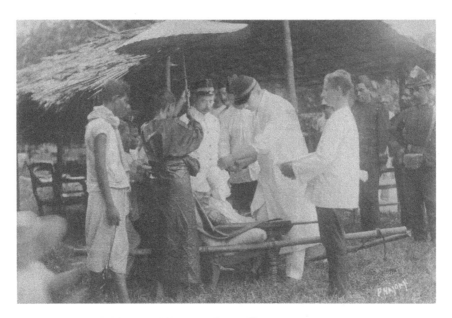

Figure 5: P. Najoan, KNIL medical officers treating civilians in an
open-air hospital following the January 6, 1898 earthquake on Ambon.
(Leiden University Library Special Collections, A1420 KITLV 4766.)

as a morbid tribute to her 1898 inauguration.[20] More significantly, many were published in an account of the disaster printed in Amsterdam.[21] Contemporary accounts such as this were significant for providing the only internationally circulating, mass-produced images of the disaster in a time when newspapers did not yet carry illustrations.

The Amsterdam account included a photograph of Najoan in action and a clear glimpse of the cumbersome photographers' tools of the period (Figure 6)—which goes some way toward explaining why there are relatively few photographs of natural disasters from Indonesia dating from the nineteenth century.[22] Before 1900, commercial and official photographers with specialized skills and equipment dominated the field. Their mobility and responsiveness to sudden disasters and volatile circumstances were constrained by the practical limitations of large, heavy cameras, fragile plates, and awkward props like the tripod. Thus, commercial photographers working before the twentieth century typically captured the aftermath of catastrophes, when conditions were stable again, or else worked at a safe distance from an unfolding natural disaster such as a volcanic eruption.

It was not until the advent of handheld cameras and roll film in the early 1900s, and the boom in amateur photography that commenced in Indonesia around 1920, that

---

[20] Leiden University Library Special Collections, KITLV A1420.

[21] Bintang Djaoeh, *Ambon voor en na de ramp.*

[22] The mystery here, of course, is, who took the photograph of Najoan? This particular image was among those published in Bintang Djaoeh, *Ambon voor en na de ramp.*

Figure 6: Photographer unknown, P. Najoan on the main street of the
Chinese quarter in Ambon town after the January 6, 1898 earthquake.
(Leiden University Library Special Collections, KITLV A1420, 4763.)

a more diffuse and diverse source of images of natural disasters, including snapshots
made by bystanders for personal use, fundamentally changed who could participate in
photographic culture as producers as well as consumers of images.[23] The eruption of
Gunung Kelud in the early twentieth century—twice, on May 23, 1901, and again on
May 20, 1919—occurred during this period. It was the latter eruption that occasioned the
first significant instances of amateur bystanders taking photographs in the aftermath of
a disaster.[24] Significantly, few collections show the KNIL's involvement, except for two.
One was a personal album by an unknown amateur photographer. Its main focus was
the impact of the volcanic eruption on local Javanese communities, but it also obliquely
identified the KNIL's role in the reconstruction process through several group portraits
of soldiers armed with spades (Figure 7). Another was a commercial album made by a
little-known studio from Bondowoso, "Promemoria," that charged customers ƒ12,50 for
their choice of twenty from a catalogue of forty photographs.[25] Much like the amateur
album, most of the focus was on the experience and response of the local population,
with one exception, an image of the military kitchen that supervised the delivery of food
aid to victims (Figure 8).[26]

---

[23] On these aspects of amateur photography's advent, see Protschky, *Photographic Subjects*.

[24] Some examples are discussed in Ouwehand, "Disastrous Encounters," 52–56.

[25] Leiden University Library Special Collections, KITLV A389.

[26] The published account by Jorissen (next n.) explains that the military had only a supervisory role in
running these kitchens, 124.

Figure 7: Photographer unknown, KNIL soldiers participating in clean-up
operations near Blitar after the eruption of Gunung Kelud in May 1919.
(Leiden University Library Special Collections, KITLV A500, 80693.)

Figure 8: Studio "Promemoria," The military kitchen coordinating food aid
for victims of the May 1919 eruption of Kelud.
(Leiden University Library Special Collections, KITLV A389.)

Contemporaneous textual sources on the 1919 Kelud eruption are clearer on the fact of the army's presence. A published account included a chapter on "the help given by the army," written by the Captain of the KNIL General Staff, C. A. Jorissen.[27] It reveals the actions and priorities of a colonial army caught in a disaster zone. Jorissen was candid about the reason for the unusually substantial KNIL presence in Kediri Residency at the time of the eruption, which was to quell unrest on local plantations. Indeed, he recounted that the KNIL's first response, during the night of the eruption, was focused on the secure relocation of hundreds of prisoners who were at risk of escape. Five brigades of the *maréchausée* (military police)—the most notorious arm of the KNIL—were deployed to the town of Blitar for "police services": principally, to protect property and halt looting.[28] One Sergeant Kretz, who was responsible for relocating his brigade to higher ground, found himself coordinating the flight of five hundred Javanese who were also on the run from the nearby village of Kali Cilik. The sergeant later led a rescue mission to the village, from which one hundred survivors and fifty-six deceased victims were retrieved. Substantial reinforcements from the garrison at Malang were sent between May 22 and 24 to undertake further such "rescue, clean-up and reconstruction work." In the days that followed, the KNIL assisted with mass burials, organized the restitution of communications and transport, and arranged the distribution of food aid and shelter. They did not stay for long. Within a week, the majority of the deployed forces had been withdrawn, leaving a single infantry company and the greater part of the engineering corps to persist with the reconstruction.[29]

Perhaps the most important part of Jorissen's account of the 1919 Kelud eruption has been overlooked by scholars of natural disaster in Indonesia. He suggests the KNIL's actions were the result of a very recent policy shift at the instigation of Governor-General J. P. van Limburg Stirum (r. 1916–21). In August 1918, a circular was issued on his behalf to regional heads of government on Java that identified the following situation within the KNIL:

> Since Dutch authority is secured everywhere in the Archipelago and large expeditions have become exceptional, the soldierly life has lost much of its appeal to the volunteer servicemen. The allure of adventure has dissipated, and the main concern has now become to qualify [the soldier] for his [new] war mission.

> It is felt necessary to take measures to keep the lesser [rank of] soldier occupied, body and soul, in his spare time, and to provide him with as much diversion and relaxation as possible, such that the monotony of his existence makes itself less burdensome. . . .

Van Limburg Stirum's solution to the dilemma was to deploy the army in "natural disasters or significant disturbances, such as earthquakes, fires, floods and the like" in order to promote "appreciation of the soldier among the general civilian population."[30] Another problem, it seems, was the army's reputation after decades of violence. For

---

[27] C. A. Jorissen, "De hulp van het Leger," in *De Kloetramp van 20 Mei 1919*, ed. J. Koning, (Surabaya: N.V. Soerabaiasch Handelsblad en Drukkerijen, 1919), 118–20.

[28] Jorissen, "De hulp van het Leger," 115–17.

[29] Jorissen, "De hulp van het Leger," 118, 122–24.

[30] Jorissen, "De hulp van het Leger," 125. The circular was also published in "In het belang van den militair," *De locomotief*, August 21, 1918.

Jorissen, the situation was repaired after the 1919 Kelud eruption, when "trust in the army [was] strengthened."[31] Yet, in the albums mentioned above, the photographers "saw" mainly Javanese and civilian authorities responding to the disaster. It was perhaps too soon for the KNIL to have developed capacity around civilian disaster-response. Much was left to local medical organizations and, in the longer term, the "Kelud Fund," a major charity drive coordinated with the Netherlands to enable the construction of an overflow tunnel for the crater lake that caused most of the damage whenever the volcano erupted.[32]

The governor-general's 1918 circular arguably demonstrates that, certainly in the *design* of a new military policy, the needs of the population in a natural disaster were incidental to his primary aims. These were, firstly, maintaining "rust en orde" (peace and order) within a military institution more recently charged with subduing defiant Indonesians and, secondly, reinforcing the army's standing in East Indies society. It is worth remembering that the Kelud eruption happened during the height of the Ethical Policy era on Java, when colonial authorities were bent on shifting the grounds of Dutch legitimacy from extraction and military might to beneficent rule and "Native" welfare. The governor-general's circular demonstrates once again how ostensibly "Ethical" directives, such as the conscious deployment of the KNIL to provide what we would now consider humanitarian assistance to civilians, readily accommodated reverence for and preservation of colonial institutions that monopolized the violence underpinning more "liberal" forms of legitimacy.[33]

The High Command: The Military Aviation Division and the Advent of Coordinated Disaster Response

On December 20, 1930, the *Indische Courant* published some of the earliest news in the world on the violent eruption of Gunung Merapi, one of Indonesia's most active volcanoes, situated in Central Java, one of the archipelago's most densely populated regions. The eruption had commenced the night before, discharging a flow of "lahar six kilometres long, two hundred metres wide and twenty metres high in various places, ravaging its way through the Blonkeng ravine."[34] The eruption, and the secondary disaster that followed in the days afterward, as surrounding rivers filled with millions of tons of pyroclastic matter and broke their banks, killed at least 1,300 and displaced more than 10,000 people. This event represents a turning point in the history of military responses to disaster in Indonesia for two reasons, each linked to technological developments in photography. First, due to the motility of handheld cameras, images of the Merapi eruption placed army personnel more decisively among the first responders to natural disaster in the active, interventionist mode augured by the governor-general's

---

[31] Jorissen, "De hulp van het Leger," 126.

[32] Schrikker, "Disaster Management and Colonialism," 244.

[33] Elsbeth Locher Scholten, "Imperialism after the Great Wave: The Dutch Case in the Netherlands East Indies, 1860–1914," in *Liberal Imperialism in Europe*, ed. Matthew P. Fitzpatrick (New York: Palgrave MacMillan, 2012), 25–46; Marieke Bloembergen and Remco Raben, "Wegen naar het nieuwe Indië," in *Het koloniale beschavingsoffensief; wegen naar het nieuwe Indië, 1890–1950*, ed. Marieke Bloembergen and Remco Raben (Leiden: KITLV Press, 2009), 1–26.

[34] *Indische Courant*, December 20, 1930.

1918 circular, but not yet visible in the 1919 Kelud eruption. Second, a military institution—the recently founded Aviation Division of the KNIL—emerged as a *producer* of new forms of knowledge about natural disaster using the novel technology of aerial photography.

To begin with the first turning point: while the first amateur photographs showing the impact of volcanic eruptions on local populations emerged during the Kelud disaster of 1919, it was the Merapi explosion that demonstrated the effect of compact, handheld cameras on how disaster victims could now be represented. The amateur as well as commercial photographs made in the wake of Merapi's explosion were almost unprecedented in their explicit, sometimes gratuitous portrayal of the modes of death that followed the eruption of noxious gases, heavy ashfalls, and streams of *lahar* (a Javanese word for "lava mixed with mud" that has now passed into standard, international usage among volcanologists).[35] Among a large set of postcards based on the work of an unknown photographer who roamed the countryside during the eruption were several images showing the interventions of the KNIL as the disaster unfolded. Soldiers were placed on watch duty to warn villagers of *lahar*, KNIL personnel and field police checked houses for the dead and wounded, and military escorts accompanied thousands of displaced villagers to refugee camps (Figure 9).[36] The first Dutch newspaper to publish images of the disaster—nine days after the first photographs appeared in Indies newspapers—included similar pictures of the KNIL at work, with a caption that marveled at the field kitchens assembled "as they were in times of war."[37] All newspapers that published photographs of the Merapi eruption, in the Indies as well as the colonial metropole, included an entirely novel representation of natural disaster in Indonesia: aerial images, taken by specialized cameras operated from aboard military aircraft.

The Merapi eruption was the first time the army's response was coordinated with an aerial action led by the Luchtvaart Afdeeling (LA), or Aviation Division, of the KNIL.[38] The LA became an official division of the colonial army in 1922, although test flights had commenced as early as 1914 and pilots were trained from 1919. It was housed at Andir air base near the West Javanese city of Bandung, which had long been the headquarters of the KNIL.[39] By the early 1930s, there was an archipelago of smaller air bases across Java as well as some of the so-called "Outer Provinces" of the East Indies such as

---

[35] With the exception of one explicit photograph in the "Promemoria" commercial album of the 1919 Kelud eruption, KITLV A389, 84490.

[36] Collection Nationaal Museum van Wereldculturen, IWI doos 23, TM-33005566, TM-33005572. These and other activities are reported at length in the official account of the campaign, given in P. G. Mantel, "Militaire bijstand na de Merapiramp, December 1930–Februari 1931," *Indisch Militair Tijfschrift* 2 (1931): 555–85, refugee figures at 574–75. Casualty figures are a conservative estimate as they refer only to those refugees interned in camps, yet there were thousands more spread throughout the district.

[37] The Amsterdam daily, *Algemeen Handelsblad*, published these images on January 7, 1931. The first Indies newspaper to publish photographs from the Merapi disaster was *Het nieuws van den dag voor Nederlandsch-Indië* on December 29, 1930 and January 2, 1931.

[38] Luchtvaartafdeeling was the official name of the colonial air force from August 1921 to March 1939, at which point it was renamed the Militaire Luchtvaart (Military Airline). In practice, it was referred to by both names from the 1930s, but for the sake of simplicity I shall refer throughout this article to the official "LA": M. van Haselen, *25 Jaar Militaire Luchtvaart in Nederlandsch-Indië* (Batavia: Koninklijke Drukkerij, 1939), 137, 163–64.

[39] Van Haselen, *25 Jaar Militaire Luchtvaart*, 137, 159, 163–64. After 1950, when Indonesia was independent and the KNIL was dissolved, the base became the Husein Sastranegara Airport.

Figure 9: Photographer unknown, KNIL soldiers accompany people displaced
by the eruption of Merapi in December 1930 to refugee camps.
(Collection Nationaal Museum van Wereldculturen, IWI doos 23, Coll. no. TM-33005569.)

Sumatra, Bangka, Sumbawa, and Timor.[40] However, it was at Andir that Indonesia's first military-industrial complex emerged, devoted not only to the planes and flying personnel of the Aviation Division—all of whom were European or Eurasian, as per the officer class throughout the rest of the KNIL—but also an infrastructure, staffed largely by Indonesian personnel, that included a technical secondary school; machinist, carpentry, and parachute workshops; a radio station; and the Phototechnisch Dienst (PTS), or Photo-Technical Service (Figures 10 and 11).[41]

The KNIL had been keen on developing a capacity for aerial reconnaissance since the 1880s, when it began monitoring French military uses of air balloons and speculating on the possible applications to the Aceh War.[42] Bizarrely, as late as 1913, there were even

[40] See the album of J. C. Koster, presented to him in 1932: Leiden University Library Special Collections, KITLV A1279, 49422-32.

[41] Van Haselen, *25 Jaar Militaire Luchtvaart*, 174, 176. See also the very detailed photograph album of H. A. van Neden, Leiden University Library Special Collections, Or.27.767. Note the PTS was also sometimes also called the Photo-Reconnaissance Service and was housed at Andir from 1923.

[42] "Verkenningen met behulp van luchtballons," *Indisch Militair Tijdschrift* 1 (1884): 490; "Stuurbare ballons," *Indisch Militair Tijdschrift* 2 (1885): 730.

Figure 10: LA-KNIL, Photo-Technical Service of the LA- KNIL at Andir near Bandung, West Java, 1928, from an album presented to Captain Adjutant H. A. van Neden. Note the white serial number at bottom right, which denotes photographs produced by the PTS. (Leiden University Library Special Collections, Album Or.27.767.)

Figure 11: The emblem of the LA-KNIL, an eagle carrying an aerial camera, from the album of J. C. Koster, 1932. (Leiden University Special Collections, KITLV A1279, 49421.)

discussions of using rockets and passenger pigeons for photographic reconnaissance.[43] In the end, however, it was the PTS, a military institution, that made the first ever aerial photographs in Indonesia and thus generated a new form of knowledge about natural disasters in ways that redefined what a position of high command entailed for armed forces increasingly oriented toward disaster.

The Aviation Division's involvement in the KNIL response to the Merapi eruption commenced on the second day after the main eruption ceased, on December 22. Its missions involved deployment of a reconnaissance plane, commandeered by Captain-(Observer) G. J. Reerink, head of the Photo-Technical Service, and First Lieutenant (Pilot) J. M. J. Wegner, to ascertain the geographical extent of the destruction, monitor further volcanic activity, and locate survivors. The LA-KNIL coordinated with the Volcanological Service to map the course of *lahar* and monitor changes in Merapi's crater over time.[44] It was also an LA-KNIL aircraft that took Governor-General A. C. D. de Graeff (r. 1926–31) on his three-day tour of the disaster zone.[45] Finally, the air force delivered food supplies by parachute drop to the entirely closed-off villages of Balong and Klampean, a feat widely reported in newspapers and referred to in the very first aerial photograph published about the disaster.[46]

The images produced by the PTS and used by the LA-KNIL were intended to assist with two goals: the planning of rescue and aid for survivors and the gathering of intelligence to warn ground forces and civilian authorities of constantly evolving threats to life and property. These included a massive section of Merapi's crater wall breaking off and triggering a fresh landslide of volcanic matter down the mountain, followed by overflowing rivers. KNIL and newspaper sources used a Dutch conjugation of the Indonesian word for "flood," *bandjiren* (to "ban[d]jir"), to describe this secondary disaster that displaced hundreds more people and lasted into February.[47] To those purposes, the LA-KNIL photographs showed elevated, distant views of the land formations around Merapi with paths of *lahar* coursing across the countryside, and aerial views of annihilated rice fields and villages (Figure 12), as well as the settlements that had been spared.[48] With the exception of the small handful of photographs released to the media for publication, the stamps on the reverse of photo prints signal they were considered classified.[49]

Outside official military uses, some of these photographs were given as gifts in commemorative albums belonging to high-ranking officers such as P. J. A. van Mourik, General Major of the Infantry, and J. C. Koster, one of the first pilots to be trained in 1919

---

[43] "Photografie van uit een vuurpijl," *Indisch Militair Tijdschrift* 2 (1913): 194–95.

[44] The *Soerabaijasch handelsblad* dedicated a whole report to the use of the LA and aerial photography in monitoring crater changes, January 31, 1931.

[45] First reported in *Het nieuws van den dag voor Nederlandsch-Indië*, December 29, 30; see also *De Tijd and Algemeen Handelsblad* on December 30, 1930.

[46] Mantel, "Militaire bijstand na de Merapiramp," 559–60, 563, 567, 580–81; Van Haselen, *25 Jaar Militaire Luchtvaart*, 75. See the photograph in *Het nieuws van den dag voor Nederlandsch-Indië* on December 29, 1930.

[47] See, e.g., Mantel, "Militaire bijstand na de Merapiramp," *Indisch Militair Tijfschrift*, 561, 563–69.

[48] See Leiden University Library Special Collections, KITLV Albums A15, A1279 and A1357.

[49] KITLV A15.

Figure 12: Technical Service of the Aerial Division (LA-KNIL), Kampung Batu Duwurs, destroyed by a *lahar* stream during the eruption of Gunung Merapi in December 1920. (Leiden University Special Collections, KITLV A1357, 123134.)

and General Major of the General Staff and Inspector of the Air Force.[50] Van Mourik earned a Knighthood in the Order of the Dutch Lion for his service during the Merapi campaign, while the two men aboard the LA-KNIL aircraft, Reerink and Wegner, were among the few officers to be made Knights in the Order of Oranje-Nassau.[51] That these men were *not* given the Military Willems Order, but instead the highest civilian orders in the Dutch royal honors system, eloquently demonstrates how the army's role was being recognized by the peak authority in the Dutch empire—the institution of the monarchy—as playing a crucial role in peacetime, perhaps even humanitarian, operations.[52]

The circulation of classified aerial photographs among military insiders as souvenirs that commemorated the careers of senior personnel reinforces the significance of the Merapi disaster as constituting what I would call a campaign memory of the kind more typically associated with wars and expeditions of conquest in colonial Indonesia. These were the first photographs to show that responses to natural disaster had been internalized as fundamental military work worthy of remembrance, an interpretation

[50] Both albums held at Leiden University Library Special Collections: KITLV A1357 (Van Mourik) and KITLV A 1279 (Koster); Van Haselen, *25 Jaar Militaire Luchtvaart*, 163–64.

[51] Mantel, "Militaire bijstand na de Merapiramp," 583–84.

[52] For an explication of the meaning of these knighthoods, see C. H. Evers, *Onderscheidingen; leidraad voor de decoraties van het Koninkrijk der Nederlanden* (Amsterdam: De Bataafsche Leeuw, 2001), 25–32.

further supported by the fact that the Merapi eruption was the first natural disaster ever reported in the primary organ of the KNIL, the *Indisch Militair Tijdschrift* (*IMT*).[53] By contrast, the journal had been completely silent on every prior major disaster, including the Krakatau eruption of 1883, which had attracted greater international attention and occasioned some military assistance.[54] Given Dutch military expansion within Indonesia had been entering a new phase of intensity in the 1880s, the journal was focused on other military expedition news, including the campaigns that commenced the long, horrific Aceh War.[55] The *IMT* also had nothing to report on military responses to the Ambon earthquake of 1898 or the two Kelud eruptions. Its lengthy and unprecedented account of the KNIL response to the 1930 Merapi eruption signals a turning point in colonial military history as well as Indonesian disaster history. Indeed, the report's author, P. G. Mantel, Captain of the Infantry, intended to provide "evidence of the great value of the organs of the defence forces in the aftermath of a natural disaster."[56] The military's role in such a context, he wrote, was

> . . . for a large number of people to be brought to action in a cohesive manner, and led by a central idea. This was best enabled by the organs of the defence force, whose performance [in these regards] was set up by its organisation, its military-hierarchical relationships, discipline, *experience*. A carriage run by a goat must be *instructed* by a coach and horses. A military organisation is best equipped for such action. . . .

> There is, above all, despite the differences, an unmistakable analogy between the tactical handling of an enemy and the lending of assistance after a natural disaster. . . .[57]

The Aviation Division's photographs also visualized the first *civilian* deployment of the colonial air force in pursuit of its major purpose: to supply intelligence to and support for ground forces. Prior to the Japanese attack on the Netherlands East Indies in 1942, colonial authorities had no plans for an air force that would perform any function other than supporting the army. While officers of the LA-KNIL hotly debated its role in a potential attack on the Netherlands East Indies (particularly, whether fighter and bomber planes should be prioritized over reconnaissance planes in preparation), the high command had no plan to defend the Indies from occupation so much as uphold the neutrality of the Netherlands in international conflicts.[58] During the Merapi eruption, in the process of carrying out the reconnaissance and supply-distribution work the air force had been bred for, albeit in "peacetime," the LA-KNIL photographs demonstrated how military aerial photography was also giving rise to new forms of colonial knowledge about natural disaster in Indonesia.

---

[53] Published between 1870 and 1942 by G. Kolff & Co., Batavia.

[54] *Java-bode*, September 13, 1883; *De locomotief*, September 18, 1883; *Sumatra-courant*, October 6, 1883.

[55] *Indisch Militair Tijdschrift* 1883, 1884, 1885.

[56] Mantel, "Militaire bijstand na de Merapiramp," 555, repeated 581–82.

[57] Mantel, "Militaire bijstand na de Merapiramp," 582. Italics in original.

[58] Van Haselen, *25 Jaar Militaire Luchtvaart*, 139, 142–43. See also Maartje Abbenhuis, *The Art of Staying Neutral: The Netherlands in the First World War, 1914–1918* (Amsterdam: Amsterdam University Press, 2006), 27. For debates among high-ranking officers of the LA on the role of the air force in a foreign occupation, see all articles published on the LA-KNIL in the 1930 and 1931 volumes of the *Indisch Militair Tijdschrift*.

The Role of the Colonial Military-Industrial Complex in the Production and Distribution of Visual Knowledge About Disaster

Had the Aviation Division's pioneering use of aerial photography in Indonesia simply heralded a new capacity for colonial military institutions to coordinate disaster response, this alone would have been a development worthy of recognition as a historic turning point. However, as has often been the case for technologies first developed by and for defense forces, the photographs produced by the Photo-Technical Service rapidly exceeded their original military purposes and began to influence other colonial forms of knowledge about disaster. Apart from producing classified military knowledge and photographic memorabilia for military gifts, the PTS also serviced civilian institutions to promote colonial science, tourism, and industry. These activities predated the Merapi eruption of 1930, which turns out not to have been the first collaboration between the LA-KNIL and the Volcanological Service. In 1922–23, the PTS photographed all the major volcanoes of Java for the service, generating what became a large archive of what I will call "crater portraits," images that profiled the distinctive geological features and activity of Java's volcanic vents and calderas at particular points in time.[59] Crater portraits were not images of disaster per se. Rather, I argue, they were forms of scientific and military knowledge that expressed evolving colonial concepts of how disaster in the East Indies might be lived with and planned for, produced by technologies that had been invested in, acquired, and developed by the colonial army for the purposes of war. These photographs, generated at the intersection of two ostensibly dissimilar disasters— conflict and natural hazards—provide a unique view into how militarized ways of seeing permeated broad areas of colonial society in early twentieth-century Indonesia.

We can surmise that the Aviation Division took pride in its crater portraits from the fact they featured prominently among the photographs reproduced in the commemorative volume celebrating the twenty-fifth anniversary of the LA-KNIL in 1939.[60] Many crater portraits were also included in presentation albums given by the Aviation Division to VIPs. Albums filled with commissioned photographs were a major component of the material and visual culture of gift-giving in elite colonial society, among both Europeans and Indonesians.[61] Aviation Division albums featured crater portraits among aerial photographs of the major cities, landmarks, and strategic industries of the East Indies, from Batavia to Borobudur to the oil concessions of Balikpapan. These were given not just to senior military figures, some of whom were detailed in the previous section, but also to retiring members of the civil service, visiting captains of industry (including an agent for Rolls Royce, builder of aircraft engines), and even the queen of the Netherlands, thereby reinforcing relationships between the military and other powerful institutions.[62]

[59] Van Haselen, *25 Jaar Militaire Luchtvaart*, 60, 129, 263. Note that some of Java's volcano craters are, technically speaking, calderas, but not the volcanoes discussed in this article, so for the sake of convenience I will refer to "craters."

[60] Van Haselen, *25 Jaar Militaire Luchtvaart*.

[61] Liesbeth Ouwehand, *Herinneringen in beeld; fotoalbums uit Nederlands-Indië* (Leiden: KITLV Press, 2009), 221–25.

[62] Leiden University Library Special Collections, KITLV Or.27.767 (Album of Captain Adjutant of the LA-KNIL, H. A. van Neden, 1928), KITLV A1085 (H. Millward, 1936); KITLV A 15 and A351 (unknown owners), KITLV A895 (Queen Wilhelmina of the Netherlands, 1926), KITLV A579 (J. J. M. A. Popelier, Resident of Krawang, 1929).

A small number of crater portraits in photograph albums held in archives are marked with a stamp that reads "Feenstra" (Figure 13).[63] This was no ordinary trademark. It refers to the work of Reserve First Lieutenant (Observer) H. C. Feenstra, who established the Photo-Technical Service as a distinct section of the Aviation Division in 1921.[64] In adopting the imprint of a commercial trader, as was typical for many photographers of the period, Feenstra envisioned possibilities for a broader distribution of images that were, strictly speaking, made "on the job" using military personnel and equipment located at the Andir air base. Other stamps on the reverse side of PTS photographs reveal the Aviation Division was all too aware of this potential. Some photographs in personal albums are stamped with copyright warnings, such as "forbidden to publish without acknowledging the [LA]-KNIL."[65]

Indeed, by the second half of the 1920s, the LA-KNIL copyright required protecting because the military complex at Andir had developed industry partners. In 1928 the well-known Batavia publisher, Kolff & Co, published a coffee-table book promoting commerce and tourism on Java to English-speaking tourists.[66] *The Importance of Java Seen from the Air* was filled with aerial photographs taken by none other than G. J. Reerink, then chief of the PTS and one of the two air force crew who would go on to conduct the Merapi operations of 1930.[67] The book was given free to Chambers of Commerce and Board of Trade members, consular officials, trade commissioners, industry clubs, and overseas libraries with the stated aim of encouraging foreign investment and tourism in the East Indies. Members of the public could also purchase the book for *f*7.50. Written endorsements by military executives and captains of colonial industry lauded Java's modern transport and communications infrastructure, plantations, factories, and stunning natural wonders and were interspersed with aerial photographs of Java's major cities, coffee estates, sugar factories, suspension bridges, hotels, hill station resorts, and volcano craters. C. W. Wormser's *Bergenweelde* (Wealth of mountains), also published in 1928, performed similar functions for the Dutch-language market.[68] Promoted by the Royal Java Motor Club, which viewed tourism as a means for members to extend the recreational use of their cars, the book discussed at length the pleasures of what scholars now call "geotourism": hiking adventures in volcanic mountain ranges, comfortably enabled by commutes on sealed roads, stays at luxury hotels, and the porting and guidance services of villagers. The holy grail for hikers on these tours was to reach the crater. To inspire enthusiasts, Wormser's book included portraits of the famous craters of Java's volcanoes, all provided with the permission of the Aviation Division.

A visual culture's vitality is determined as much by how amateur photographers produce images as it is by how professional photographs are published and consumed.[69]

[63] See an album belonging to an unknown owner, KITLV A77, as well as one that belonged to Raimond Naizare de Ruijter van Steveninck (1894–1963), one of the first instructors at Andir (KITLV Or.27.181).

[64] Van Haselen, 25 Jaar Militaire Luchtvaart, 26.

[65] Leiden University Library Special Collections, KITLV A349.

[66] H. M. de Vries, *The Importance of Java Seen from the Air* (Batavia: Kolff & Co, 1928).

[67] Van Haselen, *25 Jaar Militaire Luchtvaart*, 75.

[68] C. W. Wormser, *Bergenweelde* (Bandoeng: NV Mij. Vorkink, 1928).

[69] Protschky, *Photographic Subjects*.

Figure 13: H. C. Feenstra, Aerial photograph of the Merapi crater,
c. 1925. Note the wing tip of the plane at the left.
(Leiden University Special Collections, KITLV A77, 50352.)

Figure 14: Photographer unknown,
"Jan at the top of Bromo," June–July 1931.
(Collectie Stichting Nationaal Museum
van Wereldculturen, Netherlands,
TM-ALB-2122.)

Tourist books like those by Wormser and De Vries circulated in a growing market of amateur photographers, whose own images from the 1920s and 1930s show volcano tours replete with triumphant hikers posing by their peak destination (Figure 14). Many of the most enthusiastic geotourist-photographers were also avid collectors of volcano photographs and not only those by commercial practitioners like Onnes Kurkdjian (1851–1903) and Thilly Weissenborn (1883–1964), who specialized in sublime views of Java's famous volcanoes. Private collections also sometimes featured aerial photographs of craters that were issued by the PTS as prints.

The aerial crater portrait is a view of, over, and into the vent of a volcano that no mountaineer could generate, either from an opposite peak or at the site. Taken from the perspective of looking down through a lens, not unlike a microscope, the aerial photograph converts the height, scale, and colored variety of notorious summits to portable, perspectival, comparable, monochrome pictures.[70] Such images elide the journey and exertion celebrated in the snapshots of amateur photographers; the narrative sequence of ascending the peak that assumes such importance in personal albums and culminates in "I-was-there" images of exultant hikers posed beside the stony slopes and fizzing fumaroles of crater peaks (Figure 14). As Paula Amad has argued, the "distant, dehumanising, transcendent" aerial photograph appears "post-humanist" in its distinction from the "intimate, embodied, local" view that amateur photography more typically afforded.[71]

The aerial crater portrait not only divorced the prized view of the volcano's peak from the dangers of reaching it, it also ended European scientists' and geotourists' reliance on the labor and knowledge of Javanese guides and porters. Despite skirting close to (often active) craters, aerial photographers portrayed an environment that was not at all volatile; indeed, these pictures needed to be taken in calm, clear conditions with no clouds or turbulence.[72] Crater portraits taken with air force equipment for military and scientific purposes thus produced an image of mastery over nature, one that tourism promoters appropriated to persuade European consumers that "peace and order" reigned atop Java's summits. "No volcano was too high, no jungle or swamp too inaccessible for the graceful birds and tremendous areas have been mapped and photographed by the officers of the Military Air Force," the coffee-table tourist book proclaimed.[73] The appearance of Aviation Division crater portraits in tourist publications and private photograph collections thus exemplifies the deep imbrication between what Caren Kaplan calls the "scenic" and the "metric" in aerial photography;[74] a confluence between aesthetic and scientific ways of seeing that arose from the "fluid sites of production, influence, interpretation, and dissemination" of images produced by technologies intended for war and focused on preparation for natural disaster.[75]

---

[70] Paula Amad, "From God's-Eye to Camera-Eye: Aerial Photography's Post-humanist and Neo-humanist Visions of the World," *History of Photography* 36, no. 1 (2012): 85.

[71] Amad, "From God's-Eye to Camera-Eye," 66–69.

[72] J. R. van Diessen and R. P. G. A. Voskuil, *Boven Indië: Nederlands-Indië en Nieuw-Guinea in luchtfoto's, 1921–1963* (Purmerend: Asia Major, 1993), 14–15.

[73] De Vries, *The Importance of Java Seen from the Air*.

[74] Caren Kaplan, *Aerial Aftermaths: Wartime from Above* (Durham: Duke University Press, 2018), 147–48.

[75] Amad, "From God's-Eye to Camera-Eye," 66–69, 86.

Nowhere do these intersections between military, aesthetic, and touristic modes of seeing volcanoes become clearer than after the 1930 Merapi eruption. Exactly one month later the fledgling civilian airline, the KNILM (Koninklijk Nederlandsch-Indisch Luchtvaart Maatschappij)—founded in 1928 on the basis of military infrastructure, propaganda, and personnel—invited a journalist from *De Indische Courant* to take a flight tour of the disaster area.[76] What followed was an advertorial for disaster tourism: an account of the otherworldly wreckage left below and an incitement for others to take the tour, since the KNILM would organize more flights if there was sufficient demand.[77] No photographs were published with the report. Indeed, the Aviation Division retained a near monopoly on the production and publication of aerial photographs for the remainder of Dutch rule in Indonesia, despite the emergence of a civil aviation sector with its own capacity for photography.[78] What the military Photo-Technical Service had thus produced was a new way of seeing Indonesia's volcanic landscapes: as theaters of military heroics, advances in aviation technology, humanitarian intervention, scientific curiosity, and modes of tourism that set the sky as the new limit for intrepid explorers.

Conclusion

This article has demonstrated that, from the late nineteenth century until the end of the First World War, colonial armed forces were caught in disasters by virtue of their coincidental presence where natural hazards engulfed the garrisons and expeditionary forces conducting ever-shifting wars of conquest across the archipelago. Military responses to the plight of Indonesian communities affected by earthquakes, floods, and volcanic eruptions in this period were localized and reactive. The turning point for a more coordinated, interventionist role for the military adopting a role in natural disasters came in 1918, with a viceregal circular that heralded a new use for a colonial army whose conquering work was ostensibly behind it. Following the imposition of colonial *rust en orde* (peace and order) across Indonesia, maintaining it *within* an idling KNIL became the next concern for colonial authorities. The postwar milieu is also an important explanation for the change. Given the rise of anticolonial movements and threats to the colonial state, as well as the official adherence to the Ethical Policy on Java, the 1918 circular represented an attempt to build the military's legitimacy in colonial society by promoting its value in civilian emergencies. It was also the first instance of a modern army being deployed for ostensibly humanitarian purposes in Indonesian history.[79] For historians of the military in Indonesia, this colonial moment would seem an early precursor to the modern Indonesian army's "dual function" (*dwifungsi*) in post-independence civil society, most markedly during Suharto's New Order regime, when

---

[76] On the founding of the KNILM, see Van Haselen, *25 Jaar Militaire Luchtvaart*, 50, 63, 72, 121, 129, 132–34.

[77] *De Indische courant*, January 19, 1931.

[78] As well as the KNILM, corporate airlines of mining companies like the BPM (Bataviaasch Petroleum Maatschappij) and NNGPM (Nederlandsch Nieuw Guinea Petroleum Maatschappij) developed airlines and occasionally produced aerial photographs: Collection Nationaal Museum voor Wereldculturen, TM-Doss-25; Leiden University Library Special Collections, KITLV A161 (nos. 78612, 78613-14), A498, A499.

[79] Although, paternalistic humanitarian discourses had certainly been deployed by the military in justifying subjugation campaigns earlier: Paul Bijl, "Saving the Children? The Ethical Policy and Photography of Colonial Atrocity during the Aceh War," in *Photography, Modernity and the Governed in Late-Colonial Indonesia*, ed. Susie Protschky (Amsterdam: Amsterdam University Press, 2015), 103–32.

the Tentara Nasional Indonesia actively propagandized about its service to the people while flexing the continuing threat of coercive violence.[80]

Long after the end of Dutch rule, veterans of the KNIL themselves, in their own commemorative literature, marked the eruption of Gunung Merapi in 1930, and not that of Kelud in 1919, as the moment when military assistance in a disaster became worthy of honoring.[81] The postcolonial memory-work around the Merapi eruption in KNIL circles concurs with historical sources that show the novel development of campaign memories around this disaster within the senior ranks of the army and aviation division. The fact that it was Gunung Merapi's eruption, and not Kelud's, that signaled the full development of the military's focus on reconnaissance and humanitarian assistance in natural disaster accentuates how late a development this policy was, compared to the previously more reactive position of the military. It was almost 1920 before Indonesian victims of disaster warranted the coordinated attention of the colonial military, and it took the development of an air force with capabilities in aerial reconnaissance and photography to make this new policy a possibility: technologies that were acquired for war, fostered at the military-industrial complex at Andir, and effectively monopolized by the army, even after the development of civil aviation. The forms of knowledge about disaster generated by military airplanes, cameras, and photographers far exceeded their operational purposes and not by accident. The cooperation between the Aviation Division of the KNIL with scientific and commercial partners to assist volcanological research and geotourism arose from the military's historic role in generating ways of seeing at the intersection of the scenic and the metric that were fundamental to colonial modes of knowledge production in the Indies.[82]

Acknowledgments

The research for this article was funded by an Australian Research Council Discovery Grant (DP170100948) and a 2018 Brill Fellowship at the Scaliger Institute of the Leiden University Library (Netherlands).

---

[80] Katherine E. McGregor, *History in Uniform: Military Ideology and the Construction of Indonesia's Past* (Singapore: NUS Press and ASAA Southeast Asia Publications Series, 2007).

[81] Heshusius, *KNIL 1830–1950*, 127.

[82] Kaplan, *Aerial Aftermaths*, 147.

Plague Rat or Anopheles: Health Disasters and Home Improvement in Late Colonial Java

Maurits Bastiaan Meerwijk

Abstract

When plague broke out in Java in 1911, the Dutch responded with home improvement in an attempt to widen the distance between human residents and the rodent host of this disease. Over the following thirty years, home improvement was implemented on a tremendous scale—resulting in the reconstruction of over 1.6 million houses. After the mid-1920s, however, home improvement was gradually implicated in facilitating malaria transmission instead: effectively replacing one set of disease mortality with another. In this article, I trace how this correlation came to light and was responded to. The case of *woningverbeteringsmalaria*, I suggest, offers a case study for us to reflect on how health priorities were set, how developmentalist colonial policies designed to counter one threat often generated others, and understand how advances in understanding the human-animal relations underpinning health gradually broadened from linear transmission theories into broader ecological models.

Keywords: plague, malaria, animals, colonialism, visual, environment, health

Maurits Meerwijk is a historian of medicine and colonialism affiliated with the Centre for the Humanities and Medicine at the University of Hong Kong. I wish to thank Susie Protschky for organizing a wonderful conference on disasters in Indonesia and editing this special issue.

Between 1911 and 1942, a force of nature descended over Java. During the last three decades of Dutch colonial rule, an outbreak of plague triggered an unprecedented health intervention that impacted on Javanese cultures and ecologies with a vengeance: *woningverbetering* (home improvement). This intervention was not unique to plague in Java, but the scale of its implementation was.[1] Some 1.6 million houses would be renovated or rebuilt in an attempt to "build out the rat," the animal reservoir of plague. Millions of houses more were subjected to a periodic inspection. And furthermore, countless Javanese were exposed to a concurrent hygienic reform campaign that sought to "rat-proof" the practices of homeowners along with their dwellings. In the process, home improvement transformed and reordered the island's landscape. It contributed to the control of plague. And it facilitated new human-animal relations that were belatedly recognized to facilitate the transmission of an arguably worse health threat: malaria.

Plague had been endemic in China since the middle of the eighteenth century. Accounts of the disease sparked fear among Europeans, who equated it with the Great Plague (1346–53) that had decimated medieval Eurasia and the equally deadly Plague of Justinian (541–751) before that.[2] In 1894, plague broke out in the British colony of Hong Kong and from this key shipping hub spread around the world. By 1901, "plague ports" had been established in Southeast Asia, India, Australia, the United States, South America, Africa, and indeed Europe.[3] The response to this historically loaded disease differed from place to place: ranging from panic to denial, from lax to outright draconian control measures, and from the condemnation of specific social groups to the mockery of scientific medicine.[4] Scholars studying this so-called Third Plague Pandemic have often focused on British India, where plague prompted "an unprecedented assault upon the body of the colonized" in the form of quarantines, vaccinations, and house searches that in turn prompted unrest and resistance, but corresponding developments took place around the world.[5]

The late inclusion of the Dutch East Indies in this pandemic event caught colonial health officials off guard. Rather than establishing itself in a major port city, plague slipped into the rural interior of East Java. By the time it was recognized in March 1911, plague had already become epizootic among rodents and impossible to eradicate. On the bright side, Dutch scientists and physicians benefitted from recent advances in plague research. The outbreak offered them an opportunity to put competing transmission

[1] Branwyn Poleykett, "Building Out the Rat: Animal Intimacies and Prophylactic Settlement in 1920s South Africa," *Engagement, February 7,* 2017, https://aesengagement.wordpress.com/2017/02/07/building-out-the-rat-animal-intimacies-and-prophylactic-ssettlement-in-1920s-south-africa/.

[2] Carol Benedict, "Bubonic Plague in Nineteenth-Century China," *Modern China* 14, no. 2 (1988): 107–55.

[3] Myron Echenberg, Plague Ports: *The Global Urban Impact of Bubonic Plague, 1894–1901* (New York: New York University Press, 2010).

[4] James Mohr, *Plague and Fire: Battling Black Death and the 1900 Burning of Honolulu's Chinatown* (Oxford: Oxford University Press, 2005); Lukas Engelmann, "A Plague of Kinyounism: The Caricatures of Bacteriology in 1900 San Francisco," *Social History of Medicine* 33, no. 2 (2020): 489–514.

[5] David Arnold, *Colonizing the Body: State Medicine and Epidemic Disease in Nineteenth-Century India* (University of California Press: Berkeley, 1993), 200–39; David Arnold, "Disease, Rumor, and Panic in India's Plague and Influenza Epidemics, 1896–1919," in *Empires of Panic: Epidemics and Colonial Anxieties*, ed. Robert Peckham (Hong Kong: Hong Kong University Press, 2015), 111–29.

theories to the test and demonstrate their scientific acumen through the identification of a peculiarly Javanese plague ecology that posited the house as a "carrier" of plague.[6] Moreover, the relatively successful control of this high-profile disease through the strategy of home improvement transformed it into a signature health intervention. As plague spread over the island, home improvement was systematically rolled out across entire districts, extensively photographed, and displayed to colonial, metropolitan, and foreign audiences alike as evidence of the new "Ethical" course of colonial governance pursued after 1900.[7] Meanwhile, it is key to point out the resources devoted to plague control were disproportionate to its burden when compared to the control and impact of endemic health disasters such as smallpox, tuberculosis, and malaria most of all.[8]

This article examines how a Dutch health intervention in late colonial Java to counter plague was belatedly recognized to facilitate malaria. We may ask what this episode tells us about how acute health disasters have been negotiated alongside chronic ones and how health priorities are set more generally. If this theme is topical in the context of the ongoing pandemic of COVID-19, it is also acutely relevant as boundaries between events that precipitate death, disease, and damage as purely geophysical, biological, or man-made are becoming increasingly diffuse. Human-driven environmental change now prompts questions about the "naturalness" of floods, droughts, fires, pests, and indeed plagues. In disaster-prone regions, the beginning or end of any one such calamity may seamlessly merge into another. Finally, the case of *woningverbeteringsmalaria* is illustrative of the processes by which the role of animals and environments became implicated in the production of disease. Recently, the anthropologist Anna Tsing suggested the ecological entanglements that support life are becoming increasingly evident in part through contemporary processes of "ruination."[9] Can we extend this observation to early twentieth-century Java to say that—in the aftermath of the home improvement scheme—new but linear notions of chains of disease transmission gave way to a more complex, ecological understanding of the human-animal relations underpinning health? And how were these successive insights responded to?

This article first surveys the advances in scientific medicine that clarified the natural history of plague and malaria around 1900. Next, I discuss plague, plague control, and malaria in late colonial Java. Finally, the article traces how home improvement was gradually implicated in increased rates of malaria transmission and examines two case studies presented by contemporary authors that clarified the existence and nature of this correlation. I conclude by reflecting on the impact of and response to the phenomenon of *woningverbeteringsmalaria*.

[6] M. B. Meerwijk, "Bamboo Dwellers: Plague, Photography, and the House in Colonial Java," in *Plague Image and Imagination from Medieval to Modern Times*, ed. C. Lynteris (Cham: Palgrave Macmillan, 2021), 205–34.

[7] Susie Protschky, "Camera Ethica: Photography, Modernity and the Governed in Late-Colonial Indonesia," in *Photography, Modernity and the Governed in Late-Colonial Indonesia*, ed. Susie Protschky (Amsterdam: Amsterdam University Press, 2015), 11–40.

[8] As in other contexts, Christos Lynteris, *Ethnographic Plague: Configuring Disease on the Chinese-Russian Frontier* (Palgrave Macmillan, 2018), 1; Terence H. Hull, "Plague in Java," in *Death and Disease in Southeast Asia: Explorations in Social, Medical and Demographic History*, ed. Norman Owen (Oxford: Oxford University Press, 1987), 210–34; Arnold, "Disease, Rumor, and Panic."

[9] Anna Lowenhaupt Tsing, *The Mushroom at the End of the World* (Princeton: Princeton University Press, 2015).

Plague and Malaria around 1900

Plague is a zoonotic and vector-borne disease. Its causative bacterium, *Yersinia pestis*, was identified during an outbreak in Hong Kong in 1894 that marked the start of the so-called Third Plague Pandemic.[10] The disease primarily affects rodents and is most commonly transmitted by the bite of the so-called oriental rat flea. *Xenopsylla cheopis*, however, is induced to feed on other animals (including humans) once its usual hosts expire. This route of transmission was first proposed in 1898 but remained contentious as the main or sole method of human infection for at least another decade.[11] Malaria, on the other hand, is a protozoal disease caused by one of several variants of *Plasmodium* parasites. This pathogen was first identified as such about 1880, while its method of transmission between humans by female mosquitoes of the genus *Anopheles* was established in 1897.[12] As a rule, *Anopheles* species prefer to breed in brackish water and become active at dusk. Both diseases consequently hinge on human-animal relations that are in turn mediated by cultural, economic, and environmental conditions. Rats may live further away from or closer to humans and carry different numbers of fleas depending on their habitat, increasing or reducing the risk of plague infection among humans once an epizootic begins. The presence or absence of stagnant water in the vicinity of human residences, meanwhile, or the ability of residents to avail themselves of screens, fans, and bed nets, are factors that affect their risk of being bitten by mosquitoes and the incidence of malaria.

If such dynamics are self-evident today, the insights underpinning them were radical at the turn of the nineteenth and twentieth centuries. The so-called laboratory revolution in medicine had generated a new understanding of plague, malaria, and other diseases as a product of infection that involved specific pathogens, insect vectors, and animal hosts.[13] Such relations were gradually understood to be grounded in environmental conditions, but they would not normally be framed in the more complex network of human, animal, and environmental entanglements that we have come to refer to as "disease ecologies" only since the 1930s.[14] Rather, these relations tended to be articulated in neat, simplified, linear sequences. Plague had its "rat-flea-man" transmission scheme, for instance, while malaria went from human to mosquito to human. If anything, such chains of disease transmission would be complicated by pointing to the "dangerous" behaviors of certain social groups that were seen to facilitate particular human-animal contact, often perpetuating preexisting stigmas. Conversely, certain animals such as rats, bats, and mosquitoes have become implicated as the "epidemic villain" behind a disease, thereby appearing to absolve humans of their own role in the processes behind infection.[15]

---

[10] M. P. Sutphen, "Not What, but Where: Bubonic Plague and the Reception of Germ Theories in Hong Kong and Calcutta, 1894–1897," *Journal of the History of Medicine and Allied Sciences* 52, no. 1 (January 1, 1997): 81–113.

[11] Christos Lynteris, "A 'Suitable Soil': Plague's Urban Breeding Grounds at the Dawn of the Third Pandemic," *Medical History* 61, no. 3 (2017): 343–57.

[12] Ria Sinha, "Fatal Island: Malaria in Hong Kong," *Journal of the Royal Asiatic Society Hong Kong Branch* 58 (2018): 55, 80.

[13] Nicholas A. Evans, "Blaming the Rat? Accounting for Plague in Colonial Indian Medicine," *Medicine, Anthropology, Theory* 5, no. 3 (2018): 15, 42.

[14] Christos Lynteris and Frédéric Keck, "Zoonosis," *Medicine Anthropology Theory* 5, no. 3 (2018): 1–14.

[15] Christos Lynteris, ed., *Framing Animals as Epidemic Villains: Histories of Non-Human Disease Vectors* (Cham: Springer International Publishing, 2019).

Such sequences (and the epidemiological diagrams they inspired) were not necessarily "wrong," but often failed to pay attention to the overlapping cultural and environmental systems underpinning them.[16] They pursued simplification in an attempt to make disease actionable. After all, chains could be broken. Their simplicity, however, inspired equally straightforward responses that took little stock of other factors and processes. Indeed, the agenda of imperial tropical medicine that took shape at the end of the nineteenth century concentrated on the control and eradication of the most prominent parasitic and infectious diseases. Overwhelmingly, these interventions would be arranged in vertical and monolithic campaigns pursuing a technical "fix" that targeted one disease at a time.[17] Home improvement in late colonial Java against plague was a case in point, and the consequences of such tunnel vision in this context were especially severe.

Plague and Home Improvement in Java

When plague was recognized in Java at the end of March 1911, the disease had already attained a wide diffusion in the district of Malang. A suite of control measures covering an equal number of transmission theories was quickly implemented by Dr Willem de Vogel, the vice-director of the colonial Civil Medical Service [Dienst der Volksgezondheid, DVG].[18] While de Vogel tentatively supported the rat-flea-man transmission theory, however, his team was unable to confirm the presence of a concurrent plague epizootic among the rodent population of Malang. Their search for an animal host had concentrated on the house rat but was foiled by a failure to identify infected specimens, or, indeed, *any* specimen. The normally ubiquitous house rat was in inexplicably short supply across the plague-stricken district. A breakthrough only came several months later, in June. Could it be, ventured the bacteriologist Dr. Johannes van Loghem about this time, that the rats inhabiting a plague house had already died inside? And if so, where were their remains? The impromptu plague service initiated a "systematic investigation of the houses where plague had occurred," with dedicated brigades searching a house as soon as a patient was diagnosed. Gradually, rats (healthy, sick, or dead) as well as their nests began to be found in myriad hiding spaces: within the thatch roof made of *atap*, on ceilings, in-between double walls, and inside the hollow poles, beams, and articles of furniture made of Java's principal building material: bamboo. In short, de Vogel and van Loghem unveiled the traditional Javanese house as a vibrant space of multispecies encounters.

Elsewhere, I have argued that photographs of plague in Java were crucial for imbuing longstanding notions of the house as a space of plague infection with a new materiality.[19] Photographs of rats and nests embedded within split pieces of bamboo in particular

[16] Christos Lynteris, "Zoonotic Diagrams: Mastering and Unsettling Human-Animal Relations," *Journal of Royal Anthropological Institute* 23, no. 3 (2017): 463, 485.

[17] Michael Worboys, "The Colonial World as Mission and Mandate: Leprosy and Empire, 1900, 1940," *Osiris* 15 (2000): 207, 218; John Farley, *Bilharzia: A History of Imperial Tropical Medicine* (Cambridge: Cambridge University Press, 1991).

[18] A colonial civil medical service called the Burgerlijke Geneeskundige Dienst was established only months earlier and was later renamed the Dienst der Volksgezondheid.

[19] Meerwijk, "Bamboo Dwellers," 214–15.

helped to integrate this material, or the house in itself, as a separate link in plague's rat-flea-man transmission chain. Put differently, the traditional bamboo dwelling was recognized as a distinguishing feature of an emergent (and distinctively Javanese) plague ecology. This newly identified complexity, however, was immediately simplified again. By integrating the house into the existing rat-flea-man transmission scheme, a straightforward intervention suggested itself. Under the leadership of de Vogel and van Loghem, the DVG settled on home improvement as a control strategy in an attempt to increase "the distance between man and rat" and prevent transmission.[20] This approach was not entirely unexpected. As a physician and municipal councilor in Semarang, de Vogel had previously been involved in sanitary reform and urban planning projects to "build up" public health in this city—while van Loghem had suggested that "the construction of better houses" was instrumental to plague control in an article published mere weeks before the outbreak in Malang was identified.[21] Over the following years, as plague expanded westward, home improvement became increasingly systematic and radically transformed the landscape. The traditional Javanese house was renovated primarily in wood. The use of bamboo was strictly regulated. The traditional *atap* roofs were replaced with tiles. Additional building codes sought to prevent the creation of "dead space" where rats might nest unobserved. And while the government provided funding, home improvement was primarily financed through advances to homeowners, with little regard for their ability to repay them.[22]

Home improvement was slow, costly, almost entirely reactive, but not without success. At the landmark Bandung Rural Hygiene Conference of 1937, a committee of international health professionals praised the "excellent example" set by the Dutch colonial government of home improvement as an efficacious intervention against plague.[23] But home improvement, it is important to recognize, did not make the Javanese house intrinsically "rat-proof." In the first years of the epidemic, plague sometimes returned to previously improved districts. Meanwhile, an emergency *desa schoonmaak* (village cleaning) that involved regular inspections of the traditional bamboo house for the presence of rats was already highly effective in reducing the incidence of plague. As such, health officials recognized that the real key to success lay less in improving the houses than reforming the domestic and hygienic behaviors of their occupants. A thorough weekly cleaning, they insisted, had to become *adat* (customary).[24] Home improvement merely facilitated this inspection, but was far more *visible* as an intervention. Over the following decades, hundreds of photographs of houses, landscapes, and (to a lesser extent) peoples that had been "improved" in the name of plague control were circulated to colonial, metropolitan, and foreign audiences alike (Figure 1). These processes took place in the context of the Dutch reform period after

[20] J. J. van Loghem, "Some Epidemiological Facts Concerning the Plague in Java," in *Publications of the Civil Medical Service in Netherlands India* 1b (Batavia: Javasche Boekhandel en Drukkerij, 1912), 5–6.

[21] H. F. Tillema, "Persoonlijke Herinneringen," in *Gedenkboek der Gemeente Semarang 1906–1931* (Semarang: De Locomotief, 1931), 27, 29; J. J. van Loghem, "Over Pest," *Maandblad voor Ziekenverpleging* 21, no. 3 (1911): 150–55.

[22] Hull, "Plague in Java," 210, 230.

[23] *Report of the Intergovernmental Conference of Far-Eastern Countries on Rural Hygiene* (Geneva: League of Nations Health Organization, 1937), 97, 98.

[24] N. H. Swellengrebel, "Plague in Java," *The Journal of Hygiene* 48, no. 2 (1950), 135, 145; Dienst der Pestbestrijding, *Verslag over het Eerste Kwartaal 1915* (Batavia: Javasche Boekhandel, 1915), 197.

Figure 1: Photograph of home improvement in Java, inspection by Dr. Otten, Dr. Lumentut, and Dr. van Loon. Courtesy of Delft University of Technology Library. Image courtesy of M. Mortier Hijmans, "Een en Ander Over de Pest op Java en Hare Bestrijding," *Nederlandsch-Indië Oud en Nieuw* 2, no. 5 (1917): 153–69.

1900, customarily referred to as the *Ethische Politiek*. This civilising mission, steeped in the language of Christian responsibility, was never clearly formulated—let alone consistently implemented—but certainly involved taking responsibility for the health and well-being of local populations.[25] Simultaneously, however, it served a role in

[25] One scholar, for instance, specifically speaks of the ethical policy as "fragmented." Elsbeth Locher Scholten, *Ethiek in fragmenten; Vijf studies over koloniaal denken en doen van Nederlanders in de Indonesische Archipel (1877–1942)* (Utrecht: HES Publishers, 1981).

promoting the cause for Dutch colonial rule, which has led me to suggest elsewhere that home improvement also served as a dramatic performance of the impact of Dutch "Ethical" governance. This, in turn, leads me to refer to some of these photographs as a "living picture" designed to convey an ideal of Dutch-Javanese collaboration and an aesthetic of Calvinist productivity transplanted to a tropical setting.[26]

Malaria in the Dutch East Indies

By 1928, there had been 129,000 deaths due to plague in Java. Some 1 million houses had been rebuilt, and plague control consumed over *f.* 2 million every year.[27] It was about this time that physicians with the DVG began to notice a curious phenomenon. It seemed as though wherever home improvement was implemented, plague declined while another disease gained ground: malaria. This was no small matter, but it was not until late in 1937, mere months after the international endorsement of home improvement by the Bandung Rural Hygiene Conference, that the first of just two publications exploring this correlation was published.[28]

Malaria was the true pathogenic menace of the Indies. Whatever the reputation of plague, it was malaria that was consistently described by physicians and officials alike as the leading endemic disease in the archipelago. Already in 1908, de Vogel spoke of malaria as "the chief enemy of the population of our colonies."[29] In the government's *Koloniaal Verslag* (Colonial report) of 1928, one official declared that malaria remained "undoubtedly the worst scourge of the population of the Dutch East Indies".[30] And as late as March 1940, the Dutch Minister of Colonies reiterated the primacy of malaria over other tropical diseases in a parliamentary debate on health care in the Indies in no uncertain terms:

> I would point out that one can speak of all manner of tropical diseases, but that one must always acknowledge that malaria is in reality the principal disease. In the tropics, malaria is the chief disease and the chief underminer of the strength of the population. All other sorts of illnesses find their ultimate cause in the reduced strength of the population caused by malaria. He who combats malaria, combats also the tuberculosis and many other diseases. Consequently, a tropical country such as the Indies cannot but emphasize the control of malaria.[31]

None of these sources bothered to provide figures on the incidence of or deathrate for malaria, and any statistics that were kept in the late colonial period were limited in scale and scope. In 1954, however, a World Health Organization report on malaria in newly independent Indonesia still listed malaria as the "number one" health threat in the

---

[26] M. B. Meerwijk, *A History of Plague in Java, 1911, 1942* (Ithaca: Cornell University Press, forthcoming 2022).

[27] Meerwijk, *A History of Plague in Java.*

[28] J. W. Grootings, "Woningverbetering en Malaria," *Mededeelingen van den Dienst der Volksgezondheid in Nederlandsch-Indië* 27, no. 3 (1938): 397, 416.

[29] W. Th. de Vogel, *Malaria-bestrijding en Hygiëne in Tropische Gewesten* (Amsterdam: J. H. de Bussy, 1908), 6.

[30] *Verslag van Bestuur en Staat van Nederlandsch-Indië, Suriname en Curaçao van 1928*, no. 5 (1928, 1929): 47.

[31] "Handelingen," *Tweede Kamer 48e Vergadering*, March 5, 1940, 1281.

archipelago, with an average mortality ranging from 20 to 50 deaths per 1,000 cases in ordinary years.[32]

Malaria, in other words, was understood as the leading disease eroding the health, happiness, and prosperity of the Indies population. And, as the Minister of Colonies recognized, tackling this disease could have a considerable impact on the burden of other health threats as well. Having said that, attempts to control malaria were limited. A comprehensive history of malaria in the Indies would undoubtedly reveal a more complex story but, leaving aside a number of signature drainage projects such as those at Sibolga (a port in north Sumatra) and Tandjong Priok (the harbor of Batavia), most interventions were modest in scale and scope. Often, they relied on local and short-lived "species sanitation" efforts (i.e., the elimination of mosquitoes) and the distribution of quinine (an anti-malarial drug and prophylactic). Despite the Netherlands East Indies producing over 90 percent of the world's supply of quinine by the time of World War II, the drug was not widely accessible to local populations.[33] Meanwhile, a dedicated Malaria Bureau to coordinate anti-malarial interventions was not created until 1924, while an independent Plague Service was active between 1915 and 1921. There was a divide, then, between the prevalence of malaria and its priority to the DVG. This challenge is still with us today and has been referred to by the World Health Organization as the "10/90" problem, in which diseases that affect 90 percent of the global population attract only 10 percent of global health research as the powers that be have "accepted" their endemic presence in certain spaces—as was and continues to be the case with malaria in "the tropics."[34] That being said, it seems fair to stress that surely no one in the Dutch East Indies intended for the disease to spread.

Home Improvement and Malaria

At the end of 1937, a paper by the head of the Department of Plague Control, Dr. H. J. Rosier, first introduced the possibility of a correlation between home improvement and veritable "explosions" of malaria to a larger audience.[35] Observations of such a phenomenon, he maintained, dated back "rather recently." In fact, it had been nine years since physicians first tentatively reported a curious increase in malaria following plague control in the districts Kedu, Magelang, and Surakarta in 1928. Two years later, health officials in Surakarta first "positively ascribed" outbreaks of malaria to the renovation works. That year, 1930, a solitary article in the Indies newspaper *Soerabaisch Handelsblad*, later copied in the Dutch newspaper *Het Vaderland*, reported on this development. "Enquiring after this," the author noted, "we were told that the statistics of the last seven years absolutely confirm" that this was a recurring phenomenon. The article effectively claimed that a link between home improvement and malaria had become apparent since

[32] WHO/Mal/118. H. T. Soeparmo, "Anopheles Sundaicus and its Control by DDT Residual House Spraying in Indonesia," communication to the World Health Organization, December 2, 1954.

[33] Arjo Roersch Van Der Hoogte and Toine Pieters, "Quinine, Malaria, and the Cinchona Bureau: Marketing Practices and Knowledge Circulation in a Dutch Transoceanic Cinchona–Quinine Enterprise (1920s–30s)," *Journal of the History of Medicine and Allied Sciences* 71, no. 2 (April 2016): 197–225.

[34] Philip Stevens, *Fighting the Diseases of Poverty* (New York: Routledge, 2017).

[35] H. J. Rosier, "Woningverbetering en Malaria," *Mededeelingen van den Dienst der Volksgezondheid in Nederlandsch-Indië* 26, no. 4 (1937): 343, 344.

1923 but the story somehow failed to gain traction.[36] The subsequent seven-year interval until Rosier's publication on the subject is significant as home improvement steadily continued. It is a silence that speaks both to the priorities of health authorities and, I would argue, to the centrality that home improvement had assumed in Dutch efforts to broadcast an image of modern and benign colonial governance. In the meantime, Dutch and Indies newspapers occasionally reported on novel or startlingly severe outbreaks of malaria in districts that had only recently overcome plague.[37]

At the same time, the phenomenon began to be observed further west in Central Java. In his diary, the Dutch plague physician and prolific photographer Dr. G. M. Versteeg recounted a tour through Pekalongan in 1930, together with Rosier. On April 17, he wrote:

> Visit to the improved *kampongs* [villages]. Very orderly, but far too airy. Bad open walls, large, unnecessary ventilation holes. . . . In my opinion the unprotected houses are far too open. Rosier pointed to the malaria epidemic, which manifested shortly after home improvement. Saw several individual patients.[38]

His reference to the appearance of malaria following home improvement is offhand, almost casual, as though it was familiar and required little further explanation. If anything, it demonstrates that Rosier himself was aware of incidents in four districts in Central Java and that other members of the plague service were likewise familiar with them. Nor was discussion of a possible correlation between plague and malaria limited to health officials alone. In 1932, the outgoing *Resident* (governor) of Pekalongan wrote to his successor:

> Another curious fact is that wherever home improvement has been implemented by the plague control service, a malaria explosion occurs soon after, which slowly disappears after the distribution of quinine. It is blamed on the airier building style after home improvement. The real cause is, however, not yet known.[39]

Anecdotal and, indeed, epidemiological evidence supporting a causal link dated back even further, as we will see below. The population of Central and West Java, meanwhile, reportedly spoke of *sakit wonéng*, or "house disease," in reference to the malarial fever outbreaks that followed in the wake of plague control.

Although home improvement had achieved "excellent" results against plague, wrote Rosier, its increasingly strong connection to fresh outbreaks of malaria was cause for concern. As mentioned, the Dutch broadcast home improvement to a large and international audience, as evidence of both their scientific and governing ability. The suggestion that the colonial government's signature health intervention might facilitate the spread of what was quite possibly the deadliest disease in the Indies could "discredit" the entire operation. Other factors also came into play. As home improvement steadily expanded westward, there was the health of Dutch colonials in Batavia, Buitenzorg, and

---

[36] "Solo," *Soerabaisch Handelsblad*, September 2, 1930; "Malaria-epidemie," *Het Vaderland*, October 11, 1930.

[37] "Een Malaria-explosie in 26 Desa's in Banjoemas," *Nieuwe Rotterdamsche Courant*, May 2, 1928; "Malaria-Epidemie in de Bergen," *Het Vaderland*, March 21, 1930.

[38] Anton Versteeg, *Dagboek van mijn grootvader Gerard Martinus Versteeg*, vol. 5 (Pumbo: 2017), 137, 138.

[39] J. J. M. A. Popelier, Resident van Pekalongan, 1929, 1932, 16, 17. Nationaal Archief, Den Haag, Ministerie van Koloniën: Memories van Overgave, 2.10.39.

Bandung to consider. They were usually little affected by plague, but malaria did pose a threat. Finally, the development of an efficacious vaccine against plague by the Dutch bacteriologist Dr. Louis Otten (1883–1946) at the end of 1935 offered a viable alternative to home improvement and a new scientific breakthrough to obscure the fallacies of the old one. In short, the time had come to review the available evidence regarding *woningverbeteringsmalaria*, for which Rosier concentrated on Pekalongan, a *residentie* (province) on the north coast of Central Java.

Home Improvement: Malaria in Pekalongan and Tasikmalaya

Plague had struck Pekalongan in two waves in 1921 and 1925. Home improvement began in 1925 and was ultimately completed in 1931. Coastal parts of Pekalongan were apparently "malarious," while the more mountainous terrain where plague had entrenched itself was regarded "from experience" as malaria-free. But almost as soon as the renovations began, outbreaks of malaria were also reported. And worryingly, the previously infrequent disease persisted long after the work had been completed. When studying the available evidence, Rosier quickly concluded that a causal relation was apparent. By overlaying the routes and dates of home improvement through the district alongside the advance of malaria as arrows on a map, the latter followed the former closely (Figure 2). Both arrows circled in on themselves, revealing how the subdistrict at the center, Petungkriono, was only affected by malaria after the renovation work began in 1930, despite bordering on subdistricts where malaria first manifested five years earlier. Both the chronological order of events, and the unlikely geographical advance of malaria toward Petungkriono, concluded Rosier, implicated home improvement as the cause of these new outbreaks.

To support his case, Rosier presented several more items of evidence: both anecdotal and epidemiological. In particular, his use of imagery stands out. As well as maps, he compiled two tables that strongly suggested a correlation between home improvement and malaria. The first listed forty-four out of a total of seventy-one subdistricts where home improvement had been implemented since 1928 and where physicians had reported fresh outbreaks of malaria soon after. Affected provinces and districts included Magelang, Wonosobo, Banjarnegara, Klaten, Bojolali, Batang, Pekalongan, Brebes, Tegal, Kuningan, Ciamis [Tjiamis], and Tasikmalaya. In other words, all of interior Central Java between Yogyakarta and Bandung. A second table recorded quarterly measures of plague outbreaks in each of the districts of Pekalongan, when home improvement took place, and when malaria first manifested. In each case, the Ms indicating malaria followed the Ws for home improvement almost immediately (Figure 3). As can be seen from the first set of rows for the subdistrict Bawang, the table pushed epidemiological evidence for the existence of a correlation back by another two years to 1926.

Perhaps the most striking image in Rosier's report was a series of eight mortality statistics for each of the improved districts in Pekalongan. They suggested a harrowing probability: that plague control had *exacerbated* overall mortality. Each graph recorded overall mortality per annual quarter across a decade. Plague mortality was marked in black. In most diagrams, plague mortality was often already on the wane when home improvement began, suggesting the efficacy of the mandatory *desa schoonmaak* over *woningverbetering*. Then, we see how overall mortality substantially and enduringly

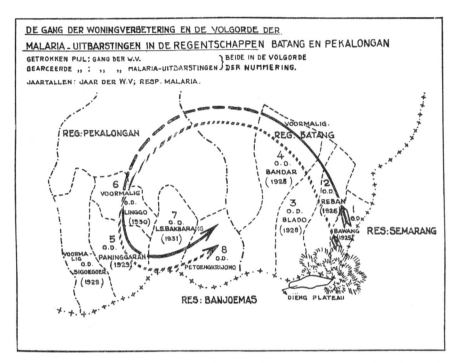

Figure 2: Map demonstrating the advance of home improvement and malaria outbreaks in the residency Pekalongan. Courtesy of the University of Groningen Library, photograph by Dirk Fennema. (Reprinted from H. J. Rosier, "Woningverbetering en Malaria," *Mededeelingen van den Dienst der Volksgezondheid in Nederlandsch-Indië* 26, no. 4 [1937]: 343–63).

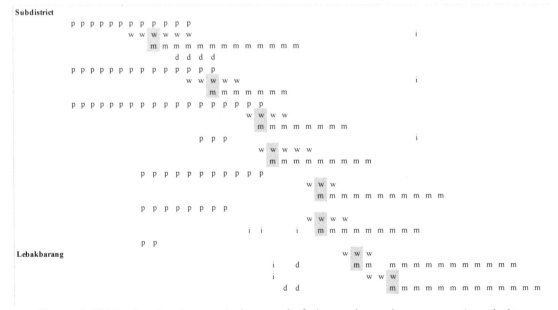

Figure 3: Table showing the quarterly record of plague, home improvement, malaria, influenza, and dysentery in eight subdistricts of the residency Pekalongan. (Table after H. J. Rosier, "Woningverbetering en Malaria," *Mededeelingen van den Dienst der Volksgezondheid in Nederlandsch-Indië* 26, no. 4 (1937): 343–63.)

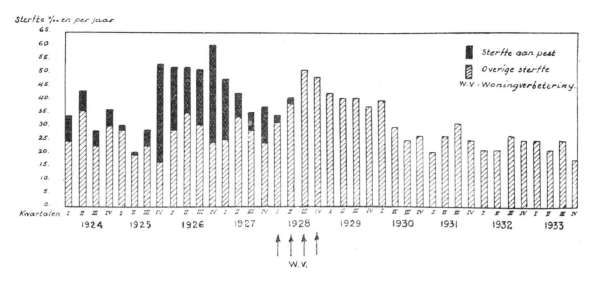

Figure 4: Table showing overall mortality (white) and plague mortality (black) in the subdistrict Blado. Courtesy of the University of Groningen Library, photograph by Dirk Fennema. (H. J. Rosier, "Woningverbetering en Malaria," *Mededeelingen van den Dienst der Volksgezondheid in Nederlandsch-Indië* 26, no. 4 [1937]: 343–63).

increased almost as soon as home improvement (w.v.) began. In the subdistrict Blado this pattern was evident from the same quarter as renovations commenced (Figure 4). The most poignant evidence, however, came once more from Petungkriono. As Figure 2 already indicated, this district never hosted plague and was improved for "tactical" reasons only. Through the early 1930s, we see a dramatic rise in overall mortality that Rosier put down to previously unheard-of outbreaks of malaria (Figure 4). Belatedly, he added: "we must remember that the epidemics described were all powerfully combated by the supply of quinine." In other words, these disturbing figures already presented "a mitigated form of the course of [malaria] without such interventions."[40]

Having established that *woningverbeteringsmalaria* was a real phenomenon, Rosier offered some suggestions to explain it. During the renovation, he observed, the population lived in temporary sheds. The village grounds were full of rubbish and demolition materials. Earth was dug up for tile production. When the rains came, a village and its surroundings were consequently filled with puddles, while ditches were blocked by debris. The local environment saw significant change by the cutting down of trees and bamboo for building materials. Such conditions favored mosquito breeding, while malaria parasites were likely introduced by the "invasion of outsiders" involved with the renovations: laborers, traders, drivers, porters, not to mention physicians and engineers. "In short, the quiet, orderly, remote and often malaria-free *desa* is disturbed in her isolation." Meanwhile, the "rejuvenated" dwellings themselves were perhaps more open to mosquitoes, as Versteeg had essentially already observed back in 1930. And finally, there was a socioeconomic side to consider. Home improvement, admitted

---

[40] Rosier, "Woningverbetering en Malaria," 362.

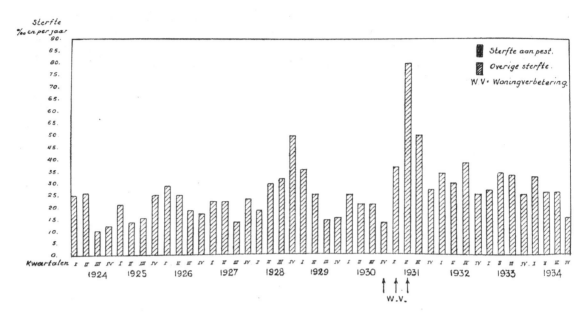

Figure 5: Table showing overall mortality in the subdistrict Petungkriono.
Courtesy of the University of Groningen Library, photograph by Dirk Fennema.
(Reprinted from H. J. Rosier, "Woningverbetering en Malaria," *Mededeelingen van den
Dienst der Volksgezondheid in Nederlandsch-Indië* 26, no. 4 [1937]: 343–63.)

Rosier, placed new financial burdens on local homeowners that could impact their ability to purchase food. Lack of vitamins and protein, in turn, could affect people's ability to resist infection.[41] But if these factors explained an immediate surge in malaria, then what caused the disease to persist?

In 1931, Dr. J. W. Grootings published a second paper on the concurrence of home improvement and malaria. His investigation concentrated on the phenomenon in the regencies Tasikmalaya and Ciamis, located further to the west in the *residentie* East Priangan. Plague began to spread in earnest through the district after 1930, although home improvement only commenced in 1933. Budget cuts across the health service as a result of the Great Depression had severely delayed the scheme. As a result, plague deaths in Priangan between 1933 and 1935 rose dramatically, ultimately exceeding the total number of plague deaths in East Java since 1911.[42] Despite the limited rollout of home improvement, Grootings's predecessor in the district, Dr. B. K. Zon, already reported in 1933 that local populations believed "the houses now contain many more mosquitoes than before."[43] An initial mosquito survey between two improved districts and one unimproved district resulted in an average yield of 6.7 and 11.1 mosquitoes per house in the former against 3.75 in the latter during one hour of searching, a significant

---

[41] Rosier, "Woningverbetering en Malaria," 359 – 360.

[42] Hull, "Plague in Java," 225.

[43] J. W. Grootings, "Woningverbetering en Malaria," *Mededeelingen van den Dienst der Volksgezondheid in Nederlandsch-Indië* 27, no. 3 (1938): 397.

difference. In his final report for 1933, Zon duly informed his superiors that "improved houses are more attractive" to mosquitoes and that home improvement consequently resulted in "a greater contact between these dangerous *anopheles* and humans." "The more severe incidence of malaria since home improvement took place," he concluded, "would partially be explained by this."[44] Zon was reassigned to Purwokerto soon after, and in the following years Grootings continued his research.

The paper by Grootings resembled Rosier's. First, it praised the efficacy of home improvement with regard to plague. Then, brushing over some of the more common financial objections to the scheme, he continued by stating that the local population was not necessarily opposed to home improvement. That is to say, if it was not for a growing sense that the renovations brought about another health challenge:

> What now is the case? In the aforementioned subdistrict the people are quite unanimously of the opinion that W.V. is necessarily followed by malaria. This opinion is not merely that of the dumb masses, but is shared by the more educated among the population and even by Native Officials.[45]

The "dumb masses" had been perceptive, "for this turned out to have in fact been the case." Drawing once more on a series of annotated maps, graphs, and tables, Grootings illustrated how malaria followed hot on the heels of home improvement across the district. The correlation was clear, and, fearful that the matter would cause the acclaimed home improvement scheme "to be placed in a bad smell," he set out to explore what caused it.

As in Pekalongan, malaria outbreaks persisted for too long after home improvement had been completed to have been only related to the immediate renovation works. Several colleagues had suggested cultural, behavioral, and environmental factors as a possible cause, but given that *woningverbeteringsmalaria* was so widespread, Grootings dismissed these theories as either unlikely or insufficient to explain the phenomenon across Java. Finally, he asked the obvious question: was there anything about the improved house itself that facilitated transmission? "Is the idea itself so absurd," he ventured, and replied to his own question: "No, it is the most logical conclusion." If all other conditions in a community either remained the same or stabilized once the renovations had been completed, the altered house itself was the only remaining explanation.

The impact of home improvement on the traditional Javanese house was tremendous. The *atap* roof was replaced with tiles. The bamboo frame was sealed off or replaced with wood. Dirt floors were replaced with tiles or concrete. Where the old dwelling tended to be dark and poorly ventilated, the improved dwelling was light and airy (Figure 6). But the crucial difference, Grootings suggested, was that the traditional bamboo dwelling had a cooking area in the main compartment, while the improved structure normally featured a separate kitchen area with a smoke vent. The improved dwelling was not just better ventilated, it was simply not as infused with smoke as its predecessor. Given that the nocturnal *Anopheles* mosquito was generally averse to smoke, the fundamental change that had taken place was that the simple act of sleeping indoors no longer provided the same protection against malaria infection as the old house had. Several

[44] Grootings, "Woningverbetering en Malaria," 410.
[45] Grootings, "Woningverbetering en Malaria," 397.

ONVERBETERD EN VERBETERD HUIS.

Belangrijk verschil in netheid en in ventilatie!

Figure 6: Photograph of an "unimproved" and an "improved" house with arrows
pointing out ventilation openings in the latter. Courtesy of the University of
Groningen Library, photograph by Dirk Fennema. (Reprinted from J. W. Grootings,
"Woningverbetering en Malaria," *Mededeelingen van den Dienst
der Volksgezondheid in Nederlandsch-Indië* 27, no. 3 [1938]: 397–416.)

photographs and sketches illustrated this transformation. They bore captions such as
"ventilation openings!" and "notice the black-sooted walls!" that curiously inverted
customary hygienic assumptions. With regard to malaria, "airiness" had become a health
hazard and "black-sooted walls" constituted a crucial defense.

As a final piece of evidence, Grootings returned to the mosquito survey by Zon. In
an expanded survey, he organized simultaneous mosquito surveys in *desa*s that featured
both improved and unimproved houses. A table of the results was clear: there had been
a nearly fivefold increase in mosquito incidence in renovated structures (Figure 7).
"Contact between man and mosquito," he concluded, "had become more intimate in an
improved dwelling."

Restoring Biological Balance

Given its invasive character, Rosier wrote in his report, nefarious "side effects" with
home improvement had been anticipated from the start but facilitating the spread of
other diseases had not been among them. It had been decided early on that the traditional

	In unimproved houses			In improved houses		
	Houses visited	No. of caught mosquitoes	No. of caught mosquitoes per 10 houses	Houses visited	No. of caught mosquitoes	No. of caught mosquitoes per 10 houses
Tjiamis	817	129	1.6	793	713	9
Tasikmalaja	467	125	2.7	313	316	10
Total	**1284**	**254**	**2**	**1106**	**1029**	**9.3**

Figure 7: Table showing the number of mosquitoes caught in "unimproved" and "improved" houses in the regencies Ciamis and Tasikmalaya. (Table after J. W. Grootings, "Woningverbetering en Malaria," *Mededeelingen van den Dienst der Volksgezondheid in Nederlandsch-Indië* 27, no. 3 [1938]: 397–416.)

Javanese house would not be "improved" with an eye to the prevention of other diseases, though comments that the scheme "visibly" improved the overall sanitary state of house and *desa* alike were common.[46] The identification of *woningverbeteringsmalaria* made such a position difficult to maintain. But frankly, it should surprise us that such a possibility had not been considered, or its occurrence not recognized sooner. Interventions in the built and natural environment that related to the prevention or inadvertent appearance of malaria (in urban areas in particular) were a staple of colonial rule. The "greening of Hong Kong" through a concerted afforestation program in the 1880s, for instance, was explicitly pursued to reduce the intensity of "fever."[47] In Hanoi, French health officials paid increasingly strict attention to where houses were being built, what materials were used, and to light, ventilation, and furnishing. "Lush gardens," meanwhile, served both as a buffer between house and city and as potential breeding grounds for mosquitoes.[48] Irrigation in India, railway construction in Hong Kong, drainage in Manila, but also land reclamation in the Netherlands itself were likewise linked to the prevention and/or accidental outbreak of malaria.[49] The identification of its mosquito vector clarified the connection between such phenomena. Still, as late as 1920, van Loghem would write in ambiguous terms over whether it was the breezy or the poorly ventilated house that was more conducive to the transmission of malaria.[50] Either way, home improvement ought to have been expected to alter the generic "environmental" or specific "human-animal" dynamics underpinning it. By the 1930s, the phenomenon of "man-made malaria" was

---

[46] Dienst Der Pestbestrijding, *Verslag over het Eerste Kwartaal* (1915), 66; "De Strijd tegen de Ziekte," *De Locomotief*, February 18, 1928.

[47] Robert Peckham, "Hygienic Nature: Afforestation and the Greening of Colonial Hong Kong," *Modern Asian Studies* 49, no. 4 (2015): 1177–209.

[48] L. Victoir, "Hygienic Colonial Residences in Hanoi," in *Harbin to Hanoi: The Colonial Built Environment in Asia*, 1840–1940, ed. L. Victoir and V. Zatsepine (Hong Kong: Hong Kong University Press, 2013), 231–50.

[49] Lies Visscher-Endeveld and Jan Peter Verhave, "Rode Kruistochten door Polderland. Jac P. Thijsse en de Nederlandse Malariabestrijding," *Gewina* 28 (2005): 132, 146; Marcus van Toor, "Polderkoorts in een Moeras: Een Nieuw-Materialistisch Perspectief op de Eerste Jaren na de Drooglegging van het Haarlemmermeer 1852, 1859" (MA thesis, University of Utrecht, 2020).

[50] J. J. van Loghem, *Vraagstukken der Indische Hygiëne* (Amsterdam: Ellerman, Harms & Co., 1920), 29, 30.

broadly recognized, even if its belated identification in the more rural context of home improvement in Java offered a fresh example.

The remark by Grootings regarding human and mosquito "intimacy" within the improved Javanese house transports us back to the early days of the plague outbreak in 1911. At that time, it had been the unsuspected proximity of human and rodent bamboo dwellers that suggested an intervention in the built environment to begin with. As researchers gradually began to uncover the human-animal relations underpinning health, Dutch scientists and physicians contributed to the debate by identifying the bamboo house as a vibrant space of multispecies encounters. These relations supported a distinctively Javanese plague ecology. But as mentioned, this newfound complexity was immediately simplified. The house was integrated into plague's existing rat-flea-man transmission scheme to form a new link where this chain might be broken. Now, the light, airy, and supposedly more hygienic, "improved" house turned out to facilitate multispecies encounters of a different kind, and that were just as damaging to health. The reductionist rationale underpinning home improvement had become tragically apparent: *woningverbeteringsmalaria* made it clear that human-animal relations were not as linear as researchers had presumed, or that chains of disease transmission did not exist in isolation. The question of what reasons delayed a more expeditious confession of this revelation is important, but more pertinently for the purposes of this paper, we may ask: did the recognition of this phenomenon generate a more nuanced understanding of the environmental entanglements underpinning human health?

According to Rosier, "home improvement malaria" constituted clear evidence of how Dutch interventions "in established natural conditions on a grand scale . . . can acutely favor malaria transmission." Rosier continued by speaking of natural balance and its disruption, and Grootings likewise wrote:

> There, where the incidence of breeding sites on the one hand, but the specific style of house construction on the other hand, created a sort of balance, a biological balance, this balance protected the population against a close contact with anopheles, this balance has been broken by home improvement.[51]

This notion of "biological balance," he stressed, had historically been "of the utmost importance" to the hygienist:

> It is a factor that one must keep a close eye on, so that one-sided hygienic interventions would not disrupt such balance and pose unexpected new problems. We humans have, however, intervened in this biological balance, and disturbed this balance. When this malaria is indeed caused by home improvement, we have an example of *man-made malaria*.[52]

In other words, Grootings suggested that Dutch physicians had taken insufficient stock of the consequences of their "one-sided" intervention, with fresh outbreaks of malaria as a result. In short, both plague physicians considered home improvement malaria to be a man-made phenomenon. How were they to proceed?

---

[51] Grootings, "Woningverbetering en Malaria," 413.
[52] Grootings, "Woningverbetering en Malaria," 413.

It is telling that rather than pursuing changes in the highly systematic roll-out of the home improvement scheme, both Rosier and Grootings advocated *further* environmental change to tackle the challenge posed by home improvement malaria. Both suggested a thorough study of malaria was in order, followed by targeted interventions in the immediate vicinity of districts undergoing improvement. The plague service could screen workmen for malaria infection, or time the renovations in response to periods of irrigation of the rice fields, but primarily a solution was to be found in eliminating mosquito breeding sites. In low-lying regions, suggested Rosier, "typical" mosquito breeding sites could be removed, while in hilly terrain afforestation offered recourse. Grootings, meanwhile, compiled a list of eight recommendations to address the problem. Despite his straightforward conclusions, he did not suggest a return to the nocturnal "balance" that had previously existed, something that could theoretically be achieved by, for instance, screening windows and doors. No: seven out of eight recommendations advocated for changes in the local environment of improved villages. These ranged from planting new vegetation, draining artificially inundated rice fields after the harvest, and releasing larvivorous fish in nearby ponds. Only the final recommendation by Grootings could be seen as an attempt to restore the status quo. "One could conduct a trial with distributing bed nets," he concluded, and thereby deny the nocturnal *Anopheles* mosquito the opportunity to feed on humans while they slept.

When considering these recommendations, it seems that Rosier and Grootings had certainly developed a better understanding of the bigger picture behind human health. They recognized the overlapping cultural and biological complexities involved in the production of plague and malaria, and Rosier made explicit note of socioeconomic conditions as well—which had also been a key point of discussion at the Rural Hygiene Conference.[53] Indeed, their suggestions could be argued to match a broader interest in methods of "biological control" that were gaining currency in Southeast Asia at the time. With various pests and parasites being "liberated" by colonial agents in plantation settings in particular to counter others, instead of resorting to social or chemical methods of control.[54] On the other hand, however, we notice a desire to immediately steer the discussion away from the interspecies encounters within the house and toward the broader environment instead. Better to drain ponds, reforest land, introduce new species, or alter harvesting practices than to screen the doors and windows of houses already being renovated. What could go wrong? While the prestige of home improvement as a plague control measure may have been a limiting factor here, it also seems that despite a growing understanding of the complexity of human-animal relations there was a pragmatic desire to continue to think linearly about chains of transmission that could be disrupted by targeted interventions. And while the recommendations by Rosier and Grootings were primarily "environmental" in nature, it is curious that neither advocated a *return* to previous conditions but rather pursued *further* environmental change.

The response to the studies by Rosier and Grootings was generally mild. No one, at least, seems to have suggested that health officials had knowingly facilitated malaria transmission for the better part of a decade, or to have somehow concealed

[53] Theodore M. Brown, "The Bandoeng Conference of 1937: A Milestone in Health and Development," *American Journal of Public Health* 98, no. 1 (2008): 42–43.

[54] Jack Greatrex, "Liberating Parasites: Biological Control in British Malaya," (paper presented at Centre for the Humanities and Medicine, University of Hong Kong, May 15, 2020).

such a possibility. If anything, the Indies newspaper *Het Nieuws van den Dag* called the correlation between malaria and home improvement "disastrous" if true and asked how desirable it was to continue with home improvement if the lives saved from plague, on the one hand, were lost to malaria, on the other.[55] When Grootings's article came out the following year, several newspapers pointed out the painful dilemma these insights posed to the DVG. Which health threat was worse, "plague rat or anopheles?" When toward the end of 1938 home improvement was suspended on the Bandung plateau on account of the threat posed by malaria, the *Algemeen Handelsblad voor Nederlandsch-Indië* actually praised the government for "the timely recognition of this danger."[56] Meanwhile, the prominent Dutch malariologist N. H. Swellengrebel acknowledged that the evidence pointed to a causal link between home improvement and outbreaks of malaria, but objected to the explanations offered by Rosier and Grootings. Nonetheless, he mused: "What should one do with a control measure for a disease that one suspects to induce a similar if not indeed higher mortality for another disease than the one being suppressed?"[57] Finally, in 1939, a three-year-long "correlation inquest" was announced to explore the matter in detail.[58] The advent of World War II brought an end to this project. In the meantime, a large-scale vaccination scheme nearly eliminated human plague from Java.

Conclusion

Between 1911 and 1942, more than 1.6 million houses in Java were either renovated or rebuilt in the name of plague control. Home improvement was slow, costly, but also highly efficacious in combination with a hygienic reform campaign. By the late 1920s, however, a fatal flaw had become apparent. The intervention designed to counter one health disaster was directly implicated in the creation of another. The social and environmental disruption that was steadily rolled out across much of rural Java either introduced or advanced malaria in settlements that were being "improved." Meanwhile, the "improved" house itself may have widened the original distance between human and rodent bamboo dwellers, but lastingly facilitated a new interspecies intimacy between humans and mosquitoes instead.

Over this period, plague killed an estimated 215,000 people: about 7,000 people a year. The mortality for malaria over that same time was both incalculable and uncalculated but certainly exceeded that for plague by an order of magnitude. If the home improvement scheme itself already demonstrated the incongruity between the burden of these diseases and their priority to colonial health actors, the decade-long delay between the identification of *woningverbeteringsmalaria* and its public acknowledgement underscored this point. Furthermore, the delay hints at the importance that home improvement had assumed in other domains than public health. As with developmentalist policies in other colonial contexts, there was an element of national and scientific pride at stake: a desire to be seen to be doing something to help defend colonial projects at large.

---

[55] "Een Bedenkelijk Nevenverschijnsel," *Het Nieuws van den Dag voor Nederlandsch-Indië*, January 22, 1938.

[56] "Vreemde Malaria-Explosies," *Algemeen Handelsblad voor Nederlandsch-Indië*, October 19, 1938.

[57] N. H. Swellengrebel, "Woningverbetering en Malaria op Java," *NTvG* 83 (1939): 105, 107.

[58] "Woning en Malaria," *Het Nieuws van den Dag voor Nederlandsch-Indië*, January 5, 1939.

This developmentalist disaster was not unique to Java, then, but its impact on rural as opposed to urban populations and its explicit origins in a health policy do make this episode stand out.

The question of how many lives were lost to malaria on account of plague, meanwhile, is impossible to answer. A previous attempt to extrapolate from the available data, however, is painfully suggestive. As the engineer W. B. Snellen wrote in 1991:

> From Grootings' curves, I have calculated the average of the maximum mortality rates in the 17 sub-districts as recorded before house improvement; this was 38 per thousand. The average of the peak mortality rate recorded after house improvement in the 8 sub-districts is twice as high: 77 per thousand. This indicates that Grootings was justified to speak in terms of "an increase of mortality to an unprecedented level."[59]

In other words, the average mortality rate in the regency Tasikmalaya in the years following home improvement had doubled in the wake of home improvement. It was a public health disaster with clear roots in human activity—and one must recall Rosier's caution that given the active distribution of quinine in affected districts, the figures presented in these studies offered a "mitigated" picture.

When we consider the analyses and suggestions by Rosier and Grootings, we notice a growing awareness of the bigger picture: an attentiveness to both the cultural and environmental forces shaping plague and malaria transmission. They speak of environmental relations, biological balance, shifting and dynamic interspecies encounters. There is criticism toward predecessors who failed to grasp these complexities and forged ahead with "one-sided" hygienic interventions. Through their use of the phrase *woningverbeteringsmalaria*, both physicians acknowledged the man-made origins of this biological disaster, or, at any rate, the entanglement of cultural and biological processes in the production of health and disease. On the other hand, we may question their newfound insight. Was their failure to advocate for alterations in the home improvement scheme a result of pragmatic concerns or concerns for international prestige? Were their suggestions for further environmental and cultural interventions in the Javanese landscape evidence of a broadening perspective (that allowed for methods of biological control) or of a continued tendency to think linearly and a continued failure to oversee the consequences of such interventions? And what, we may ask, would physicians, officials, and local populations ultimately regard as the real health disaster in Java: plague or plague control?

---

[59] W. Takken et al., "Environmental Measures for Malaria Control in Indonesia, an Historical Review on Species Sanitation," *Wageningen Agricultural University Papers*, 90, no. 7 (1991): 124.

The Public Politics of Supplication in a Time of Disaster

Julian Millie and Dede Syarif

Abstract

The research explores supplications—acts and utterances seeking divine relief—as responses to disaster in Muslim Indonesia, focusing specifically on the way these are facilitated in public communication at events held by political actors and holders of public office. Two contrasting Islamic perspectives on disaster responses are examined, namely the ritual practices observed by the elites and followers of the traditionalist Nahdlatul 'Ulama civil society organization and the disaster relief NGO and associated theodicy established by the modernist organization known as the Muhammadiyah. The article observes that collective supplications seeking divine relief—practices typical of traditionalist practice but objected to on doctrinal grounds by modernists—have become dominant in public events, even where the audience is plural in terms of its Islamic affiliation. In explaining the expanding dominance of traditional styles of supplication, we propose two reasons: first, that the modernist repertoire lacks techniques and ritual styles suitable for the collective supplications that audiences demand in times of crisis such as the COVID-19 pandemic, and second, that the styles of the traditionalist current, oriented to group supplication, are favored by the political actors who mobilize Islamic messaging in political communication. Supplications are approached analytically not simply as requests seeking divine assistance, but also as genres of public communication that are influenced by the dynamic nexus of Islam and politics in Indonesia.

Keywords: Islam and politics, Islamic communication, Nahdlatul 'Ulama, Muhammadiyah, ritual and worship, religion and COVID-19, religion and disaster relief

[Julian] Millie is Professor of Indonesian Studies at Monash University. Dede Syarif is a sociologist lecturing at the Sunan Gunung Djati State Islamic University, Bandung. The research on which this article is based was funded by the Australian Research Council Future Fellowship grant FT140100818 titled "Deliberation and Publicness in Indonesia's Regional Islamic Spheres."

Recent literature has revealed the importance of religion in responses to disaster, especially in Southeast Asia, which has been the site of repeated disasters in recent decades.[1] We focus here on a specific category of response, Islamic practices of supplication, and their place in public life. By *supplication* we mean combinations of acts and utterances that are intended as requests for divine intervention and assistance. In Indonesia's Muslim communities, as is the case with religious communities elsewhere, natural and man-made disasters are responded to with supplication practices. There are specific ritual observances for supplicating, such as the *istisqah*, a ritual performed by the Prophet to plead for rain in times of drought. Others are more routine: simple supplications are conventionally verbalized at the commencement and conclusion of the Friday sermon. In pandemic-afflicted Indonesia, preachers make sure they use these brief opportunities for supplicating on behalf of those gathered. The COVID-19 pandemic has led communities to hold dedicated supplications in novel forms, for example those that involve digitally enabled sociability: after a number of staff members at the university where one of the authors of this article works was afflicted by COVID-19, staff held an online "Special Collective Prayer." Staff logged on to listen and respond as a colleague provided a sermon that included a prayer for the health of sick colleagues.[2]

For two reasons, it is important to put the spotlight on supplications as responses to disaster. First, this discussion highlights the limitations of overtly materialist conceptions of disaster aid.[3] Embodied and performative practices of religion provide responses to disaster in which people facing crisis and hardship mobilize tools, techniques, and methods that are validated by their cosmological and religious traditions and are readily available for use without the need of assistance from outside parties or agencies. They are resources called on when everyday life is disturbed and threatened and should not be underrated on the grounds that they leave unresolved critical problems concerning the material welfare, safety, and health of populations.

A second reason for placing attention on supplication practices is the considerable differences emerging in the way Indonesians perceive supplications, their propriety, and efficacy. This is a theme that we expand on in what follows. One's preferred supplication might not match the preference of one's neighbor. In fact, one's neighbor

[1] The literature has several foci, including the recent growth of Islamic NGOs in the disaster relief sector, for example Philip Fountain, Robin Bush, and R. Michael Feener, "Religious Actors in Disaster Relief: An Introduction," *International Journal of Mass Emergencies and Disasters* 33 (March 2015): 1–16; the "proximity" between the beneficiary community and the aid organization, for example, J. Benthall, "Have Islamic Aid Agencies a Privileged Relationship in Majority Muslim Areas: The Case of Post-tsunami Reconstruction in Aceh," *Journal of Humanitarian Assistance* 15 (June 2008), http://sites.tufts.edu/jha/archives/15; the overlap between relief programs and those dedicated to religious renewal, for example, R. Michael Feener and Patrick Daly, "Religion and Reconstruction in the Wake of Disaster," *Asian Ethnology* 75, no. 1 (2016): 191–202; and the role of religion in the remaking of self and society in the aftermath of disaster, for example, Annemarie Samuels, *Disaster Narratives and the Remaking of Everyday Life in Aceh* (Honolulu: University of Hawai'i Press, 2019) and David Kloos, *Becoming Better Muslims: Religious Authority & Ethical Improvement in Aceh, Indonesia* (Princeton: Princeton University Press, 2018).

[2] By practices of supplication, we do not mean that the practices discussed here are totally understood as instrumental requests for divine help: the anthropology of religion recognizes supplication practices as having a number of efficacies in addition to the hoped-for divine intervention: ritual practices offer opportunities for affirmation of social solidarity; the joint enunciation of aspirations, grief, and hopes provides relief for grieving communities; the chance for Muslims to participate in ethical practices that affirm notions of virtue and propriety.

[3] Fountain, Bush and Feener, "Religious Actors in Disaster Relief," 4

might not even believe that supplications of any kind are efficacious. These differences mark religious, social, and political borders within Indonesian societies and point to social, institutional, and sectarian divides. Different perspectives on the propriety and legality of supplications are among the clearest points of difference between the religious outlooks cultivated and developed within the civil society organization known as the Muhammadiyah, a vehicle for Muslims with a contemporary, reformist bent, and those nurtured within "The Rising of the Scholars" (Nahdlatul 'Ulama or NU), a vehicle for the segment generally referred to as "traditional."[4] While diverse forms of supplication are everyday practice for tradition-oriented Muslims, modernist doctrine sees them as lacking in religious validity.

This diversity is not a problem per se, for public Islam in Indonesia has more or less facilitated a non-sectarian status quo in which the major currents of Islam coexist for the good of the greater community.[5] The online prayer for university staff just mentioned was acceptable to all staff because of its form—it avoided specific supplicatory practices that point to any specific Islamic current. It succeeded because it avoided sectarian preferences. Yet we have noticed significant changes in the nature of Islamic public communication over recent decades. Since the end of the authoritarian period in 1998, when the rule of the government of Suharto ended, political aspirants and holders of office have been the agents of a marked increase in the public staging of piety. Piety has become a part of public communication with voters and constituencies in ways that it had not been during the authoritarian period, when candidates did not play to voters' symbolic affinities. The arrival of COVID-19 has added a new dimension to public piety; a pressing need for collective supplication has emerged. We have noticed that at this time, when the political stage requires pious display in greater volumes, religious styles and techniques of group supplication associated with the NU have gained ascendancy. Explicitly supplicatory forms that are characteristic of traditional Islam have a public presence they previously lacked. We argue that the supplicating styles associated with NU have gained an ascendancy in public performance, a trend that has been more visible because of the pandemic-induced public demand for group prayer. In what follows, we convey the variety of Islamic responses to disaster by comparing the responses preferred and implemented within NU and Muhammadiyah practice and doctrine and then explore the ascendancy of traditional styles that has recently become apparent in public events held by office-holders and political actors.

Our article falls into two parts. In the first, we explore the differentiation of Islamic practices, placing them in the historical context of the emergence of the two civil society groups. This part continues with illustrative examples of religious responses to disaster and the COVD-19 virus. Specifically, we discuss the radically contrasting

---

[4] The Muhammadiyah and NU are civil society organizations. We use these terms interchangeably with the descriptive labels traditionally attached to the demographics they represent, namely modernist (Muhammadiyah) and traditional (NU). There is not perfect synonymity between the terms, for the categories of modernist and traditionalist are broader than the civil society organizations. Furthermore, the organizations are not active across the entire territory of the Republic of Indonesia. Nevertheless, this article focuses not only on populations, but also on doctrinal statements and authority structures, and these themes point to the organizations, for these are institutions that publicly advocate for distinctive forms of Islamic belief and practice. Accordingly, it suits this article to use the terms interchangeably.

[5] Jeremy Menchink, *Islam and Democracy in Indonesia: Tolerance without Liberalism* (Cambridge: Cambridge University Press, 2016).

understandings about techniques for group supplication that are cultivated within these groups. The first example, characteristic of NU practice in response to disaster, is the circulation of Arabic supplications composed and authorized by revered Islamic leaders. Our second example is the establishment by the Muhammadiyah of the Muhammadiyah Disaster Management Center (MDMC). We contextualize this center within the group's theological understanding of the religious meanings of disaster.

In the second part, we shift our attention to the public meanings of practices in contemporary public communication. For the purposes of this article, public means practices facilitated by representatives of the state and holders of governmental office. We describe an event held in 2020 in the city of Bandung, organized by the Governor of the province of West Java. We note the many political agendas of the event, which was held as a response to COVID-19, and note the supplication performed within it. What is striking about this event is the domination of the religious part of this event by the group supplication technologies favored within the NU. We connect this dominance to recent trends in public performance of supplication.

Supplication in a Plural Islamic Community

We take the two organizations Nahdlatul Ulama (NU) and Muhammadiyah as a frame for exploring the contrasts in Islamic styles that are central to this article. These are civil society organizations that publish and advocate for contrasting Islamic outlooks. They both have influential institutional presences in religious, political, and educational settings, and they both connect with grassroots followings. The contrasting religious projects of the two groups can be conveyed through a brief historical treatment of the groups' emergence. The NU emerged as a network of the institutions of learning known as *pesantren* (Islamic schools). The leaders of these schools (*kyai*) form the group's hierarchy, and the traditions of Islamic learning and practice cultivated in these institutions reflect a distinctive Islamic program frequently referred to as "traditional."[6]

Traditional Islam is a broad and varied repertoire of concepts and practices, for the broader NU demographic includes Muslim communities who continue local practices, something generally tolerated within NU doctrine and practice. We can characterize the NU styles with three generalizations: first, the demographic includes practices that are highly material, relying for efficacy on specific formulations of words or conditions concerning place; second, NU encourages Muslims to participate in collective gatherings structured around routines and cycles of commemoration and practice (Islamic and civic calendars, life cycle). In other words, people should come out of their homes to worship and supplicate together, and third, the identity of individual Muslims is significant in NU practice. The presence of an Islamic teacher from a celebrated lineage is highly desired at gatherings and is frequently considered to add to the efficacy of the observance. Also, deceased Muslims such as the Prophets, saints, and caliphs are favored as intercessors, and for this reason, are conventionally honored in group supplications.

---

[6] Key sources on NU and traditionalist Islam include Martin van Bruinessen, *Kitab kuning, pesantren dan tarekat: Tradisi-tradisi Islam di Indonesia* (Bandung: Mizan 1999); Zamaksyari Dhofier, *The Pesantren Tradition: The Role of the Kyai in the Maintenance of Traditional Islam in Java* (Tempe: Arizona State University, 1999); Greg Fealy, "Ulama and Politics in Indonesia: A History of Nahdlatul Ulama" (PhD diss., Monash University, 1998).

The Muhammadiyah was formed in Yogyakarta in 1912.[7] Its founders had a distinct religio-political vision—they observed that around the globe Muslim populations lived under non-Muslim colonial regimes. They saw that Muslim populations around the world were suffering from deficits in wealth, technology, education, etc. This observation led the founders to take the position that the Islamic practices that had the greatest popularity in the Indies, including those just described, were in fact holding its Muslim populations back. Their program was one of renewal—the established practices, in which clerical elites held privileged positions, needed to be replaced with simpler religious styles based on models found in the Qur'an and traditions. These practices did not need the hierarchies and material conditions that the NU Muslims implemented in their observances. Also, Islamic obligation did not require Muslims to gather in groups to celebrate events such as the Prophet's birthday. In the Muhammadiyah program, political and economic progress required those conditions be made redundant. The real mission of Islam was not to give service to locally specific traditions, but to strive for prosperity for all citizens within the framework of the modern nation-state and its institutional infrastructure. The movement's egalitarian, rationalizing outlook has led its members to be described as "Muslim puritans."[8] They might equally well be described as "Weberians."

The traditional elites who headed the Islamic boarding schools were worried by the formation of an organization that struck at their foundations. In 1926, those elites met at an Islamic school in East Java where they formed the Nahdlatul Ulama (the Rising of the Scholars). Both NU and the Muhammadiyah remain strong in contemporary Indonesia, working within different institutional contexts. As noted, the institutional core of the Nahdlatul Ulama is based at the Islamic boarding schools, while the Muhammadiyah maintains a growing stable of social infrastructure: orphanages, schools, universities, and hospitals. It also runs a disaster-relief NGO called the Muhammadiyah Disaster Management Centre (MDMC) (described in more detail below).

At a general level, the contrasts between the groups' religious programs may be described as follows: NU practice foregrounds human capability to call on divine power in this-worldly situations. According to Nahdlatul Ulama doctrine, religious practices performed collectively according to the specifications laid down by doctrine and tradition can be used to access divine power. It is beneficial to gather in groups to make supplications under the leadership of elite Muslim teachers, and these supplications ought to show respect to saints, Prophets, and other deceased Muslims, for these figures are capable of interceding on behalf of the supplicant. According to Muhammadiyah doctrine, these notions are based on incorrect interpretations of revelation. Authentic Islam doctrines do not, the group contends, make such specifications and in fact, the doctrine of Allah's singularity (*Tauhid*) forbids many such notions. Allah's power cannot be coerced into action through specific human acts and words but is immanent in the world. No individuals, dead or alive, can act as channels for divine power, and all

[7] Key sources on the Muhammadiyah include James L. Peacock, *Muslim Puritans: Reformist Pscyhology in Southeast Asian Islam* (Berkeley: University of California Press, 1978); *Mitsuo Nakamura, The Crescent Arises over the Banyan Tree: A Study of the Muhammadiyah Movement in a Central Javanese town c.1910–2010.* 2nd edition. (Singapore: ISEAS, 2012).

[8] See James L. Peacock, *Muslim Puritans: Reformist Pscyhology in Southeast Asian Islam* (Berkeley: University of California Press, 1978).

humans have the same capacity as religious subjects. And it is a religious duty on all Muslims, not just elites, to gain knowledge and access to the Qur'an's truths. In contrast to the Nahdlatul Ulama's preference for mass gatherings, Muhammadiyah doctrine recognizes little need for mass gatherings. According to the group's doctrine, many of the feasts marked by enthusiastic celebration by NU followers are human creations invented by traditionalist Muslims. The true mission is to work for the material and political welfare of the national population.

The civic accommodation between these two Islamic currents is a great accomplishment of modern Indonesia. On the one hand, the Muhammadiyah's religious program requires Muslims to strive within the homogenous civic order defined by the modern nation-state, so its religious program would appear to be more at home in the era of national modernity. Its Islamic mission has a this-worldly, rational-bureaucratic character. Features of NU religion such as mysticism, charismatic leadership, intercession, sanctity, sacrality of space, clerical hierarchies, efficacious words . . . these sit uneasily within postcolonial, bureaucratic modernity. But even so, public life in Indonesia is greatly influenced by the other-worldly orientation of the traditionalist segment. Its repertoire of observances continues to underpin religious life for many communities, especially rural ones, and its elites have great political influence. As a result, neither has dominated the other in political contexts. Public Islam in Indonesia has featured a non-sectarian ethic where preference for specific styles is generally avoided. Of course the need to avoid preference has differing levels of urgency according to context. In settings such as the NU "heartlands" in East Java, where NU affiliation is assumed to be shared by all participants, public performance might replicate NU styles. Nevertheless, in settings where shared affiliation cannot be assumed, care needs to be taken to avoid specific religious technologies that betray a practice as belonging to one or the other segment. A status quo of mutual tolerance is respected, so the differences in worship preferences are avoided. We now look at responses to disaster from the two groups in more detail.

A Prayer for Circulation

On November 29, 2020, it was reported that the Chairman of the NU executive, Said Aqil Siradj, had on the previous day tested positive for the COVID-19 virus. Siradj, a nationally known figure and respected Islamic authority, was initially hospitalized, but recovered and left hospital on December 7. He had resumed duties by January of 2021. At the time of the chairman's illness in December of 2020, the parents of one of the authors of this article received the paper fragment reproduced in Figure 1. They received it while attending a gathering for prayer and study (*pengajian*) at an Islamic school in Garut, West Java, and later showed it to author Syarif, being aware of their son's professional interest in such practices. The text of the fragment is a photocopy of a supplication formula written in Arabic (*wirid* or *doa*). The Arabic text may be rendered in English as follows:

> In the name of Allah, upon mention of whose name everything on the Earth and the heavens poses no danger, and He is All-hearing and All-knowing. 3x
>
> Morning 3x
>
> Afternoon 3x

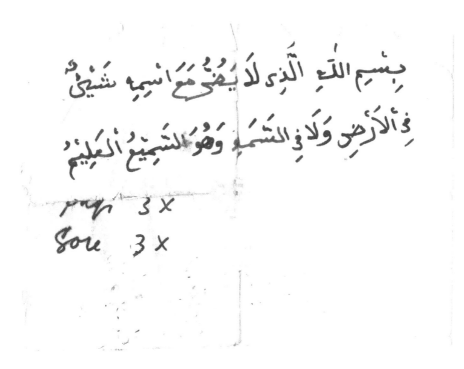

Figure 1: Supplication in response to the threat of COVID-19.
Photo by Dede Syarif, taken in Garut, December 2020.

The writing is by the hand of the *kyai* of the Islamic school at which the gathering was held. Like many leaders of Islamic schools, he serves as a local official within the Nahdlatul Ulama organization. The text in Figure 1 is a photocopy he distributed among participants. The *kyai* informed the gathering that he had received this supplication from Said Aqil Siradj with an endorsement for its use. He used the term *diijazahkan* (literally, "to be licensed to someone") to describe this process. The great leader had affirmed the value of the prayer by recommending its use. As noted above, in NU's cosmological vision, the identity of the teacher matters: for many traditionalist Muslims, individual clerics are considered as sources of blessings, and in some locations, physical contact with a *kyai* or his personal effects is considered as a source of blessings (Arabic: *tabarruk*).

After receiving it, the *kyai* had written it out and photocopied it for circulation among those attending his gatherings. The prayer and others like it are recited by participants in collective gatherings such as the one attended by the parents of author Syarif and are also recommended for recitation at home. The text also includes specifications about times for reciting the supplication and the number of repetitions to be completed. Implicitly, compliance with these details assist the efficacy of the supplications. In some texts of this kind, beside the words of the prayer appears an attribution of the prayer to one of the well-known compilations of Prophetic traditions, indicating that the supplication was used by the Prophet Muhammad himself. One version has "HR Abu Dawud dan

At-Turmudzi" written after the supplication. These are famous collectors of accounts of the Prophet's practice, so their naming on the fragment has the effect of affirming that this formula was the Prophet's practice. After the COVID pandemic spread throughout Indonesian populations, Siradj promoted this supplication as an authorized, authentic response to the virus. His promotion of the prayer led to its adoption across Indonesia. A report of his recuperation published in a NU news outlet mentioned that he had "recited this one particular practice" (see Figure 1) during his period as a COVID patient.[9] Not surprisingly, supplications of this kind also circulate through social media.

This example displays a number of features of Nahdlatul Ulama supplication styles. It is premised on the conviction that divine power can be swayed by human efforts, as long as the correct forms of text and performance are adopted. That is to say, performance of these words will be efficacious above other possible combinations. Apart from that, the prayer's efficacy is connected to the roles of distinguished humans in its production (i.e., it DOES matter who wrote and authorized the text). Finally, the text was circulated through a classic medium of NU sociability—gathering for group prayer.

A final qualification is necessary for this ethnographic sketch of this circulating prayer. The NU is sometimes criticized for favoring mystical efficacy above the rationalism encouraged in Muhammadiyah circles. Although Said Aqil Soradj promoted the use of this specific supplicatory technology, he did not neglect the bio-scientific aspects of COVID-19. In fact, in all his media engagements during the pandemic, he has emphasized the importance of the messages promoted by the Indonesian government for stopping the spread of the disaster (washing hands, social distancing, wearing a mask, etc.). Official NU media has also supported the government's biomedically based COVID-19 instructions.[10]

Muhammadiyah's Theology of Disaster

The Muhammadiyah's religious response to disaster consists of services and infrastructure mobilized to give material assistance to communities afflicted by disaster. Its response engages with disciplines from outside the field of religion such as medicine, engineering, and the social sciences. It does not include acts and utterances designed to appeal for divine intervention, nor does it presume the existence of audiences gathering to do such things. It does not advocate techniques of group supplication. We mention here the two primary features of the Muhammadiyah response: its theodicy, which is published in a document titled *The Jurisprudence* [fiqh] *of Natural Disaster*,[11] and its establishment of an NGO specifically dedicated to providing practical disaster assistance, known as the Muhammadiyah Disaster Management Centre (MDMC).

[9] Abdul Rahman Ahdori, "Amalan Cepat Sembuh dari COVID-19 Menurut Kiai Said Aqil Siroj," *NU Online*, December 9, 2020, https://www.nu.or.id/post/read/125187/amalan-cepat-sembuh-dari-covid-19-menurut-kiai-said-aqil-siroj last accessed?.

[10] At the time of writing (December 2021), NU was preparing for its peak level assembly, held once every five years. NU media carries instructions and reminders explaining the biomed-based procedures to be implemented in order to make the meeting COVID-safe (see: https://nu.or.id/search/covid). The heavy emphasis placed on these instructions is partly explained by the refusal of a small number of NU leaders to comply with biomedically based protocols.

[11] Pimpinan Pusat Muhammadiyah, Fikih Kebencanaan, Tuntunan Shalat (Pimpinan Pusat Muhammadiyah: Yogkakarta, 2018).

The religious platform for the establishment of the MDMC is thoroughly laid out in *The Jurisprudence of Natural Disaster*. This jurisprudential treatise was prepared as a textually based, legal-rational response to decades of natural and man-made disasters experienced by Indonesian communities. It sits alongside many other publications in which Islamic sources are used to provide logical and coherent explanations of worldly realities. Indeed, publication of such explanations is considered part of the Muhammadiyah's public mission. It has published a journal named *Suara Muhammadiyah* (The voice of Muhammadiyah) since 1915, which is now available online (*suaramuhammadiyah.id*), and its various committees publish many one-off publications. Its affiliated intellectuals produce books and articles. At Muhammadiyah's 29th "Deliberative Consultation" (*musyawarah tarjih*) in 2015, the organization resolved to produce a treatise on the Islamic jurisprudence of disasters; this was published in 2018.

Much discussion within the treatise is devoted to a perennial question faced by followers of religion, namely the question of theodicy: If the Divinity is ever merciful, then why does God wreak havoc on creation in the forms of tsunamis, earthquakes, floods, landslides, and pandemics? The resulting theodicy is a complex one in which many verses and traditions are considered. At the expense of the elegance and thoroughness of the treatise, it might be summarized as follows: when a person ignores God's will and injunctions, by sinning or by failure to pay proper respect to the natural world, God afflicts that person with disaster (In the Qur'an: *'iqab, nazilah, azab*).[12] But when a Muslim of piety (*salih*) is afflicted by a disaster, this is not a punishment, but an ordeal designed to test the quality of the person's faith (*bala'*). The Muslim's acceptance of this ordeal and her efforts to overcome it earn her a closer position at Allah's side.[13] By this reasoning, any disaster is in fact an example of God's goodness and mercy.

According to this treatise, should Muslims respond to disasters with specific technologies of supplication? No. The treatise is clear that Muslims are obliged to regularly perform a number of practices under the category of *'ibadah* (worship, service), but disasters are not averted nor ameliorated in their effects by specific supplicatory technologies. This position can be understood in part by referring to the specific history of Muhammadiyah. The organization was established by traders in the city of Yogyakarta, a city that is exceptional in the era of Indonesian democracy because it is under the formal governance not of an elected governor but of a genealogically entitled Sultan. The courtiers of the Sultan maintain cycles of ritual that implement a uniquely Javanese Islamic cosmology. In times of disaster, such as the earthquake of May 27, 2006, which caused the death of some six thousand people, local residents resort to local myths for explanations. Many residents blamed the Sultan for the disaster, citing his failure to maintain customary ritual practices.[14] These interpretations of ritual causation are a source of ongoing concern for Muhammadiyah members and are cited in Muhammadiyah literature as examples of baseless interpretations of disaster.[15]

[12] Pimpinan Pusat Muhammadiyah, *Fikih Kebencanaan, Tuntunan Shalat*, 20–40.

[13] Pimpinan Pusat Muhammadiyah, *Fikih Kebencanaan, Tuntunan Shalat*, 35–36.

[14] Judith Schlehe, "Anthropology of Religion: Disasters and the Representations of Tradition and Modernity," *Religion* 40, no. 2 (2010): 112–20.

[15] Zakiyuddin Baidhawy and Azaki Khoirudin, *Etika Muhammadiyah & Spirit Peradaban* (Yogyakarta: Suara Muhammadiyah 2017), 404–7.

The treatise underpins its position on supplication with two bases, both of which are typical of the organization's theology and ideology. First, the treatise is dismissive of ritual practices performed specifically for the aversion of natural disaster. Muhammadiyah recognizes practices as Islamic only when they have clear precedent in the Qur'an or the practice of the Prophet. On this basis, many of the rituals well-established in Indonesian tradition, such as the ritual offerings, dances, and parades of heirlooms performed in response to the disasters in the Yogyakarta area, are very objectionable: they are not religious and therefore performance of them is "irrational." Second, in the Muhammadiyah view, those practices turn to efficacies other than those vouchsafed by the Qur'an and traditions. It is irrational to perform "mystical rituals that from a scientific point of view do not have any connection with the disaster, which give rise to the attribution of God's power to other parties (*shirk*)."[16]

The Jurisprudence includes also reasoning that is characteristic of the Muhammadiyah's modernism: in understanding and responding to disasters, Muslims should pay heed to and gain expertise in the natural sciences and secular disciplines of learning. The treatise's reasoning is full of Qur'anic verses that justify the treatise's statements, but these sit alongside many references to publications in Indonesian and English from the field of disaster management. The treatise argues that engagement with the sciences is essential for understanding the operation of God's will on Earth, and care for the natural environment then becomes a religious duty.[17] Failure to care for the environment and treat it with proper consideration of the risks involved is in fact sinful behavior. The broadening of the range of sources beyond religious ones to include secular disciplines of learning is a feature of Muhammadiyah's jurisprudential methodology.[18]

Against the background of this scientific orientation, it is not surprising that the Muhammadiyah has established resources for responding to disaster with practical action. After the 2004 tsunami, it established its Muhammadiyah Disaster Management Centre (MDMC). The center plays a leading role in practical responses to disaster, facilitating responses including emergency medical aid, securing hospitals from shocks and disturbances, coordination of volunteers, and rehabilitation of communities.[19] It has played a bridging role between NGOs, implementing a strictly non-confessional approach to aid that has made it an effective mediator between Muslim communities and non-Muslim aid providers. Its success in this regard has been so great that Robin Bush has written of it: ". . . in the international humanitarian world, Muhammadiyah and its disaster response unit MDMC is the wave of the future."[20]

The contrast between the religious responses to disaster described above are striking. In Muhammadiyah's treatise on the jurisprudence of disasters, revelation is mobilized to explain worldly phenomena of the greatest gravity—the suffering of Muslim populations is reasoned as something that does not challenge our conception of a merciful God. Its theodicy is abstract in a way that is typical of the modernizing currents within world

---

[16] Pimpinan Pusat Muhammadiyah, *Fikih Kebencanaan, Tuntunan Shalat*, 10.

[17] Pimpinan Pusat Muhammadiyah, *Fikih Kebencanaan, Tuntunan Shalat*, 73–89.

[18] Nadirsyah Hosen, "Revelation in a Modern State: Muhammadiyah and Islamic Legal Reasoning in Indonesia," *The Australian Journal of Asian Law* 4, no. 3 (2002): 232–58.

[19] Zakiyuddin Baidhawy and Azaki Khoirudin, *Etika Muhammadiyah*, 415–28.

[20] Robin Bush, "Muhammadiyah and Disaster Response," 46.

religions, which provide logical and coherent, overarching explanations of hardships, while drawing back from specific embodied responses to individual instantiations of hardship.[21] Although it provides nothing for the victim wishing to make an embodied request for relief alongside friends and family, its MDMC has set a global standard for religious responses to disaster. It provides material assistance to victims in dire need and is a model for its commitment to providing charity without regard to the creed or victims. The NU vision leaves the development of scientifically informed responses to disaster to experts, instead approaching disaster as a moment for supplication using specific verbal formulations appropriate to the goal being sought, that are validated by their provenance, and that come with conditions concerning performance. Islamic tradition supplies resources to be performed with the bodies and tongues of individual worshippers. Where the Muhammadiyah's response has the same bureaucratic-rational character as the state's own infrastructure for disaster relief, the NU provides embodied supplications sanctioned by religious authority, that enable victims to supplicate in embodied forms alongside fellow victims.

Contemporary Politics of Public Supplication

We have described two contrasting religious responses to disaster. In reality, these two options do not sit together in a static embrace. Their public salience is subject to the rules of public communication, and over recent decades, the conditions for public Islamic public communication have changed dramatically. A major point of change was the commencement of electoral democracy after the end of the Suharto era in 1998. In 2004 Indonesians began to vote in open elections for government at national, provincial, and municipal levels. Media expression and public participation had been liberalized after the decline of Suharto, and in the campaigns leading up to elections, candidates brazenly mobilized religious and cultural symbols. In areas where Muslims formed majorities, campaigns became heavy with Islamic messaging. Candidates competed to project pious impressions, even when they were running for parties with nationalist rather than Islamic platforms.[22] And so, campaign stages were erected to enable the delivery of messages in Islamic forms. In local elections in the present, candidates will hold events such as *istighotsah* (joint supplication), *istisqah* (supplications for rain), *silaturahmi* (affirmation of social ties), and *tabligh akbar* (large preaching event) featuring local Islamic elites. Traditionalist and modernist religious styles are not equal in their suitability for this expanded stage, for NU practices are oriented to large gatherings, while the Muhammadiyah's religious platform distances it from them. In an environment where Islamic messaging was in such high demand, is it surprising that NU practices would come to dominate political stages?

We wish to describe here a recent event that reflects this ascendancy of traditional Islam in public Islamic messaging. On October 21, 2020, civil and religious dignitaries in Bandung, the capital city of Indonesia's West Java Province, were invited to a state-owned mosque to attend an event entitled "Large-Scale Supplication" (*Istighotsah Kubro*)

---

[21] Clifford Geertz, "Internal Conversion in Bali," *The Interpretation of Cultures: Selected Essays* (New York: Basic Books, 1973): 170–89.

[22] Robin Bush, "Regional Sharia regulations in Indonesia: Anomaly or symptom?," in *Expressing Islam: Religious life and politics in Indonesia*, ed. Greg Fealy and Sally White (Singapore: ISEAS, 2008), 174–91.

for Divine Help featuring the Governor of West Java and Habib Luthfi'. The event was held by the office of the Governor of West Java Province.[23] Dignitaries including the governor and the famed Sufi teacher Habib Lufthi bin Yahya (b. 1947) sat on a stage erected in the mosque while a small number of attendees sat in appropriately distanced spots marked on the mosque's floor. The program started with the reading of Qur'anic verses, then continued with singing of blessings on the prophet. After that, speeches were heard from the provincial head of Social Development and Services, the Head of the Provincial Office of the Ministry of Religion, and the Governor of West Java.

All these dignitaries mentioned two goals for the event: to seek divine help in the face of the COVID pandemic and to stimulate introspection about the failings and shortcomings of the community. The event was not only about these things, for there were political agendas involved also. This event was a chance for the government to announce progress on a policy initiative designed to support the Islamic community: Four and a half thousand students of the Qur'an would receive government scholarships with the goal of providing a *hafidz* (a person who has memorized the Qur'an) for every village in the province. The program is named "One village; one memorizer." A selection of three recipients were ceremoniously awarded their logoed jacket. The provincial government was taking every opportunity to broadcast its commitment: the event was streamed online throughout the province. The MC of the event stated the hope of the governor that one million students of Islam would join in the supplication to follow. A further political agenda, mentioned briefly by the governor, was the need to calm tensions in the province concerning the return to Indonesia from Saudi Arabia of a high-profile Islamic figure, Muhammad Rizieq Shihab, the leader of the "Islamic Defenders' Front" (FPI). This man was at the time being investigated by authorities for various offenses, and to many Muslims in West Java, this was a politically motivated investigation.[24] As is common in situations of political tension, the local government authorities sought to quell unrest by holding a meeting of public figures.

After the dignitaries had spoken, the microphone was taken up by Habib Luthfi, a nationally famous sufi preacher of Arabic descent based in Central Java. This man, widely admired for his inspiring sermons, travels across Indonesia responding to invitations to give sermons at all kinds of events. So greatly is he admired that among his followers he is readily referred to as a "saint" (*wali*).[25] Like Said Aqil Siradj, he is also regarded as a teacher of sufficient stature to authorize supplications. Luthfi's followers receive Arabic supplications for dealing with COVID-19 from him, complete with authorizations in his name, and then recirculate them online.[26]

On this day, he gave a sermon lasting for ten minutes about everyday morality and piety, but it was what followed the sermon that is of interest to us. The microphone was taken up by another man who commenced the supplication technology of the *istighotsah*

[23] The provincial government posted a video of the event on YouTube: https://www.youtube.com/watch?v=0V7Y8AjCWbo.

[24] See Greg Fealy and Sally White, "The Politics of Banning FPI," *New Mandala*, June 18, 2021, https://www.newmandala.org/the-politics-of-banning-fpi/.

[25] Ismail Fajrie Alatas, "Dreaming Saints: Exploratory Authority and Islamic Praxes of History in Central Java," *Journal of the Royal Anthropological Institute* (N.S.) 26 (2019): 67–85.

[26] A recently circulated example can be downloaded at https://iqra.id/ijazah-shalawat-dari-habib-luthfi-agar-terhindar-dari-penyakit-menular-seperti-corona-236210/.

(Arabic: a request for succor). During the opening five minutes, the gathering recited the first chapter of the Qur'an, while this man used a formulaic Arabic text to gift the divine benefit of the recitation to Islamic notables.[27] The parties to whom the benefit of the recitation was gifted included the prophet Muhammad, his companions, the four "Rightly Guided" caliphs, and famous Muslims and sufi saints. The hope behind this gifting, which is conventional practice among traditional Muslims, is that the recipients of the gifts will intercede on behalf of the reciters. After that, another leader took the microphone for the *istighotsah*: a series of chants, prayers, and Quranic verses, all delivered as supplication for divine mercy. The event, which lasted around seventy-five minutes in total, concluded with formulaic recitations in the style of the sufi movements that have large followings in all of Java.

The governor is not a person known to belong to any particular Islamic current. He is the elected leader of a diverse Muslim community. This was a civic event held in state Islamic infrastructure as a response to the COVID pandemic. All of these facts suggest that it would be appropriate to provide a program acceptable to all Muslim persuasions, yet it was striking how much the event's religious content resembled an NU gathering: the invited speaker's identity as a famous sufi teacher of Hadhrami descent, the offerings to deceased Muslims of the benefits of Qur'anic recitation, the hope for intercession though these Muslims, the collective chanting of blessings on the Prophet, the explicit naming of intentions before the supplication, the verbalization of a compilation of Arabic formulas valued for their efficacy; all these belong to the same Islamic outlook as the slip of paper given to the elderly couple in Garut. To put it bluntly, this was an Islamic performance that was objectionable for modernist Muslims. The obvious question to ask is: given that these styles are so closely associated with one segment of Indonesia's Islamic community, and are known to be objected to by other segments, how did this performance come to take place at an event held by a government seeking to benefit all Muslims of the province?

We see a confluence of two things behind this, both of them noted already in this article. First, NU's Islamic vision includes a repertoire of practices that Muhammadiyah lacks. In a time when the public cries out for tangible methods for seeking divine intervention, it is traditionalist Islam that has the tools. This religious current embodies a ritual sociability that draws people out of their homes to gather at events busy with ritual, chants, and sermonizing. NU sociability encourages collective responses in group prayer, while Muhammadiyah's repertoire is lacking in this kind of sociability. NU styles offer action-oriented content where Muhammadiyah offers reflection. The second factor is the increase in the volume and frequency of Islamic communication brought by open electoral contest in Indonesia. When a political candidate seeks to impress voters with their piety, and requires a frame of embodied sociability to do so, NU's repertoire provides a suite of embodied practices that engage believers in Islamic practice. And the candidate is on safe ground in mobilizing those technologies, for in many locations, especially rural ones, practitioners of traditionalist Islam outnumber the followers of styles associated with the Muhammadiyah.

[27] Julian Millie, "Supplicating, Naming, Offering: *Tawassul* in West Java," *Journal of Southeast Asian Studies* 39, no. 1 (2008): 107–22.

If the content of the Bandung event and other events is dominated by traditional styles, it might be asked whether this draws criticism from Muslims feeling that their preferences are not being respected. In fact, public Islamic actors such as Muhammadiyah are generally reluctant to openly criticize the public performance of NU supplication techniques. In a country where such broad support exists for public religion, to make sectarian objections about public practice creates the risk of appearing to care for one's own theological preferences above the public interest. Nevertheless, occasional criticisms of the politicization of practices are heard from actors outside the political status quo. The poet and political satirist Acep Zamzam Noor has been a vocal critic of group supplications. In his view, the holding of group supplications (*istighotsah*) by NU power brokers wishing to further political careers has meant that this particular ritual has "slowly lost its sacredness. . . . it has become a political tool giving [candidates] access to the traditional Islamic schools, and has given birth to political brokers from those Islamic schools."[28]

Concluding Words

This article is an attempt to understand a recent development in public Islam, namely the adaptation by political actors of supplications in traditional Muslim styles. This was a development that predated the COVID-19 but has been exacerbated by it. After all, group supplications provide the opportunity for collective expression of piety in a time of great insecurity. Political actors recognize the value of these styles for public display. The problem with this development is that it gives public piety a sectarian orientation that might exclude Muslims with theological objections to supplicating in traditional forms.

There is some irony in this development. The Muhammadiyah's responses to disaster replicate the policies and dedication to secular science and infrastructure that the national government provides. They aim to safeguard the physical and material well-being of Muslim communities, resulting in a religious response that takes a bureaucratic-rational form appropriate for policies designed to benefit the citizen population. The group's responses to disaster harmonize closely with the aspirations of Indonesian governments. Yet on the public stage, embedded as it is in political agendas, the styles and doctrine of traditionalist Islam are privileged. Public communication relies on the materiality and collectiveness of those styles in preference over the abstract reflection of modernist Islam.

---

[28] The statement is in the essay "Istighotsah" on Noor's blog at http://budaya-acepzamzamnoor.blogspot.com/2009/07/artikel-2.html.

Review of Farabi Fakih. *Authoritarian Modernization in Indonesia's Early Independence Period: The Foundation of the New Order State (1950–1965).* Leiden: Brill, 2020. 316 pp.

Mattias Fibiger

The 1950s have long sat uneasily in the historiography of Indonesia. The palace historians of the Suharto regime branded the decade one of political chaos, institutional decay, and economic stagnation, a characterization that justified the army's assumption of national leadership in the wake of the September Thirtieth Movement. Nugroho Notususanto's final volume of the *Sejarah Nasional* argued that ceaseless political turnover and economic deterioration in the 1950s "proved that liberal democracy did not comport with conditions in Indonesia."[1] The trope of the vanishing state inflected scholarship on the 1950s as well. No less a figure than Benedict Anderson famously claimed the 1950s were a decade of "the penetration of the state by society"—a curious interregnum between the triumphs of the *state-qua-state* in the late colonial period and the New Order.[2]

Onto this well-worn terrain steps Farabi Fakih, a historian at Gadjah Mada, who sees an entirely different landscape underfoot. He contradicts the prevailing wisdom by arguing that the state did not disappear in the 1950s. Far from it: the decade was one of profound innovation in which a "new managerial class" established the institutional and ideological foundations for the New Order developmental state. In the civil service and the military, Indonesian elites tapped into transnational circulations of capital and expertise that emphasized the creation of a powerful state capable of charting a course toward modernity. Such managerial ideas found a particularly hospitable terroir in Indonesia, where countervailing ideologies of liberalism and individualism possessed shallow roots compared to longstanding traditions of collectivism and feudalism. Inasmuch as it focuses on how Indonesian elites adopted the premises of managerial ideologies within their particular context, the book marks a step forward from the analysis of modernization theory in Brad Simpson's pathbreaking *Economists with Guns.*[3] But it sustains Simpson's emphasis on the importance of the United States. "Indonesianization,"

---

[1] Sartono Kartodirdjo, Marwati Djoened Poesponegoro, and Nugroho Notosusanto, *Sejarah Nasional Indonesia, Jilid VI: Jaman Jepang dan Jaman Republik Indonesia* (Jakarta: Departemen Pendidikan den Kebudayaan, 1975), 92.

[2] Benedict Anderson, "Old State, New Society: Indonesia's New Order in Comparative Historical Perspective," *Journal of Asian Studies* 42, no. 3 (May 1983): 483.

[3] Bradley Simpson, *Economists with Guns: Authoritarian Development and U.S.-Indonesian Relations, 1960–1968* (Stanford: Stanford University Press, 2008).

Fakih writes of efforts to transcend the legacies of colonialism, "was Americanization" (88). In this respect Fakih's book might be put into conversation with David Bourchier's tremendously insightful genealogy of the organicist ideologies that undergirded the New Order, which despite their indigenist pretensions possessed similarly international origins.[4]

Fakih is to be commended for his creative use of source material, including seldom-consulted sources like journals of education and administration (including *Bulletin Lembaga Administrasi Indonesia* and *Madjalah Manager*). A particularly engaging chapter in this vein traces the rise of educational programs in public and business administration. Dutch programs in public administration hewed toward legalistic-juridical thinking, which some Indonesian elites considered inimical to efforts to establish an effective managerial state. In much the same way, Dutch programs in business administration focused almost entirely on the firm, which some Indonesian elites believed elided the role of the state in economic development. Postcolonial Indonesian elites thus contracted with US public and business administration specialists to train faculty, translate texts, and establish new educational programs in the American mold. Seminars replaced the lectures that predominated in Dutch educational programs—part of an effort to achieve what State Administrative Academy chief Prajudi Atmosudirjo called "changes in the spirit of our civil servant," from "one who 'merely follows the rules'" to "one who has an entrepreneurial spirit which embodies the spirit of the 'managers of the state'" (155–56). Though the content of these new educational programs was not adapted to the Indonesian milieu, leaving trainees conversant in jargon but no more effective as managers, Fakih argues their emphasis on dynamic managerialism contributed to the erosion of the *trias politica* (separation of powers) and the rise of authoritarianism under Sukarno.

Among the key findings in the book is that the ideological footprint of aid was not necessarily isomorphic with the financial footprint of aid. Soviet aid dwarfed American aid in monetary terms and undergirded a particular constellation of political and economic power in Indonesia. But it did little to change the ideological orientations of Indonesian elites, meaning its gravitational force waned rapidly following the collapse of Guided Democracy. American aid, by contrast, ignited a change in outlook on behalf of Indonesian elites that acquired a momentum of its own—one divorced from the flow of aid itself. Still, one wishes that Indonesia's engagement with other Third World states was more richly textured in Fakih's account. The book offers some tantalizing clues about Indonesian engagement with the likes of Yugoslavia, Pakistan, and more, but it mostly hews to a diffusionist model of managerialism that makes it difficult to see Indonesian ideologies of state-building as anything but a derivative discourse.[5]

Casting the 1950s as a decade of state-building allows Fakih to make a number of other bold interpretive moves. Guided Democracy emerges not as the apotheosis of Sukarno's political thought on the structure of Indonesian society but rather as a rearguard action designed to subject new technocratic forms of power-knowledge to democratic authority. Indonesia's experience becomes comparable to Burma's—where Lucian Pye unearthed

[4] David Bourchier, *Illiberal Democracy in Indonesia: The Ideology of the Family State* (London: Routledge, 2015).
[5] Partha Chatterjee, *Nationalist Thought and the Colonial World: A Derivative Discourse* (Minneapolis: University of Minnesota Press, 1993).

a similar conflict between "administrators" and "politicians"—and representative of postcoloniality more broadly. In Indonesia as elsewhere, newly independent peoples sought to realize the promise of freedom while also constructing states that engaged in the kind of "techno-politics" that Timothy Mitchell has so brilliantly elucidated in the Egyptian context.[6] Future scholars might productively extend Farabi's elite-centered analysis in Mitchell's direction, for instance by examining how new managerial ideas both emerged out of and simultaneously reshaped projects that inflected the lives of ordinary Indonesians and the environments they inhabited. The steel facility in Cilegon represents one of many possible sites for such an analytical effort.

Looming like an unseen (and generally unmentioned) specter over Farabi's account of state-building in the 1950s are the mass killings of 1965–66. He gestures toward the implication of managerial ideas in the violence of that tumultuous period, suggesting that they endowed the state with a sense of responsibility for remaking the Indonesian person. The same impulse that animated the indoctrination and "retooling" (purges) in the civil service then fueled the effort to purge Indonesian society of communism following the September Thirtieth Movement. Doubtless there is a measure of truth to the claim that managerialist ideas encouraged Indonesians to see (and act) "like a state."[7] But Farabi's analysis elides the depth of ideological contestation happening between competing high modernist projects for control over of the Indonesian state apparatus—of which the events of the morning of October 1, 1965 were only the most visible manifestation.

Farabi Fakih is to be commended for authoring a powerful reinterpretation of Indonesia in the Sukarno era. Attentive to both local contexts and international dynamics, it reveals the profound interrelationships between sweeping global trends and the twists and turns of Indonesian politics.

---

[6] Timothy Mitchell, *Rule of Experts: Egypt, Techno-Politics, Modernity* (Berkeley: University of California Press, 2002).

[7] James Scott, *Seeing Like a State: How Certain Schemes to Improve the Human Condition Have Failed* (New Haven: Yale University Press, 1998).

The Javanese Travels of Purwalelana: A Nobleman's Account of His Journeys Across the Island of Java 1860-1875. (Hakluyt Society, Third Series, volume 36). Translated with an introduction and notes by Judith E. Bosnak and Frans X. Koot. London: Hakluyt Society, 2020. 272 pp.

Peter Carey

As one might expect from a Hakluyt Society publication, this is a sumptuous book that gives us an English translation and edition of four remarkable journeys across the length and breadth of Java in the mid-19th century. Originally published as *Lampah-lampahipun Radèn Mas Arya Purwalelana* (The travels of Purwalelana) in 1865–66 (reprinted 1877–80, the text used here), the present edition's exceedingly well chosen full color plates and seventy-three black-and-white images, many by renowned 19th- and early 20th-century professional photographers of the Indies,[1] enable us to journey with the author through Java in 1860–75 (in fact 1857–79, dating that will be discussed below) at a time when Javanese society was undergoing profound changes as it entered the modern world.

The author who takes us on these magical mystery tours is a Javanese *priyayi* (member of the Javanese administrative elite), Raden Mas Arya (post-1871, Adipati Arya) Candranegara V (1837–85), who adopted the pen name of "Purwalelana," literally "the original traveler," the name we will use throughout this review. This was a modern take on the *satria lelana* (wandering noblemen) of *ancien regime* (pre-1800) Java, where celebrated historical figures, like Prince Diponegoro (1785–1855), traveled incessantly on foot to places of spiritual power to find inspiration and direction for their lives and that gave us great works of the Javanese "wandering student romance" literature such as the *Jaya Lengkara Wulan, Serat Centhini* (1814) and *Serat Cabolang* (1815). In Purwalelana's case, these 'guardian deities' no longer resided in caves, graveyards, mountains, and distant seashores, but in the modern roads, bridges, dams, architecture, port facilities, steam engines, railroads, and sugar factories of Java under the Cultivation System (1830–70), which had transformed the island into a vast cash-crop plantation. The author thus chronicled what Max Weber later called the *"entzauberung der Welt* [disenchantment of the world],"[2] a process that occurred between 1830 and 1930 when Java moved from a Weberian "enchanted garden" with just six million inhabitants and 75 percent of the land area primary jungle/forest to one in which science, modernity, and human agency ruled supreme. By this time, 38 million inhabitants crowded into one of the most densely populated areas on Earth with less than 20 percent of the land still uncultivated forest. Purwalelana's text reflects this fundamental change. "Out with the old in with the new" could be his motto. In this modern world, everything of value must be capable of being measured, weighed, and assessed. Only then can knowledge be deemed "scientific." Anything based on traditional beliefs must be dismissed out of hand.

---

[1] These include the Englishmen Walter Woodbury (1834–85) and James Page (1833–65), the Belgian Isidore van Kinsbergen (1821–1905), and the pioneer Javanese court photographer Kassian Céphas (1845–1912).

[2] Max Weber, *The Sociology of Religion*, ed. Ephraim Fischoff and Talcott Parsons (1920; London: Methuen, 1971), 270.

Contemplating the tradition that the famed Margawati horses of hilly Temanggung in northern Kedu owed their strength and beauty to the sacred water they imbibed from an ancient earthenware pitcher (*kenthèng*) atop one of the only tree-shaded summits of the Temanggung hills, the author of the *Travels* is contemptuous: "I believe this is just rainwater. The horses here are indeed robust and have good hooves, . . . [but this] should not be attributed to this water, but to the fact that from time immemorial they must climb and descend day and night because there is not a single piece of flat ground here. The daily walking on the rocky ground makes their hooves very strong. The grass that grows on this stony ground is mountain grass and this [also] makes the bodies of the horses powerful . . ." (206–7).

One of the first generation of Dutch-educated Javanese administrators and related by marriage to the Mangkunegaran royal house in Surakarta, Purwalelana served first as *bupati* (regent) of Kudus (1858–80) and then as regent of Brebes (1880–85) until his early death at the age of forty-nine in 1885. A pioneer of his generation, the young Purwalelana was a child prodigy, able to read and write Javanese in the original *aksara Jawa* (Javanese letter) script at the age of five and later fluent in Dutch and French as a result of his schooling in a Dutch-language primary school in Semarang from the age of ten and then by private tutors, who also taught his three younger brothers, one of whom, Raden Ario Sasraningrat, later *bupati* of Jepara (1881–1905), would be the father of the famous Javanese women's rights activist and educationalist, Raden Ajeng Kartini (1879–1904).

"A man of the utmost refined culture, with a clearly developed intellect, who knows how to engage in discussion . . . [on] all subjects which bear witness to scrupulous Western civilization,"[3] in the words of Purwalelana's obituary notice, what is striking is that, despite his Dutch education, he retains a very Javanese aesthetic vision. What Western travel writer, for example, would describe the modern dry dock in Tanjung Perak harbor in Surabaya as being like "a floating structure that resembles . . . the wooden chest for storing *wayang* puppets, but without a cover" (87); or dismiss the regent's dwelling in this selfsame East Java port city as "a tasteless building [constructed] in the style of a Dutch mansion [and] . . . therefore impossible to identify as the palace of a regent!" (83)?

There is also a distinctly lyrical quality to some of Purwalelana's descriptions of nature, which recall the shadow-play puppeteer (*dhalang's*) traditional narrative (*kandha*) in a *wayang kulit* performance describing one of Arjuna's sons returning to his father's palace at Amarta and the harmony between the young *satria* (nobleman) and the natural world:

> The *satugalak* (wild animals), *sardula* (tigers), and *singa* (lions) make way for him with the words—"peace be with you!" The *kutu-kutu walang-ataga* (various sorts of insects) sing, as it were, a congratulation for [him]. The birds chirp as if they want to show the beautiful young man [*bambang*] the way . . .[4]

---

[3] *De Locomotief* (Semarang), May 18, 1885, quoting the Dutch travel writer and ethnographer M. T. H. Perelaer (1831–1901): "*een man van de uiterste fijn beschaving, van heldere verstandsontwikkeling, die niet alleen met u voort in het zuiverste Nederduitsch en Fransch, maar alle onderworpen die van zorgvuldig westersch beschaving getuigen, weet te behandelen.*"

[4] Boedihardjo, "Grepen uit de Wajang," *Djåwå* 2 (1923): 28.

Unlike Diponegoro, who befriended tigers while hiding out in the Gowong mountains of southern Kedu in the last year of the Java War (1825–30),[5] Purwalelana's relationship with the natural world did not include consorting with carnivores.[6] But his appreciation of the beauty of Java's landscape gives rise to some of his most lyrical passages. Overnighting in a government guesthouse in the foothills of Mount Lamongan, he writes (104):

> Behind the building [guesthouse] stretches a vast and deep lake [Lake Klakah], which makes a stay here a delight. Its far end touches the foot of a steep mountain [Mt Lamongan], which looks like a *kukusan* [rice steamer]. The mountain's reflection in the lake enhances the beauty of the scene. In the dry season, the mountain uninterruptedly spews fire from its crater [and] during the night, when it is dark, an incessant stream of fire sprouts from the mountain like gigantic fireworks. The beauty of this phenomenon is intensified by its reflection in the lake, as if flowers of fire are being expelled from both above on the mountain and below on the lake. I have never experienced anything so strikingly beautiful as this . . .

Later, the magnificent panorama of the Jambu hills, Rawa Pening and Ambarawa move Purwalelana to a fifty-seven-verse poem, a form of Javanese sonnet in *macapat* metre (197–205).

However, while there is much to admire about this volume and the skill of the editors in making available Purwalelana's text in English translation, a number of questions arise. First, why is there a need for a new translation when the *Travels* have already been the subject of a quite recent (1986) scholarly publication by the leading French scholar of Javanese society, Marcel Bonneff? Titled *Pérégrinations javanaises: les voyages de R. M. A. Purwa Lelana : une vision de Java au XIXeme siècle (c. 1860–1875),*[7] this publication was given the highest praise by Ann Kumar in her 1987 review,[8] who concluded that "its distinction far surpasses what one might expect in a pioneering work. The outstanding quality of its scholarship, and the seriousness and intelligence of its discussion, set a standard which not only French scholars will find hard to maintain." Kumar notes "the superb standard of this edition, in which everything possible has been done to illuminate the text for the reader. Each of the author's four voyages is preceded by a map which shows not only his itinerary, but also the places at which he spent most time. Another map shows all four voyages, and there are plans of the cities visited: the notes on these cities, summarizing a truly formidable range of sources, provide much greater depth to Purwalelana's description. For each voyage there is also a resume of

[5] Peter Carey, "Diponegoro dan Alam: Sekilas Hidup Ekologis pada Tatanan Lama Jawa (1785–1855)," in *Benantara: Bentang Alam dalam gelombang Sejarah Nusantara*, ed. Bukhori Masruri (Jakarta:Kepustakaan Populer Gramedia, 2021), 16.

[6] Sighting paw marks in the sand as he walked along the beach at Bajulmati on the last leg of his journey to Banyuwangi through the densely afforested northern shore of Java's Eastern Salient (*Oosthoek*), he noted that "I hurr[ied] back to my coach to resume my journey. I am actually really terrified by the idea that this animal is still hiding near where I strolled" (112).

[7] Paris: Éditions de la Maison des Sciences de l'Homme, Etudes Insulindiennes / Archipel 7, 1986 (382 pages).

[8] *Archipel* 34: 236–37.

the itinerary, including cities, public buildings, mosques, *pesantren* [religious schools], ruins, agriculture, and the author's reflections on various subjects. The (considerable) differences between the first and second edition are also meticulously noted (the translation is based on the second). The introduction is elegantly balanced, and while performing the usual tasks of distillation and commentary on the text also sets it in context in a way which invites consideration of larger questions of historical change as attested in a succession of Javanese sources."

Such meticulous scholarship is lacking in the present publication. Even the dating of Purwalelana's travels is left up in the air. The title tells us that the young *priyayi*'s journeys took place in 1860–75. But this cannot possibly be correct. This is because the introduction (11) states that Purwalelana's first period of extensive traveling took place when he was about twenty years old in 1857. At that time, at the behest of his father, Candranegara IV, the regent of Demak (in office, 1850–66), the young Purwalelana was invited to accompany the Dutch government officer and Inspector of Cultures (Cultivation System cash crops), Herman Kleijn van de Poll (1818–98), on a seven-month journey through the island of Java and part of Sumatra. So, the starting point of the author's journeys must be at least three years before the date given in the title. Then, at the end of his work, during his fourth and last journey, when Purwalelana is describing his meeting with the regent of Magelang, we are told by the editors that this high official was called "Raden Tumenggung Danakusuma (sic, Danukusuma)" (208). Since Danukusuma only took up his post on February 17, 1879,[9] then the *terminus ad quem* of Purwalelana's travelogue must be at least four years after the end date of the title (1875). These are intriguing details that indicate that Purwalelana was revising his second edition with new data almost up to the time of its publication by Messrs Ogilvie & Sons in Batavia in 1880. Yet nowhere are these chronological issues relating to the date of composition discussed by the editors.

Throughout the text there is a similar lack of fastidiousness with regard to accuracy and the willingness to include appropriate editorial annotations. Some of these are quite minor, such as the mistranslation of the motto of the Royal Netherlands coat of arms, *je maintendrai*, as "I will overcome" (49) rather than "I will uphold/maintain." At other places, a simple editorial addition in square brackets into the text clarifying the name of a geographical feature might have been in order. Hence, it would have helped on p. 76 when Purwalelana's text speaks of the house of the assistant-resident of Brebes being situated "west of a big river," and that of the regent east of it, that the name of said river, Sungai Pemali, was given by the editors. In still other places, it would have added value to the text if the editors had gone the extra mile and taken the trouble to inform readers about just who exactly is being referred to when names of prominent individuals are mentioned. Thus, on pages 92–93, there are references to a certain "Mr Hofland," a great benefactor to the local community in Pasuruan in East Java. This was Peter William Hofland (1802–72), the Madras-born Eurasian coffee planter and estate owner, who became the largest landowner in Java when he acquired, with his brother, the Tjiasem en Pamanoekan Landen in Subang in West Java in 1858. His path to stellar riches, and equally stellar downfall in the second generation of his family—the subject of

[9] Heather Sutherland, "Notes on Java's Regent Families. Part II," *Indonesia* 17 (April 1974): 32.

P. A. Daum's *"Ups" en "Downs" in het Indische Leven* (1890)—lay through Pasuruan where he arrived in 1830, becoming a government cash-crop contractor in 1833, before moving on to West Java in 1840.[10]

Other prominent individuals—both Chinese—might also have been identified. The first is Liem Yoe Kiong, *Letnan Cina* (1865–77) and *Kapitan Cina* (1877–1924) of Lasem (Figure 52, p. 130), the longest serving Chinese officer in the history of the Dutch East Indies whose biographical details can be consulted in the late Steve Haryono's (Yeo Tjong Hian, 1957–2018) magnificent work on marriage strategies among the Peranakan Chinese elite in Java in the late 19th and early 20th centuries.[11] The second is the Chinese officer (*Mayor Cina*), landowner, and regent of Besuki, Han Tik Ko (also known as Han Kik Ko, 1766–1813; in office 1811–13), whose "imposing mansion" with its signature Tou-Kung roof frame had become, by the time of Purwalelana's visit, the official residence of the Dutch Resident of Besuki (106). Han Tik Ko's remarkable career as a Chinese regent (*Babah Tumenggung*) and major landowner in Besuki and Probolinggo, as well as his tragic end in a popular revolt on May 18, 1813 is the subject of the last chapter of Sri Margana's 2007 Leiden doctoral thesis.[12] Finally, in the footnote on Trowulan as the site of the fourteenth-century royal capital of Majapahit (118n1) the editors show a lack seriousness of purpose when they reference a newspaper article (*Jakarta Post*, January 7, 2011) and not the slew of recent scholarly articles on this topic.[13]

So, the present publication is a paradox. Handsome and well-presented though it is, its principal justification seems to be that it presents Purwalelana's text in English. But the question arises: if Marcel Bonneff has produced the definitive edition (minus the full translation of Purwalelana's fifty-seven-stanza poem on pages 197–205), why reinvent the wheel? Why not just translate Bonneff's clearly superior textual edition and have done with it? The answer, I suspect, lies in what is now fashionably called the "Anglosphere," that entirely arrogant and self-regarding conceit that just because a text does not exist in English it doesn't exist for the scholarly community tout court. Here one can only speculate what might have happened if, in the late 18th century, the tides of history had produced an entirely different outcome, and Britain had been the loser in the Revolutionary and Napoleonic Wars, and the Atlantic world had become Francophone. Then there would have been no question of ignoring a benchmark text in what would have been the Western world's premier language. And this would have had the signal

[10] Pian Siopianna, Muhammad Noer Faturrachman, and Mardani Mardani, "Peran Peter William Hofland dalam Mengelola Tanah Partikelir Pamanoekan en Tjiasem Landen Subang Tahun 1802–1874," *Historia Madania* 4, no. 1 (2020): 61–72; Ulbe Bosma and Remco Raben, Being "Dutch" in the Indies; *A History of Creolisation and Empire* (Singapore: NUS Press, 2088), 138–39.

[11] Steve Haryono, *Perkawinan Strategis: Hubungan Keluarga Antara Opsir-Opsir Tionghoa dan 'Cabang Atas' di Jsaw pada Abad ke-19 dan 20* (Rotterdam: Privately Printed, 2017), 95.

[12] Sri Margana, "Java's Last Frontier: The Struggle for the Hegemony of Blambangan, 1763–1813," translated as *Ujung Timur Jawa, 1763–1813: Perebutan Hegemoni Blambangan* (Yogyakarta: Pustaka Ifada, 2012), 290–308.

[13] Amrit Gomperts and Arnoud Haag, and Peter Carey, "Stutterheim's Enigma: The Mystery of His Mapping of the Majapahit Keraton at Trowulan in 1941," *Bijdragen tot de Taal-, Land- en Volkenkunde* 164, no. 4 (2008): 411–30; Amrit Gomperts and Arnoud Haag, and Peter Carey, "Mapping Majapahit: Wardenaar's Archaeological Survey at Trowulan in 1815," *Indonesia* 93 (April 2013): 177–96; Amrit Gomperts and Arnoud Haag, and Peter Carey, "The Archaeological Identification of the Majapahit Royal Palace: Prapanca's 1365 Description Projected onto Satellite Imagery," *Journal of the Siam Society* 102 (2014): 67–118.

advantage that other equally deserving Javanese texts, including Prince Diponegoro's autobiographical the *Babad Dipanagara* (1831–32), now (June 18, 2013) recognized as a Memory of the World manuscript; Yasadipura I's (1729–1803) peerless *Babad Giyanti* (pre-1803); Raden Mas Said's (Mangkunagara I) autobiographical *Babad Pakunegaran* (1779) and the *Serat Centhini* (1815), might have found their translators instead of languishing as at present in the relative obscurity of recondite manuscript collections and century-old Dutch text editions.

CPSIA information can be obtained
at www.ICGtesting.com
Printed in the USA
LVHW071920130423
744283LV00009B/274